Understanding the Sustainable Development of Tourism

Edited by

Janne J. Liburd and Deborah Edwards

(G) **Goodfellow Publishers Ltd**

(G) Published by Goodfellow Publishers Limited,
Woodeaton, Oxford, OX3 9TJ
http://www.goodfellowpublishers.com

British Library Cataloguing in Publication Data: a catalogue record for this title is available from the British Library.

Library of Congress Catalog Card Number: on file.

ISBN: 978-1-906884-13-0

Copyright © Goodfellow Publishers 2010

Design and typesetting by P.K. McBride, www.macbride.org.uk

Printed by Marston Book Services Ltd, www.marston.co.uk

Cover design by Cylinder, www.cylindermedia.com

Contents

Contributors

David Beirman, PhD, School of Leisure, Sport and Tourism, University of Technology, Sydney, email: David.Beirman-2@uts.edu.au

Larry Dwyer, PhD, Qantas Professor of Travel and Tourism Economics, School of Marketing, Australian School of Business University of New South Wales, email:l.dwyer@unsw.edu.au

Deborah Edwards, PhD, Senior Research Fellow, School of Leisure, Sport and Tourism, University of Technology, Sydney, email: deborah.edwards-1@uts.edu.au

Jeffrey Faux, PhD, Associate Dean, Victoria University, email: jeffrey.faux@vu.edu.au

Tracey Firth, PhD, School of Marketing, University of New South Wales, email: t.firth@unsw.edu.au

Anne-Mette Hjalager, PhD, CEO and Associate Professor, Advance/1, Incuba Science Park

email: hjalager@advance1.dk

Janne J. Liburd, PhD, Director, Centre for Tourism, Innovation and Culture, Associate Professor, Institute of History and Civilization, University of Southern Denmark, email: liburd@hist.sdu.dk

Kevin Lyons, PhD, Newcastle Business School, University of Newcastle, email: kevin.lyons@newcastle.edu.au

Rajka Presbury, PhD, Australian International Hotel School (AIHS), email: rajka.presbury@aihs.edu.au

Suzanne Leigh Snead, PhD, Newcastle Business School, University of Newcastle, email:ssnead@csu.edu.au

Camelia Tepelus, PhD, Secretariat Coordinator, Code of Conduct for the Protection of Children from Sexual Exploitation in Travel and Tourism, email: camelia.tepelus@thecode.org

Stephen Wearing, PhD, School of Leisure, Sport and Tourism, University of Technology, Sydney, email: stephen.wearing@uts.edu.au

About the editors

Janne J. Liburd is an Associate Professor and Director of the Centre for Tourism, Innovation and Culture at the University of Southern Denmark. She is a cultural anthropologist and her research interests are in the field of sustainable tourism development. She has published on national park development, open innovation and Web 2.0, tourism education, tourism crisis communication, events, NGOs and accountability. Janne has conducted a number of research projects relating to competence development for tourism practitioners and tourism educators. She is the chair of the BEST Education Network and steering committee member of the Tourism Education Futures Initiative.

Deborah Edwards is a Senior Research Fellow in the School of Leisure, Sport and Tourism at the University of Technology, Sydney. Her interests are in sustainable tourism management, spatial mapping of tourists, urban precincts, tourism planning, volunteers in tourism attractions and the impacts of events. She has published extensively in the area of sustainable tourism and destination management. Deborah is an executive member of the BEST Education Network.

Foreword

Sustainable development and the application of its principles to tourism are more important now than ever. Tourism industry leaders must be stewards over the environmental and socio-cultural resources upon which their institutions depend, and educating future tourism leaders with these principles is essential. To respond to this need, in 2000, a group of educators, researchers and industry leaders formed an international consortium to address this key philosophical shift in tourism development. This group, called Business Enterprises for Sustainable Tourism Education Network (BEST EN) is an innovative group committed to knowledge creation about sustainable tourism development and to disseminating that knowledge to students through a series of educational activities. The educational chapters presented in this volume are one representation of their collective work.

BEST EN meets for annual Think Tanks at consortium universities around the world. Think Tanks have been held in South Africa, Hawaii, Costa Rica, Girona, Spain, Esbjerg, Denmark, Arizona, US, Izmir, Turkey, Singapore and Vienna, Austria. Each chapter in this volume represents the outcome of one of these Think Tanks. BEST EN Think Tanks have two main objectives: 1) to develop knowledge outcomes on a specific aspect of sustainable tourism and 2) to develop a research agenda to expand the knowledge base of that particular aspect of sustainable tourism.

To create responsible future leaders for the tourism industry, one of BEST EN's co-founders, Professor Abraham Pizam, states that 'sustainability should be integrated into all aspects of the undergraduate tourism/hospitality curriculum, and sustainable tourism principles need to be practiced in all aspects of tourism operations'. Therefore, BEST EN chose to prepare knowledge outcomes relevant to existing subject matters rather than one comprehensive course on sustainable tourism. In this way, each tourism/hospitality student will be exposed to sustainable tourism practices applicable to the subject matter they are studying.

Each Think Tank extracted the collective wisdom of the group in such a way that the outcome reached beyond individual perspectives and program or temporal constraints. Each time about 40-50 participants were divided into groups led by facilitators. Groups engaged in discussion sessions on the chosen topic of sustainable tourism using the Nominal Group Technique (NGT). On the last day of each Think Tank a comprehensive report was drafted, which was then forwarded to a small sub-group of volunteers who produce the final knowledge outcomes.

Another important innovation is successfully woven into this book. Each chapter has carefully integrated recent work from the Tourism Education Futures Initiative (TEFI) to ensure that key values underlying responsible stewardship and tourism leadership are incorporated. TEFI identified five value sets that tourism students must imbibe in order to be successful future leaders of a fragile industry in uncertain times. They are ethics, stewardship, professionalism, knowledge and mutual respect. The integration of these values into the chapters has given them a strong foundation upon which to build sustainable tourism curricula. It is our hope that the book will be a resource to inspire colleagues in tourism institutions around the world to advance the cause of sustainable tourism practices for generations to come.

Pauline J. Sheldon,
Former Chair, BESTEN
Co-founder with Daniel Fesenmaier of Tourism Education Futures Initiative
President, International Academy for the Study of Tourism

1 Introduction to Sustainable Tourism Development

Janne J. Liburd

Rationale

One of the most important challenges facing the world of today is educating the leaders of tomorrow. In order to create challenging vistas and avoid blind reproduction where students simply learn to reproduce the world that exists (Minogue, 1973), these future leaders should be equipped with a holistic understanding of the values and principles of sustainable development. Students are hereby challenged not only to think about the means to current problem solving but to reflect philosophically upon the ethics and ends in the context of desirable futures. Reflecting upon the kind of tourism we wish to have does not imply moving away from industry needs and demands of the marketplace, as well as meeting those of society, which well-trained tourism graduates must continue to satisfy. More fundamentally it raises the issues of stewardship, the kind of tourism to be developed (by whom and how it should be governed) and what the end objectives behind these activities should be.

Throughout this book, sustainability is shown to be a dynamic process of change, rather than a static goal to be achieved. This chapter will first introduce the antecedents to the concept of sustainable development and then elaborate on its application to tourism. Particular attention is next paid to the meaning of complex adaptive systems in tourism. Drawing on the Tourism Educator Futures Initiative (TEFI), interrelated values of ethics, knowledge, professionalism and mutuality will be outlined to further substantiate how sustainability should be treated as a managerial philosophy rather than a subject matter taught in one comprehensive course.

Learning outcomes

On completion of this chapter the student should be able to:

+ Explain the principles of sustainable tourism development
+ Understand the difference between sustainable development and sustainable tourism development
+ Examine sustainability as a managerial philosophy and a process of transformation
+ Explain the meaning of complex adaptive systems
+ Critically reflect upon values related to sustainability
+ Reflect upon desirable futures for travel and tourism.

Sustainable development

Current ideas of sustainable development can be traced to a variety of antecedents. The following will provide a brief historical outline to set the scene for the still evolving perspectives and conceptualisations of sustainable development. Frequently mentioned are Western environmental and conservation movements, international organisations and conferences such as the 1972 UN Stockholm Conference on the Human Environment and the 1980 World Conservation Strategy. In addition, influential publications such as Carson's *Silent Spring* (1962) and Hardin's *Tragedy of the Commons* (1968) should be mentioned. By emphasising the relationship between human beings and our use of nature, these movements, organisations and publications are pointed to as having successfully forged the links between the environment and development, which are central to contemporary notions of sustainable development. During the era of industrialisation in Europe and the United States, humankind demonstrated their ability to conquer and exploit nature. In an analysis of American environmentalism, Rothman (1998: 34) describes how 'taming rivers in the United States was both sport and mission'. Such behaviour was firmly rooted in modernity's unprecedented belief in human rationality, as seen in economic growth models (Rostow, 1952) and the political agenda following World War II. President Truman's inaugural address to the US Congress in 1949 is illustrative.

Truman's inaugural address to US Congress 1949

The inaugural address by US president Truman (1949) is characteristic of this way of thinking following World War II:

> More than half the people of the world are living in conditions approaching misery. Their food is inadequate, they are victims of disease. Their economic life is primitive and stagnant. Their poverty is a handicap and a threat to both them and more prosperous areas. For the first time in history, humanity possesses the knowledge and skill to relieve the suffering of these people… I believe that we should make available to peace-loving peoples the benefits of our store of technical knowledge in order to help them realize their aspirations for a better life… What we envisage is a program of development based on the concepts of democratic fair dealing… Greater production is the key to prosperity and peace. And the key to greater production is a wider and more vigorous application of modern scientific and technical knowledge.

With issues of underdevelopment, elimination of poverty and economic growth dominating the international agenda of the industrialised nations during the 1950s and 1960s, more direct and disciplinary practices of development were institutionalised. Exemplified by the World Bank, the International Monetary Fund, the United Nations Development Programme (UNDP) and bilateral aid agencies, institutional practices were complemented by the power of knowledge. New development theories of modernisation and underdevelopment were introduced alongside a new geo-political imagery. Hereby, the world was neatly ordered in binary oppositional forms, namely the First and Third World, centre and periphery, North and South developed and underdeveloped countries. In brief, modernisation theory visualises development as a progressive movement toward more institutionalised complex forms of 'modern' society, which can be facilitated by a series of economic and technological interventions. The benefits hereof, it was professed, will eventually 'trickle down' via the middle class to the underdeveloped masses.

Highly sceptical of modernisation theory and capitalist penetration into the Third World, theories of dependency and neo-imperialism evolved during the 1960s and 1970s, imparting changes in socio-economic development practices. Dependency theorists, of whom Frank (1967) became a widely recognised example, argue that development is an unequal process through which wealthy First World nations, labelled 'centres' or 'cores', get richer and the poor 'peripheries' of the Third World even poorer. Subscribing to the Marxist conceptual framework of capitalism as exploitative, dependency theory perceives underdevelopment as embedded in particular political structures. It points to the inherent expansionist nature of capitalism and the continuous need for new markets and increased capital accumulation. Processes of exploitation are entrenched in the constant supply of raw materials and unequal trade relationships. This is eminently illustrated by the dominating approach to tourism in the post-World War II era in which tourism was typically seen as an economic panacea that would lead to modernisation of underdeveloped, peripheral areas as foreign exchange would filter through the economy and elevate standards of living, education, health, etc. The potential negative impacts were largely unquestioned as the 'industry without chimneys' was highly reproducible. Generally, little upfront investment was required by local authorities who, lured by fascinating growth potentials, provided lucrative incentives to foreign investors and multinational corporations to set up operation in their destination (Poon, 1993; Patullo, 1996). Unfortunately they became entrenched practices that are still used upon naive and ill-informed destinations to satisfy private agendas.

Tourism researchers such as Smith (1977), Cohen (1978), de Kadt (1979) and Britton (1982) in their seminal works, argued that tourism, instead of benefiting peripheral destinations, in many cases led to new forms of dependency and acculturation. Drawing parallels between service and servitude in neo-colonial contexts, the economic value of tourism was fundamentally questioned. Frank and other dependency theorists (Emmanuel, 1972; Wallerstein, 1974; Amin, 1976) argued that peripheral countries fail to establish their own manufacturing basis and market relations as a consequence of exploitative practices and unequal relations, practices which accelerate environmental degradation and the gap between rich and poor.

Acknowledging the global significance of the intertwined problems and challenges of development and the environment, in less than a decade (1977–84) the UN established three independent commissions. Chaired by three former prime ministers, Germany's Willy Brandt, Sweden's Oluf Palme and Norway's Gro Harlem Brundtland, the commissions were established with separate mandates to report on aspects of 'the interlocking crisis of the global commons' (WCED, 1987: 4). In addition to the growing awareness of environmental degradation and major discrepancies between the rich, industrialised nations and the poor, developing countries, these commissions identified a number of factors that would have a profound negative effect on the ability of all people to sustain continued progress for generations to come. These factors included increasing world population, ecological depletion of the ozone layer, air and water pollution, soil degradation, deforestation, loss of biodiversity, hunger, poverty, illiteracy and uneven development.

Mass tourism, characterised by rigidly standardised package holidays, appeared to not only capture but directly contribute to these societal ills (Turner and Ash, 1975; McElroy and de Albuquerque, 1996). Ostracised in favour of more alternative forms of tourism development that generally embrace smallness of scale, education of tourists, localism and environmental conservation, mass tourism was easily rejected as an 'old' form of tourism (Krippendorf, 1982; Smith and Eadington, 1989; Poon, 1993). Jafari (1989) refers to the change from mass tourism and the 'advocacy' platform towards an 'adaptive' or 'alternative' tourism platform. In retrospect, the 'alternative' tourism platform has done little to address the overall 'problematique' of mass tourism while it reproduced a contemptuous view of the majority of people who travel (Miller and Twining-Ward, 2005).

Entitled *Our Common Future*, the WCED report (1987) identifies two sources – both cause and effect – of the interlocking crisis: Third World poverty and overconsumption by the First World. Frequently referred to as the Brundtland Report, *Our Common Future* (WCED, 1987) builds on the core recommendation of the two Brandt Reports to increase industrialisation, production and thus economic growth in the Third World. This was arguably a surprise given the apparent failure of kindred development schemes and well-established critique of the underlying modernisation theory and unequal exchange (Frank, 1967; Sachs, 1974; Wallerstein 1974; Escobar, 1995). The Brundtland commission also carried through Palme's participatory approach and concerns of security, which were not limited to global disarmament. Civil and ecological survival were emphasised *through* the importance of inter-and intra-generational equity, combating poverty, creation of intersectoral linkages, maintenance of the ecological resource base and empowerment of smallholders, women, indigenous people, rural farmers and local communities (WCED, 1987: 63, 116, 143). The Brundtland Report affirms a need for an integrated understanding of the world as a whole, where the wellbeing of man and nature, future development and environmental issues are inextricably linked. Given this lens, the Brundtland Report introduces limits to growth and defines sustainable development as 'development that meets the needs of the present without compromising the ability of future generations to meet their own needs' (WCED, 1987: 43).

Effortlessly embraced as a good idea of making things last, the report was met with enthusiastic support by governments, non-government organisations and academics alike. The now well-established definition of sustainable development hinges on a holistic integration of economic, environmental, social and cultural development. The Brundtland Report emphasises that meeting present and future needs not only involves economic growth in poor countries but being able to sustain it through the strengthening of international cooperative efforts. The concept of sustainable development implies both equity and ethics within and between generations, emphasised in the overview entitled 'From one earth to one world' (WCED, 1987: 1). Unfortunately, both the issues of ethics and equity have received very limited attention in the growing volume of publications on sustainable development and sustainable tourism development, which will be addressed later in the chapter.

It is important to note that the Brundtland Report concentrates on sustainable development through economic growth, effective international cooperation, strategic long-term planning and maintenance of the resource and productivity base beyond narrow institutional and national concerns. Tourism is not mentioned in Our Common Future despite being a hallmark of modern society and having a vested interest in protecting the very resource base on which it depends.

Sustainable Tourism Development

Following Jafari's (1989) idea of academic platforms occupied by tourism researchers, the late-1980s were characterised by a quest for knowledge about tourism's potential impacts – environmental, socio-cultural and economic – in tourist destinations around the world (Smith, 1977, 1989). Initially focusing on different types of tourism, notably ecotourism, the concept of sustainable development only slowly gained attention in tourism research. The relation between tourism and sustainable development was not programmatically specified until 1997 through the *Agenda 21 for the Travel and Tourism Industry* (Agenda 21) (World Travel and Tourism Council, World Tourism Organization and the Earth Council, 1997).

Agenda 21 draws on the outcome from the 1992 UN Conference on Environment and Development, also known as the 'Rio Earth Summit'. Setting out the priorities for sustainable development in the 21st century, Agenda 21 recognises tourism as a model form of economic development that should improve the quality of life of the host community, provide a high quality of experience for the visitor, and maintain the quality of the environment on which both the host community and the visitor depend. Agenda 21 identifies several measures and objectives that can be undertaken by governments and the tourism industry worldwide. These include strengthening of institutional cooperation, improved water waste management, training and education favouring minorities, and the exchange of information, skills and technology related to travel and tourism. The interrelated environmental and socio-economic elements are captured in the definition by the World Tourism Organization (1998: 21): 'Sustainable tourism development meets the needs of present tourists and host regions while protecting and enhancing opportunities for the future. Sustainable tourism is envisaged as leading to management of all resources in such a way that economic, social and aesthetic needs can be fulfilled while maintaining cultural integrity, essential ecological processes, biological diversity, and life support systems'.

Conceptual definitions and practical concerns of sustainable tourism development and sustainable tourism have received considerable academic and government attention and have been exposed to substantial criticism (Bramwell and Lane, 1993; Butler, 1998; Hall and Lew, 1998; Mowforth and Munt, 1998; Cohen, 2002; Dwyer and Sheldon, 2005; Miller and Twining-Ward, 2005). A few of the principal concerns will be addressed here to illustrate briefly how the field of inquiry has taken form during the past three decades and set the scene for the remainder of this chapter. In the context of practical concerns, there has been a relative neglect of how to implement the laudable principles in tourism and address the very reasons why individual businesses and governments should consider their environmental, social and cultural performance rather than their financial bottom line. In particular, a conceptual perplexity exists within the literature where narrow sectoral concerns and tourism's contribution to broader sustainable outcomes are at odds.

Sustainable tourism is centred on the viability of tourism and balancing industry and environmental impacts (Hunter, 1995). Sustaining tourism implies that management of the net productive value of the 'natural' capital is calculated in order to implement compensating resource replacement and substitution strategies (Hughes, 1995). Meant to provide enjoyment for tourists and residents alike and becoming a source of local income, paradoxically, conservation efforts to maintain absolute equilibrium mean that the environment, including social and cultural aspects, should be kept in an unimpaired state for present and future generations. Such an anthropocentric approach rests on static conceptualisations that neglect contemporary knowledge about the dynamics of the environment and culture. Sustainable tourism is hereby reduced to maintaining a 'natural' equilibrium as a measurable state toward which intervention strategies can be applied as an economic trade-off between present utilisation and presumed future needs.

Regulation and conservation efforts tie closely into this managerial perspective where irregularities and problems are addressed in causal, linear relationships. Butler's (1980) famous adaptation of Plog's (1974) life-cycle model into the tourism area life cycle that demonstrates how 'destinations carry within them the potential seeds of their own destruction' represents both a cautionary approach and also a belief in managerial intervention techniques if decline is to be avoided.

Without repeating Habermas' (1987) comprehensive deconstruction of the value-laden progress of Western science, the role of objective science in ideas about environmental management and sustainable tourism persevere. Hunter (1997) warns against the tourism-centric and often marginal concerns of sustainable tourism that appear to be separated from the sustainable development debate. When the tourism industry is considered in isolation, its activities may run counter to other sustainable development initiatives, preservation efforts and overall quality of life issues. These are noticeable, among other things, in the industry's notorious low-skill, low-wage structures and long working hours. Drawing on Butler (1999), Moscado (2008: 6) argues that 'tourism cannot be sustainable in its own right'. Tourism does not operate in a spatial vacuum and must be understood as a total social and economic phenomenon (Theobald, 2005) and therefore as part of other elements of society and the economy. When the fundamental interdependence between regions and socio-economic activities are acknowledged, tourism is a potential contributor to the broader societal aims of sustainable development.

A frequent claim made in the literature is that sustainable tourism development can be achieved. Arguing that sustainability is achievable over a period of time fails to understand that change and ever-evolving processes are the norm rather than the exception. Students will easily recognise how choice in life style, cultural preferences and patterns of consumption and communication are not the same between generations and that these are rather unpredictable. Similarly, it is not feasible to assume that tourism that stays the same 'will go on forever' (Hall and Butler 1995: 102). These arguments indicate that the very idea of striking a balance in which the environment, economy and social and cultural elements are in equilibrium can be seen as an oxymoron. Appreciating the complexities of socio-cultural values, quality of life aspirations, and the biophysical and economic systems in which tourism takes place over time calls for an integrated approach to sustainable tourism development. Consequently discarding the notion of sustainable development as a goal that can be achieved, a processual and holistic understanding of sustainable tourism development is introduced in the following.

Complex adaptive systems

Tourism can be seen as a complex adaptive system. Complex adaptive systems are defined as systems with non-linear dynamics, which can cause complex and changing outcomes that are hard to predict (Malanson, 1999; Gunderson *et al.*, 2005; Miller and Twining-Ward, 2005). Illustrated by a reclining figure 8, Holling's (1986) adaptive cycle demonstrates how this complex system of ongoing transitions works and how it can be adapted into sustainable tourism development: see Figure 1.1.

Figure 1.1: Complex adaptive systems (Gunderson et al., 2005)

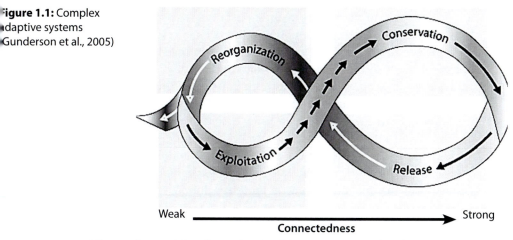

The cycle explains how the 'sudden surprises' that have various impacts on a destination may affect the destination's resilience and/or vulnerability. These changes might reinforce the destination after 'the incident' or make it weaker, in which case, then, the destination managers and stakeholders learn from the event and rebuild the destination through, for example, the introduction of innovations, as suggested by Russell and Faulkner (1999). Butler's (1980) tourism area life-cycle model can be recognised in the 'exploitation' and 'conservation' stages. Coupled with the collapse of the system, entitled 'release' and new 'reorganisation' in Holling's (1986) adaptive cycle, it becomes a dynamic model well suited for understanding the transformational processes, power and unpredictability in sustainable tourism development. A complex adaptive system is a dynamic network of many agents, or actors, (which may represent cells, species, individuals, firms, nations) acting in parallel, constantly acting and reacting to what the other agents are doing (Holland, 1994). Law (2004: 2) describes the world as a web of relations: 'Continuous, discontinuous, configured, ragged. And those relations have no status, no shape, no reality, outside their continued production. This means that the concern is with process. It is with how particular realities get made and remade. And then how they sometimes, possibly often, get themselves embedded so that they become obdurate and resistant.' The embedded ability of tourism to adapt to change, which includes occurrences outside the network's control, implies that the system is in a constant learning process to improve the system's resilience and capitalise on phases of self-organisation and reorganisation (Miller and Twining-Ward, 2005).

Complex adaptive systems can be seen as a valuable contribution to Jafari's (1989) 'knowledge-based' platform. It encourages thinking about tourism's performative ability and relations between elements in addition to coping with future uncertainty. It effectively escapes causal, linear explanations and simple accounts of tourism's 'impacts', which according to findings by Moscado and Pearce (1999) only too often are imposed on respondents by those conducting research or undertaking development. Increasingly, notions about sustainable tourism development are linked to systems thinking about managing and facilitating change (Bell and Morse, 2003) which is underpinned by a holistic understanding of sustainable development that cannot be determined by single components. Therefore, the relational understanding must not be mistaken for one of impact or inter-action, which Emirbayer (1999: 285) describes as merely resembling billiard balls colliding and reacting without affecting the interior properties of the entities in question. Rather a relational and holistic understanding sees sustainable tourism development and the entities of analysis as constituted in and through constantly unfolding processes in which different relations of power and values are always at stake.

Adding to the research platforms of advocacy, cautionary, alternative (or adaptive) and knowledge-based, a new values-based platform is introduced. It is attributable to the Tourism Education Futures Initiative which, although focused on tourism education futures, can assist in exposing the fundamental characteristics of sustainable development and transitions towards sustainable tourism development.

Guiding values in sustainable tourism development

Now housed by BEST EN, the Tourism Education Futures Initiative (TEFI) was born in 2007 out of a concern for the future of tourism education. About 70 scholars and industry leaders began a process of rebuilding the education process so that tomorrow will be shaped by people educated to commit to a sustainable world (Sheldon et al., 2008). An important outcome of the TEFI process is a set of five values-based principles that tourism students should embody upon graduation to become responsible leaders and stewards for the destinations in which they work and/or live. The five value sets are: Ethics, Knowledge, Professionalism, Mutuality and Stewardship. Underpinned by a holistic and relational perspective, the values are portrayed as interlocking value principles because of their interconnectedness and their permeability. In the following sections, these interrelated values are revisited in the context of sustainable tourism development.

Ethics

Ethics is concerned with distinguishing between behaviour that is right and behaviour that is wrong. It is the basis for good action and provides a framework for judging actions that are questionable. Ethical behaviour means striving for actions that are deemed 'good' based on principles and values. It also involves making such principles and values explicit and rendering the decision-making processes transparent. Recognising that good actions do not occur in a vacuum but are derived from specific value systems further requires understanding and respect for actions based on different systems e.g. teleology and deontology. Following Tribe (2002b), by examining ethics we can further clarify the values of sustainable tourism development as they relate to good and just tourism. In the Brundtland Report (WCED, 1987) intergenerational equity is the defining, albeit grossly overlooked value. Cohen (2002) points to the misuse of the concept in 'ecotourism' as a marketing gimmick and, more fundamentally, the unequal power relations at stake in tourism development. Seeing everyone as impartially situated as equals (Rawls, 1971) good and just tourism is not only for the few and wealthy who can afford to travel to safe havens before the crowds get there.

Moreover, local populations in developing countries are often marginalised when external agents such as private or state entrepreneurs take control over valuable sites or attractive cultural practices in the name of sustainability. Local communities are frequently depicted as the ones damaging the environment due to 'traditional' practices. The ethical principle of intergenerational equity is easily masked behind the rhetoric of involving locals as participants in the development phase and perhaps as service personnel. A very different connotation of equity is to address locals as users and stakeholders, which also secures local accessibility to valued environments (Cohen, 2002: 273). Examples of local displacements are manifold, and only two will serve to illustrate the point about equitable access here. In many parts of the eastern Caribbean, prime beach-front properties are occupied by all-inclusive hotel complexes and condominiums. Consequently, claims of trespassing are made if locals attempt to enjoy their place in the sun. In the South African game reserves, it is well known that 'locals poach' while 'tourists hunt'. Students will appreciate the ethical distinction between right and wrong behaviour in these examples and the need to uncover the meanings behind ethical behaviour in sustainable tourism development. The Global Code of Ethics approved by the World Tourism Organization in 1999 on the sustainable development of tourism is also of interest to serious tourism students.

Knowledge

Knowledge can be described as: expertise and skills acquired by a person through experience or education; the theoretical or practical understanding of a subject; what is known in a particular field; facts and information; or awareness or familiarity gained by experience of a fact or situation. This implies that knowledge is more than data (summary descriptions of parts of the world around us) and more than information (data put into a context). Knowledge comes in both explicit and tacit formats. In most instances, it is not possible to have an exhaustive understanding of an information domain so knowledge is ceaselessly incomplete. Knowledge is information connecting to existing knowledge. Knowledge is created through processes of selecting, connecting and reflecting. Knowledge is always already predicated by existing knowledge, which means that knowledge involves interpretation and contextualisation. In due course, the knowledge of others should be recognised, and existing knowledge that may be taken for granted should be challenged.

The dissemination and development of knowledge takes place in social environments that are characterised by information sharing and social interaction. Access to social and educational networks can create or assist in refining the use of knowledge. Networks and knowledge repositories are opening up as a consequence of the development of technical and institutional remedies connected to the social media. Hereby, problem solving and identification increasingly take place through sharing and cooperation in open knowledge systems, where providers and users of knowledge meet and exchange information. Tourism students and higher education institutions must understand and address the issues of open knowledge sources and open innovation. Chesbrough (2003) and von Hippel (2005) state that innovation resources are not restricted and should not be restricted to local and close networks, which are in contrast to knowledge hoarding, protection and monopolising in closed learning environments. Bridging such networks can link different repositories of knowledge and potentially enable the transition to sustainable tourism development.

Professionalism

'Professionalism' is a rather nebulous term as it implies not only a profession and the skills, competencies or standards associated with it, but also an attitude and behaviour that reflect these. It has been defined as the ability to align personal and organisational conduct with ethical and professional standards that include a responsibility to the customer or guest and community, a service orientation, and a commitment to lifelong learning and improvement (Hoyle and John, 1995). Professionalism incorporates leadership, practicality, attention to services, concern for the relevance and timeliness of evidence, reflexivity, teamwork and partnership building skills, and proactivity. These elements of professionalism expose the need for a holistic approach to tourism education similar to Tribe (2002a) where broader aims of the industry and society are explicitly addressed in tourism curricula.

Tourism education also needs to provide students with a dynamic learning experience that will enable them to operate sustainably and effectively in a fast-changing and service-intensive sector, which Tribe (2002a) refers to as 'philosophical practitioners'. The delivery of education embedding the value of professionalism towards the tourism industry and the world in which it operates calls for new learning structures and methods that are flexible in response to external change.

It involves dynamic approaches to teaching that integrate Web 2.0 learning opportunities within the classroom, the laboratory, the library, the Internet and the workplace (Liburd and Hjalager, 2010).

Stewardship

Stewardship implies the responsibility to care for something and the accountibility to exercise responsibility. As the editors of the present volume contend that the value of stewardship is deeply reflected in sustainable development, only a brief introduction to stewardship is provided here. The TEFI value of stewardship implies that the earth is a divine gift which we are permitted to use and take care of for the benefit of future generations. This definition also suggests that tourism faculty and students should learn to take leadership in three distinct aspects of stewardship:

♦ Sustainability

♦ Responsibility

♦ Service to the community.

All stakeholders have responsibility for the environment and the society, but to exercise responsibility power and/or influence are necessary. Responsibility also implies the existence of rights. If all stakeholders are to take responsibility for the future of the planet in tourism, empowerment of those who are currently power-less is necessary, as is the restraint of power of other groups. Service to the community is one way that stakeholders can demonstrate their commitment to taking responsibility.

Mutual respect

Within the TEFI framework, mutual respect has been initially defined as diversity, inclusion, equity, humility and collaboration. Equality requires different opinions, philosophies of life and cultures to be met with tolerance and mutual respect on the basis of universal human rights. Mutual respect is a value grounded in human relationships that requires attitudinal developments that are evolving, dynamic and involve acceptance, self-awareness of structural inequalities, open-mindedness, empowerment and ability to revisit one's cultural understanding of the world. Tourism education is a medium through which mutual respect can be promoted. However, mutuality is seen as a process that starts from the self. Therefore it cannot be taught directly as a subject but rather facilitated through the whole variety of general self-awareness and conflict resolution courses that should be part of tourism education.

Uncovering the values in sustainable tourism development

Revisiting the Brundtland Report's (WCED, 1987) conceptualisation of sustainable development, one can appreciate how the values of mutuality, equity and ethics can be approached from both an individual and societal perspective. Each of the three UN Commissions established in less than a decade were chaired by politicians with deep roots in Scandinavian Labour/Social Democratic parties whose ideologies have shaped the approach to equity in sustainable development. The Scandinavian countries of Norway, Sweden and Denmark have been strongly influenced by labour governments and tenacious union activity during the 20th century, which implies a particular understanding of equity. With little variance, the Scandinavian countries are built on a thorough welfare system that is controlled by relatively large and powerful government sectors and financed by the whole society in which the tax rates are among the highest in the world. The system provides security for the individual citizen through a mutual insurance and obligation under a democratic government.

In the Principles and Action Programmes of the Scandinavian Social Democratic/ Labour parties from the 20th century onwards, free-flowing capitalist market forces are represented as inherently self-destructive. Whether addressed in a national or international context, a certain amount of political control and central regulation by the state are seen as needed in order to secure both welfare and the environment for everybody. To mention but some, the principles of equity are represented in the redistribution of income, social services, education and protection of environmental resources. These values are, of course, subject to change as are the political parties constituting Scandinavian governments. Still, the fundamental ideas of equity, unity and fairness as ethical principles of doing good have longstanding merit over personal independence and self-centred fulfilment (c.f. the Norwegian Labour Party, 2005). Based on such understanding of equity and mutual respect, sustainable tourism development hereby becomes a vehicle for individual and collective fulfilment, mutual understanding and respect between people. This also highlights how sustainable development involves a complex web of ethics, beliefs and values, including the underpinning Western concepts of freedom and democracy (Macbeth, 2005).

Truly global in reach and aspiration, it is important to be mindful of the dynamic nature of tourism and sustainable development which means that the objectives, power relations and aspirations are constantly changing over time and as they are subjected to different contexts across the globe. As individuals we act in webs of relations in accord with mutually accepted regulative principles and values. Mutual respect, rational and reasonable behaviour should not be mistaken by notions about local participation and local communities as homogenous groups of people that easily reach consensus. Whereas local groups of limited size permit relatively easy liaison building, it also actualises intense face-to-face personalism, ethnicity and kinship ties of participating individuals and stakeholders. The range of stakeholders, networks and actors in tourism destinations, which, of course, also include non-government organisations, are multiple as are their aspirations and needs. By adopting a place-based approach towards sustainable tourism development, socio-cultural, environmental and economic changes that are acceptable for the destination community must be identified to determine what is to be sustained for whom and how by the people whose habitat it is, or may become, the object of tourism development (Liburd, 2007).

Also translating the broader aims and values of sustainable development to a specific location, on a sectoral base, sustainable tourism must contribute to the specific development needs and quality of life in the destination. Only thus is one able to judge whether specific practices are likely to be transformative and facilitate the interests and needs of a group of people. Applicable to all destinations engaged in transitions towards sustainable tourism development, ongoing monitoring and indicator development will help destinations build resilience to ensure that they are on the right track as they – as professionals – learn from new experiments and failures as an essential part of adaptive management. Students who will be the future professionals are hereby challenged not only to think about the means to current problem solving but to philosophically reflect upon the ends in the context of desirable futures and the kind of tourism and society we wish to have.

Future challenges and issues

A move towards values-based learning may demand a new paradigm and methodologies that transcend traditional disciplinary boundaries. Following Coles *et al.* (2006), an epistemological space exists within studies of tourism for post-disciplinary approaches based on even greater flexibility, plurality, synthesis and synergy. As a phenomenon, industry, career and lifestyle tourism constitutes exceptional learning opportunities. Greater inter- or post-disciplinary research and exchange of ideas can help expand the current knowledge base on values, complex adaptive systems management and networks in sustainable tourism development. The proposed values-based platform calls for further research and in-depth understanding about cultural interpretations and contextualised meanings of ethics, knowledge, professionalism and mutual respect. This will also assist in exposing the complexities and inherent dynamics in complex adaptive systems. Understanding what works also means understanding the 'othering' and what is made absent and silenced in this process. Wearing *et al.* (2010 p. 195) offer further perspectives on 'offering' in the context of volunteer tourism. In short, relations of power must be integral to critical enquiry about how the systems and networks are connected, released and reorganised.

Tourism's status as a hallmark activity of contemporary society means that it should not be considered in isolation from other socio-economic and environmental phenomena. International in scope and reach, Murphy and Price (2005) have argued that tourism is well positioned to take a lead in the transition towards sustainable development as it already operates beyond narrow sectoral concerns. Still, several fundamental challenges remain. At the industry level, one of these is to alter the thinking of service providers from short-term marketing and funding problems towards long-term development and research needs of the tourism industry (Jago, 2004). The importance of planning for transitions and adopting more sustainable practices into the core of tourism operations in order to secure transparency and accountability cannot be overstated. Representing a business case for CSR, tourism's financiers and notably pension funds, banks and insurance companies may embrace the challenge of socially responsible investments (known as SRI funds) to drive the pursuit of sustainability.

At the consumer level, a major challenge is how to create a concerned demand for sustainable tourism. Current practices tend to exclude holidays as part of responsible consumption patterns as documented in recent studies from England

(National Consumer Council, 2006). Just as tourism firms have started to assume responsibility for sustainable operations, as seen in triple bottom line reporting (Chapter 6) and acts of corporate social responsibility (Chapter 7), so will individual citizens need to internalise the values of sustainability and express these in their demand for sustainable travel and tourism services. In this process, social acceptability and social learning play a major role in encouraging new behaviour, as do the media and NGOs in mobilising a relentless criticism of 'green washing', unfair and inequitable practices in tourism.

Another challenge is directed at governments at all levels as they have the tools to facilitate and substantiate changes towards sustainable development. Bramwell (2005: 410) lists four types of policy instruments: government encouragement of voluntary changes in behaviour; government financial incentives; government expenditure on actions taken directly by public authorities; and government regulations that can be considered. The choice and potential mix of government instruments for sustainability are subject to ethical, political ideology, available knowledge and economic issues that are context-specific and will affect their use. Throughout this book, students will recognise different approaches to the role of government driving sustainable tourism development.

Understanding the importance of sustainability in tourism development, the concept, its values, uses, attempts at implementation and consequences must be subjected to ongoing critical analysis. The gap between scientists, who provide knowledge, and policymakers, who use this knowledge, is at times wide and must be narrowed in order to secure a sufficient basis for the decision making of tomorrow. In short, given the multiple dimensions and public and private sector interrelatedness, stakeholders must be enabled to act together in order to meet the many challenges of sustainable tourism development.

Review

This chapter set out to introduce the concept of sustainable tourism development. The widely known definition of sustainable development and its subsequent adaptation to tourism are attributable to the Brundtland Report (WCED, 1987). It was argued that while sustainability in tourism is often criticised as a vague concept (e.g. Sharpley, 2000) the concept is not value-free. The dominating and highly selective reading of sustainable development as a continuous endorsement of a free market economy with environmental constraints has been rejected. Sustainable development cannot be understood in isolation from the socio-political context in which it was born nor from the spatial context in which it is adopted as a managerial philosophy. A number of challenges were indentified to further inspire students as future leaders to understand the potential drivers for sustainable tourism development. Students are hereby challenged to reflect upon the grounds, theoretical foundations and thereby also upon the values we apply when making our decisions for sustainable tourism development without reducing applicability and action. Action must be based on philosophical reflection upon desired presents and futures and, more fundamentally, on equitable participation in order to move towards sustainable development.

Review questions

1 What is the difference between sustainable development and sustainable tourism development?
2 Can sustainability be achieved?
3 What is a complex adaptive system?
4 What are the guiding values in sustainable tourism development?
5 Why should the spatial and socio-political context be taken into account when implementing sustainable tourism development?

Further reading

For more detail on these value sets and how they can be incorporated into the learning experience See Sheldon et al. (2008) and the TEFI White Paper (2009 – available from http://www.tourismeducation.at). Students are referred to the extensive reference list of this chapter for further reading.

References

Amin, S. (1976) *La nation Arabe: Nationalisme et luttes de classes*, Paris: Minuit.

Bell, S. and Morse, S. (2003) *Measuring Sustainability: Learning from Doing*, London: Earthscan Publications.

Bramwell, B. (2005) 'Interventions and policy instruments for sustainable tourism', in W.F. Theobald (ed.), *Global Tourism*, 3rd edn, Oxford: Elsevier, pp. 406-425.

Bramwell, B. and Lane, B. (1993) 'Sustainable tourism: an evolving global approach', *Journal of Sustainable Tourism*, **1**, 1-5.

Britton, S. (1982) 'The political economy in the Third World', *Annals of Tourism Research*, **9**, 331-358.

Butler, R.W. (1980) 'The concept of a tourism area cycle of evolution: implications for the management of resources', *Canadian Geographer*, **24**, 5-12.

Butler, R.W. (1998) 'Sustainable tourism – looking backwards in order to progress?', in C.M. Hall and A. Lew (eds), *Sustainable Tourism: A Geographical Perspective*, New York: Addison Wesley Longman, pp. 25-34.

Butler, R.W. (1999) 'Problems and issues of integrating tourism development', in D.G. Pearce and R.W. Butler (eds), *Contemporary Issues in Tourism Development*, London: Routledge, pp. 65-80.

Carson, R. (1962) *Silent Spring*, Greenwich, CT: Fawcett.

Chesbrough, H. (2003) *Open Innovation: The New Imperative for Creating and Profiting from Technology*, Boston, MA: Harvard Business School Press.

Cohen, E. (1978) 'The impact of tourism on the physical environment', *Annals of Tourism Research*, **5**, 215-237.

Cohen, E. (2002) 'Authenticity, equity and sustainability in tourism', *Journal of Sustainable Tourism*, **10** (4), 267-276.

Coles, T., Hall, C.M. and Duval, D.T. (2006) 'Tourism and post-disciplinary enquiry', *Current Issues in Tourism*, **9** (4 & 5), 293-319.

de Kadt, E. (ed.) (1979) *Tourism – Passport to Development? Perspectives on the Social and Cultural Effects of Tourism in the Developing Countries*, Oxford: Oxford University Press.

Dwyer, L. and Sheldon, P. (2005) 'Introduction: sustainability and mass destinations: challenges and possibilities', *Tourism Review International*, **9**, 1-7.

Emmanuel, A. (1972) *L'échange inégal : Essai sur les antagonismes dans les rapports économiques internationaux*; Préface et "remarques théoriques" de Charles Bettelheim, Paris: Maspero.

Escobar, A. (1995) *Encountering Development. The Making and Unmaking of the Third World*, Princeton, NJ: Princeton University Press.

Frank, A.G. (1967) *Sociology of Development and Underdevelopment of Sociology*, Stockholm: Zenit.

Gunderson, L.H., Holling, C.S., Pritchard, L. and Peterson, G.D. (2005) 'Resilience of large-scale resource systems', in L.H. Gunderson and L. Pritchard, Jr (eds), *Resilience and the Behavior of Large-Scale Systems*, Washington, DC: Scope 60/Island Press, pp. 3-18.

Habermas, J. (1987) *The Philosophical Discourse of Modernity*, Cambridge: Polity Press.

Hall, C.M. and Butler, R.W. (1995) 'In search of common ground: reflections on sustainability, complexity and process in the tourism system – a discussion between C. Michael Hall and Richard W. Butler', *Journal of Sustainable Tourism*, **3** (2), 99-105.

Hall, C.M. and Lew, A. (1998) *Sustainable Tourism: A Geographical Perspective*, New York: Addison Wesley Longman.

Hardin, G. (1968) 'Tragedy of the Commons', *Science*, **162**, 1243-1248.

Holland, J. H. (1994) *Complexity: The Emerging Science at the Edge of Order and Chaos*, Harmondsworth: Penguin.

Holling, C.S. (1986) 'The resilience of terrestrial ecosystems: local surprise and global change', in W.C. Clark and R.E. Munn (eds), *Sustainable Development of the Biosphere*, Cambridge UK, Cambridge University Press, pp. 292-317.

Hoyle, E. and John, P.D. (1995) *Professional Knowledge and Professional Practice*, London: Cassell.

Hughes, C. (1995) 'The cultural construction of tourism', *Tourism Management*, **16** (1), 49-59.

Hunter, C. (1995) 'On the need to re-conceptualize sustainable tourism development', *Journal of Sustainable Tourism*, **3**, 155-165.

Hunter, C. (1997) 'Sustainable tourism as an adaptive paradigm', *Annals of Tourism Research*, **24**, 850-867.

Independent Commission on Disarmament and Security Issues (1982) *Common Security: A Programme for Disarmament*, London: Pan.

Independent Commission on International Development Issues (1980) *North–South: A Programme for Survival*, Pan, London.

Independent Commission on International Development Issues (1983) *Common Crisis: North–South*, London: Pan.

Jafari, J. (1989) 'An English language literature review', in J. Bystranowski (ed.), *Tourism as a Factor of Change: A Socio-cultural Study*, Vienna: Centre for Research and Documentation in Social Sciences.

Jago, L. (2004) 'Destination Australia: A research agenda for sustainable tourism. Building capacity for innovation in the 21st century', B.E.S.T. Education Network Think Tank IV Conference Proceedings, Sydney, Australia: University of Western Sydney.

Krippendorf, J. (1982) 'Towards new tourism policies', *Tourism Management*, **3**, 135-148.

Law, J. (2004) *After Method. Mess in Social Science Research*, London: Routledge.

Liburd, J. J. (2007) 'Sustainable tourism, cultural practice and competence development for hotels and inns in Denmark', *Tourism Recreation Research*, **32** (1), 41-49.

Liburd, J.J. and Hjalager, A.-M. (2010) 'Changing approaches to education, innovation and research in tourism', *Journal of Hospitality and Tourism Management*, **17**, 12–20.

McElroy, J.L. and de Albuquerque, K. (1996) 'Sustainable alternatives to insular mass tourism: recent theory and practice', in L. Briguglio, B. Archer, J. Jafari and G. Wall (eds), *Sustainable Tourism in Islands and Small States: Issues and Policies*, London: Pinter, pp. 47-60.

Malanson, J.P. (1999) 'Considering complexity', *Annals of the Association of American Geographers*, **89**, 746-753.

Miller, G. and Twining-Ward, L. (2005) *Monitoring for a Sustainable Tourism Transition: The Challenge of Developing and Using Indicators*, Wallingford: CABI Publishing.

Minogue, K.R. (1973) *The Concept of a University*, Berkeley: University of California Press.

Moscado, G. (2008) 'Sustainable tourism innovation: challenging basic assumptions', *Tourism and Hospitality Research*, **8** (1), 4-13.

Moscado, G. and Pearce, P.L. (1999) 'Understanding ethnic tourists', *Annals of Tourism Research*, **26** (2), 416-434.

Mowforth, A. and Munt, I. (1998) *Tourism and Sustainability: New Tourism in the Third World*, London: Routledge.

Murphy, P.E. and Price, G.G. (2005) 'Tourism and sustainable development' in W.F. Theobald (ed.), *Global Tourism*, 3rd edn, Oxford: Elsevier, pp. 194-212.

National Consumer Council (2006) *I Will If You Will. Towards Sustainable Consumption*, London: Seacourt.

Norwegian Labour Party (2005) *The Norwegian Labour Party – A brief presentation*. http://arbeiderpartiet.no/Kontakt/Information-in-English, accessed 18 October 2009.

Patullo, P. (1996) *Last Resorts: The Cost of Tourism in the Caribbean*, London: Cassell.

Plog, S. (1974) 'Why destination areas rise and fall in popularity', *Cornell Hotel and Administration Quarterly*, **14**, 55-58.

Poon, A. (1993) *Tourism, Technology and Competitive Strategies*, Wallingford, CABI International.

Rawls, J.B. (1971) *A Theory of Justice*, Cambridge, MA: Belknap Press.

Rostow, W.W. (1952) *The Process of Economic Growth*, New York: W.W. Norton.

Rothman, H.K. (1998) *The Greening of a Nation: Environmentalism in the United States Since 1945*, Fort Worth, TX: Harcourt Brace College Publishers.

Russell, R. and Faulkner, B. (1999) 'Movers and shakers: chaos makers in tourism development', *Tourism Management*, **31**, 411-423.

Sachs, I. (1974) 'Environment and styles of development', *African Environment*, **1**, 9-33.

Sharpley, R. (2000) 'Tourism and sustainable development: exploring the theoretical divide', *Journal of Sustainable Tourism*, **8** (1), 1–19.

Sheldon, P., Fesenmaier, D., Woeber, C., Cooper, C. and Antonioli, M. (2008) 'Tourism education futures, 2010-2030: building the capacity to lead', *Journal of Travel and Tourism Teaching*, 7 (3), 61–68.

Smith, V.L. (ed.) (1977) Hosts and Guests. *The Anthropology of Tourism*, Philadelphia: University of Pennsylvania Press.

Smith, V.L. (ed.) (1989) Hosts and Guests: *The Anthropology of Tourism*, 2nd ed., Philadelphia: University of Pennsylvania Press.

Smith; V.L. and Eadington, W.R. (1989) *Tourism Alternatives: Potentials and Problems in the Development of Tourism*, Philadelphia: University of Pennsylvania Press.

TEFI (2009) White Paper at http://www.tourismeducation.at, accessed 18 October 2009.

Theobald, W.F. (ed.) (2005) *Global Tourism*, Burlington, MA: Elsevier Butterworth-Heinemann.

Tribe, J. (2002a) 'The philosophic practitioner', *Annals of Tourism Research*, **29** (2), 338-357.

Tribe, J. (2002b) 'Education for ethical tourism action', *Journal of Sustainable Tourism*, **10** (4), 309-324.

Truman, H.S. (1949) *Public Papers of the Presidents of the United States: Harry S. Truman*, Washington, DC: U.S. Government Printing Office.

Turner, L. and Ash, J. (1975) *The Golden Hordes: International Tourism and the Pleasure Periphery*, London: Constable and Co.

United Nations Environment Programme (1972) Report on the United Nations Conference on the Human Environment, at http://www.unep.org/Documents. Multilingual/Default.asp?documentID=97, accessed on 2 November 2009.

von Hippel, E. (2005) *Democratizing Innovation*, Cambridge, MA: MIT Press.

Wallerstein, I. (1974) *The Modern World System, vols 1 and 2*, New York: Academic Press.

WCED (World Commission of the Environment and Development) (1987) *Our Common Future, (the Brundtland Report)*, Oxford: Oxford University Press.

Wearing, S., Lyns, K. and Snead, S. (2010) Volunteer Tourism in Liburd, J. and Edwards, D. (eds) *Understanding Sustainable Tourism Development*, Oxford: Goodfellow Publishers, 188–204

World Conservation Union (1980) *World Conservation Strategy: Living Resource Conservation for Sustainable Development*, Gland, Switzerland: World Conservation Union.

World Travel and Tourism Council, World Tourism Organization and the Earth Council (1997) *Agenda 21 for the Travel and Tourism Industry: Towards Environmentally Sustainable Development*, Madrid: WTO.

World Tourism Organization (1998) *Guide for Local Authorities on Developing Sustainable Tourism*, Madrid: WTO.

World Tourism Organization (1999) *Global Code of Ethics*, Madrid: WTO, available at http://www.unwto.org/ethics/index.php, accessed 2 November 2009.

2 Sustainable Tourism Planning

Larry Dwyer and Deborah Edwards

Rationale

Tourism not properly planned and managed can leave permanent footprints on the physical, social, cultural and economic environments of destinations. Tourism development can be alienating to local residents, overcrowded, noisy, architecturally tasteless, and place pressures on infrastructure. Inappropriate types and scales of development may arise due to laissez-faire tourism policies and a lack of national, regional or local planning and regulation. Governments and stakeholders in the tourism sector have a responsibility to ensure that in the development of tourism long-term prosperity and the quality of life of future generations are not placed at risk.

Sustainable tourism development requires a process of planning and management that brings together the interests and concerns of a diverse group of stakeholders in a sustainable and strategic way. It is this complexity that demands a planning approach which is multidimensional and is purposely integrative. Tourism planning requires an understanding of the meaning of sustainable development and the guiding values for promoting sustainable tourism. It requires that communities be made to be sufficiently aware of the tourism industry and enabled to understand its impacts, as well as the various processes to integrate and engage in participatory planning, consensus building and conflict resolution among all stakeholders.

This chapter has a number of major emphases including the critical role that the community can play in the achievement of sustainable tourism development through the importance of leadership and skills enhancement, and the role of different stakeholders in strategy implementation. The chapter also highlights the importance of evaluating performance in achieving sustainable practice in tourism planning and addressing future challenges and issues associated with how tourism planning can contribute to the achievement of sustainable tourism development.

Learning objectives

The objectives of this chapter are to:

♦ Describe the nature of a sustainability approach to tourism planning and the essential role of the community in tourism planning
♦ Classify the positive and negative impacts of tourism development
♦ Identify the interrelations between the types of destination, different forms of development, types of tourists and tourism impacts

- Evaluate economic, social and environmental impact assessment techniques and their application to sustainable tourism planning
- Implement appropriate processes to integrate and engage stakeholders in participatory planning and consensus building in the planning process
- Explain the role of different stakeholders in strategy implementation including industry, government and community including the establishment of 'codes of practice'
- Promote a better understanding of the importance of evaluating progress and monitoring tourism development to achieve sustainable practice in tourism planning.

Sustainability approach to planning

The expected outcomes from tourism planning is tourism development which:

- Is sensitive to environmental, social and cultural attributes of the destination
- Provides quality tourism and leisure experiences valued by visitors and residents
- Is valued by business, government and the community.

Subsequently there are several guiding principles that underpin planning for sustainable tourism development. These include: responsibility, commitment and leadership, cooperation, education, social creativity and freedom.

Responsibility to protect natural and cultural/heritage environments

The tourism industry shares with local residents, governments and all people the obligation to protect and maintain the heritage resources of our planet, which are required both to sustain economies and to be passed on unimpaired to future generations. This recognises the importance of the continuity of natural resources and the continuity of culture and the balances within culture (Wall, 1993): to think globally, act locally.

Commitment and leadership

Destinations require strong, committed and effective leadership by business, government and community leaders at all levels. A proactive role by stakeholders, rather than a passive one, is necessary to ensure that heritage values are fully sustained. More good community projects fail due to leadership breakdown than for any other reason.

Cooperation

Since all industries share responsibility for heritage and natural resources protection, coordination and support between all stakeholders is crucial to the achievement of sustainable tourism. Stakeholders are the people and organisations who are or will be affected by tourism development either in the present or in subsequent years (Morra-Imas and Rist, 2009). We can distinguish four different stakeholders groups concerned with tourism within any destination:

- Government authorities – with responsibility for planning the resources and maintenance of basic municipal infrastructure
- Local business community – who derive an income from the operation of commercial enterprise (this group includes owners, employees and suppliers)
- Local community – who share their area with each other and visitors; and
- Visitors – who make tourism viable.

(Bushell and Staiff, 2003)

Each of these stakeholder groups has different members with different values, aspirations and needs. The planning process requires an understanding that the need for cooperation and possible compromise among all stakeholders in multi-levels and sectors is vital to success in achieving responsible standards and goals for the tourism industry.

Education

Sustainable tourism development involves the establishment of education and training programmes to improve public understanding and to enhance business and professional skills. The tourism industry in any region depends on a stable pool of skilled employees who can progress in their careers to higher levels of employment. Businesses and communities must work together to inform, educate and inspire in everyone, stewardship and appreciation for the natural and cultural heritage and its protection through responsible conduct.

Tourism plans should encompass appropriate training and capacity building at national and local levels, and amongst communities to ensure that local people have access to the full range of jobs in the local tourism industry (UNEP, 2003).

Social creativity and freedom

Some regulation of every industry is inevitable, but sustainable tourism is best achieved as the product of a community sharing a vision for its economic, physical and social character. There is a need to strike a balance between economic, environmental and social imperatives. This recognises that development is a process that enhances the quality of life, a broader notion than economic prosperity. In the context of sustainability, *development* is best described as a change process which can be physical change, attitudinal, and/or cultural change.

Impacts of tourism development

As different types of tourists place different demands upon the resources of the destination, so the impacts and effects will vary in type, location and significance. Tourism impacts can be classified into four types – economic (Table 2.1), environmental (Table 2.2), social (Table 2.3), and cultural (Table 2.4).

The quality of the environment, both natural and man-made, is essential to tourism. However, tourism development involves many activities that can have adverse environmental effects that can gradually destroy the environmental resources on which it depends. Many of these impacts are linked with the construction of general infrastructure such as roads and airports, and of tourism facilities, including resorts, hotels, restaurants, shops, golf courses and marinas.

The social impacts of tourism refer to the manner in which tourism and travel effect changes in the collective and individual value systems, behaviour patterns, lifestyle and quality of life of the host community (Hall, 2008).

Change or loss of local identity and values may result from several closely related influences. Certain types of society (small, unsophisticated, isolated) are very vulnerable to the pressure for cultural change brought about by tourism.

Elements of culture include handicrafts, language, traditions, gastronomy, dress, art, architecture, leisure activities, music, dance, belief systems, types of work engaged in and technology used, etc.

Table 2.1: Economic impacts of tourism

(Possible) positive economic impacts of tourism development
Stimulates local production contributing to household incomes and standard of living
Generates investment in new businesses, growth of local businesses and business profits
Increases employment opportunities
Generates foreign exchange earnings for national economy
Improves development and infrastructure spending in areas such as water, sewerage systems, roads, electricity, telephone, information technology and public transport networks
Increases governments' tax base
Expands an economy's export base
Assists in the development of remote areas
Offers additional livelihood opportunities for local communities
Locally owned small enterprise development facilitates diversification of the local economy
Self-financing mechanism for natural and heritage attractions and so serve as tool for environmental preservation
Provides economic support for preservation of local culture through sale of culturally inspired handicrafts produced by the local community
Tourism can be a good employer of women and disadvantaged groups and can upgrade their economic status

(Possible) negative economic impacts of tourism development
Increases prices and shortages of goods and services
Increases price of land and housing beyond local affordability
Increases demands on public services and facilities
Increases cost of living/property taxes
Increases economic dependency on one industry
Can increase economic vulnerability of an area
Decline of other industries as resources flow into tourism industry
Higher levels of public debt and/or higher taxes to pay for increased infrastructure and services
Can lead to reduced public expenditure on essential community services
Local employment can be low-level or unskilled, seasonal, low-wage, part-time with little opportunity for advancement.

Table 2.2: The environmental or ecological impacts of tourism

(Possible) positive environmental impacts

Be a relatively 'clean' industry

Foster conservation and preservation of natural resources

Encourage community revitalisation and beautification

Raise revenues for establishing administrative and planning controls to maintain quality of environment

(Possible) negative environmental impacts

Has a substantial carbon footprint with contribution to global warming (particularly aviation)

Adverse effects on water quantity, quality and use, air quality

Waste production, recycling practices, efficiency of resource use, scenery degradation and degraded quality of natural sites

Introduction of non-native species, toxins and pollutants

Habitat destruction, direct impact on individual wildlife

Table 2.3: The social impacts of tourism

(Possible) positive social impacts

Can lead to removal of social or national prejudices

Can promote better understanding and positive social change

May encourage civic involvement and local pride in a destination

Can play a supportive force for peace

Foster pride in cultural traditions

Improves quality of life of locals

Increases availability of recreation facilities/opportunities

Improves quality of police protection

(Possible) negative social impacts

Increased prostitution, drug taking and crime

Increasingly hectic community and personal life

Seasonal nature of tourism promotes immigrant workforce and attendant social problems

Competition and conflict between tourists and residents for available services, facilities and recreational opportunities

Tourists out of ignorance or carelessness can fail to respect local customs and moral values

Visitor behaviour may be perceived to be 'intrusive' by locals

Table 2.4: Cultural impacts of tourism

(Possible) positive cultural impacts

Facilitates intercultural understanding and global communication.

Improves understanding and image of different communities and cultures

Promotes cultural exchange

Facilitates meeting visitors (an educational experience)

Preserves cultural identity of host population

Increases demand for historical and cultural exhibits

Leads to the preservation and revitalisation of local ethnic and cultural identity such as cuisine, music, dance, dress, handicrafts, art and suchlike

(Possible) negative cultural impacts

Commodification: Can turn local cultures into commodities when religious rituals, traditional ethnic rites and festivals are reduced, sanitised and performed on demand to conform to tourist expectations

Commercialisation and bastardisation: Reduce or destroy the cultural value of traditional cultural events, arts and crafts, to both host and guest

Standardisation: Standardisation occurs in the process of satisfying tourists' desires for 'familia' facilities.

Loss of authenticity and staged authenticity: Adapting cultural expressions, rituals, performances to the tastes of tourists or performing shows as if they were 'real life' constitutes 'staged authenticity'

Cultural deterioration: Due to vandalism, littering, pilferage and illegal removal of cultural heritage items. Degradation of cultural sites when historic sites and buildings are unprotected, the traditionally built environment is replaced or virtually disappears, or structures or places of religious/spiritual significance are displaced or desecrated to make way for tourist facilities

The effects listed in the tables are not related exclusively to tourism. There are various powerful external and internal forces leading to changes in the natural environment from industrialisation and urban development. There are also cultural changes worldwide, from sources such as television, cinema, the Internet and written media that act independently of the tourism industry.

Factors that determine the nature and extent of tourism-related impacts

The factors that determine the nature and extent of tourism-related impacts on a destination can be divided into four groups:

1. Factors relating to the characteristics of the destination
2. Factors relating to the characteristics of tourists
3. Factors relating to the type of tourism development
4. Factors relating to destination management.

As displayed in Figure 2.1, interrelationships between the elements of these characteristics determine the types of impact, their scale and whether, on balance, they are positive or negative in their effect. Recognising these interrelationships can assist in the formulation of guidelines for types and sizes of developments appropriate for particular destinations and in the formulation of measures to mitigate adverse impacts.

Characteristics of the destination

Typically, the aesthetically pleasing environments to which tourism is linked are among the least resilient, including fragile natural areas and ecosystems, historic cities, heritage sites and ancient monuments. The more 'developed' is a destination prior to tourism development in general, the smaller the economic, environmental and socio-cultural impacts of any given expansion of tourist facilities.

Social and cultural characteristics

The strength of the local culture, and general education levels can help cushion adverse socio-cultural impacts and reinforce the positive impacts of tourism development. The social and cultural characteristics of the tourists can also influence the social impacts on the host community. The more alike are the host community and the tourist in their social and cultural characteristics, the less chance for clashes to occur.

Political, religious and nationalistic feelings among local population can cause hostility to tourism development, particularly projects involving foreign ownership. Residents may also develop hostile attitudes towards immigrant labour which may expand in the tourist season.

Carrying capacity

Carrying capacity (CC) is the maximum number of people who can use a destination without an unacceptable alteration to the physical environment, an unacceptable decline in the living environment of the community and an unacceptable decline in the visitor experience (Mathieson and Wall, 1982). There are at least two dimensions of CC within this definition.

- ◆ The **physical capacity** of a destination or site is determined by availability of space, the form of the landscape and the CC of the land. It recognises that there are physical limits to increasing tourism numbers. This notion is related to that of ecological capacity which focuses on the demands on the landscape, and requires tourism levels which do not damage the soil, plants or animals. At some point reduced environmental quality occurs due to overuse of environmental resources, resulting in adverse impacts such as increasing pollution (noise, water, waste discharges), wear and tear on historic sites, loss of flora and fauna, degradation of scenery, destruction of wildlife habitat, etc.

- ◆ **Social-psychological capacity** is determined by residents' lifestyles and interests, and their attitudes towards tourism, as well as the possible activities, behaviour and attitudes of visitors. This notion of capacity recognises that there is a limit based on the tolerance of visitors by the host population. At some point, increasing visitor numbers can lead to resentment or even hostility by residents (O'Reilly, 1986). From the visitor perspective, large numbers of tourists may reduce the quality of their visitation experience (crowding, congestion, etc.).

Characteristics of tourists

The number of visitors and their length of stay play an important role in determining the nature of impacts on communities within the host destination. For example, a small number of visitors to an area with a large population may have minimal impact while the higher the number of tourists to an area, the more chance there is that the host community will be inconvenienced through increased prices and competition for shared amenities and attractions.

In general, large visitor numbers can be expected to magnify the adverse environmental and social impacts of tourism as well as enhancing the economic contribution of tourism to a destination including the preservation of flora and fauna, historic areas and cultural activities as a result of increased revenues for admission tickets to tourism attraction and facilities. However, a concentration of large numbers relative to resident population can lead to overcrowding of attractions and place excessive demands on existing infrastructure. Increasing tourism numbers can magnify tensions between visitors and residents.

Potentially these factors are magnified by the tourists' length of stay. The longer a tourist stays at a particular destination, the greater chance for tourists to penetrate more deeply into an area in economic and social terms.

Relative economic status of residents and tourists

Differences in economic status between tourists and residents can foster resentment by locals as well as raising their aspiration levels beyond that which is realistically achievable. A 'demonstration effect' can increase aspiration levels beyond the destination norm. This occurs where residents seek to copy tourist behaviour and spending patterns. Differences are likely to be less noticeable in developed countries than in undeveloped countries.

Yield

The amount of expenditure injected into a destination will determine the economic impacts of the activity. The greater the average expenditure per tourist, the greater will be the economic impacts, other things being equal. The net benefits of tourism are normally significantly lower than the aggregate expenditure of the tourists, because it is necessary to give up real resources, goods and services to provide for these tourists (Dwyer and Forsyth, 2008). Planners need to recognise that existing industries in the host destination (including, sometimes, a national economy) may be unable to meet all the additional demand at existing prices. In reality, economies experiencing an increase in tourism expenditure will face labour, land and capital constraints. When the economy is at or near full employment, with no spare capacity in some key sectors, increased tourism demand imposes cost pressures as the prices of scarce resources are bid up. In such circumstances, tourist expenditure will result in increased prices rather than increases in output, income and employment.

In this competition for scarce resources, increased costs will tend to reduce the competitiveness of other sectors in the economy, particularly export-oriented and import-competing industries. Price increases may particularly affect trade-exposed sectors that face world prices for their products. Firms will be unable to pass on cost increases without losing market share. Any loss of market share by domestic producers means that the net gain to the economy from further tourism will be lower (Dwyer et al., 2004).

Visibility and activities of tourists

Features of tourists themselves can influence impacts on the natural, social and cultural environments. The greater the differences of visitors in appearance, language and culture, the greater the potential for adverse social impacts such as resident hostility, mutual misunderstanding and social tensions to result. Some regard the transient social relationships of the type inherent in some forms of tourism as incapable of providing meaningful contact between hosts and visitors (Smith, 1989).

Types of tourism development

The types of tourism development appropriate for different destinations are as varied as the number of destinations and dependent on the size and inherent characteristics of the destination. Three configurations of tourism resources can be identified, each with its own development potential. These are nodal, linear and extensive resources (Wall, 1993).

♦ **Nodal resources** are specific sites that draw tourists to particular localised places. Because they attract large numbers of tourists to a small area, they have a high potential for commercial development. But these may be fragile and can easily be overdeveloped.

♦ **Linear resources** such as coasts and excursion routes have considerable commercial potential and may have more resilience than many nodal resources. But there is a danger of resource deterioration. The appropriate development strategy may be to concentrate development in a series of developed nodes connected by relatively undeveloped links.

♦ **Extensive resources** are often natural areas such as national parks, and they may also be cultural landscapes (e.g. Bali irrigated rice fields). Such resources cannot cater for large numbers of visitors.

Type of tourism products

Firms emphasising short-run profit-maximising behaviour are likely to invest for maximum capacity and density as close to environmentally valued attractions as possible, with low expenditure on repairs and maintenance and resulting deterioration of tourism plant.

Firms that emphasise long-run profits are more likely to take account of environmental considerations in their decision making. Recognising that long-term profitability depends on the preservation of attractive features of the environment, these firms are likely to undertake lower density tourism development and aim for less than capacity usage with less adverse environmental impacts. Smaller-scale projects have better potential to blend more harmoniously with socio-cultural and environmental features. Smaller developments can also be designed with sufficient flexibility and variety to meet changing demand.

Fully integrated resorts (tourism enclaves) can minimise contact between residents and tourists with possible lower social impacts, but can also alienate sites from local access, reduce possibilities for meaningful interactions between hosts and guests, reduce local involvement in the industry, and reduce the economic contribution of tourism to the resident population.

Accommodation type is a key element in the tourism system with implications for the characteristics of tourists, the built environment, economic impacts, degree of local involvement and other critical environmental and sustainability factors, such as capital, land, water, energy and waste disposal requirements. There are strong relationships between tourist types and accommodation types and the quantity and types of accommodation may be controlled by zoning systems, height regulations and other complementary planning regulations (Wall, 1993).

Degree of local involvement in ownership and operation of tourism facilities

Forms of local ownership are varied and may include independent ownership, franchise/chain, quasi-government and non-profit. Local entrepreneurs are perhaps more likely to invest for the longer term than outsiders. The stronger are the financial linkages between tourism firms and local industry generally the more supportive local firms and residents will be towards tourism development.

Destination management

Although destination management practices could be considered under characteristics of the destination, they can be treated as a separate category. The extent of the impacts, positive or negative, will depend in large measure on the framework of policies, regulations and instruments that comprise destination management. Among the activities of the public sector we would find the development of national tourism strategies, marketing by the national tourism organisation, national and regional education and manpower programmes, environmental protection legislation, zoning laws, etc.

Included among the activities of the private sector we would find those of tourism/hospitality industry associations, industry involvement in and funding of destination marketing programmes, industry training programmes, industry recycling practices, adoption of 'green' tourism operations etc.

A sustainability approach to tourism planning

Taking a sustainability approach to tourism planning requires planners to be:

♦ **Goal-oriented**, with clear recognition of tourism's role in achieving broad community goals

♦ **Integrative**, including tourism planning issues in the mainstream of planning for the economy, conservation, parks, heritage, land use and infrastructure

♦ **Market-driven** – planning for development that meets the needs of people in order to trade successfully and maintain attractiveness in the marketplace

♦ **Resource-driven**, developing assets which build on the destination's inherent strengths whilst protecting and enhancing the attributes and experiences of tourism sites

♦ **Consultative**, with meaningful community input to determine what is acceptable to the local population; and

♦ **Systematic** – drawing on, or undertaking research to provide conceptual or predictive support for planners, in particular, the experience of other tourism destinations (Tourism South Australia, 1991: 29).

Community orientation to tourism planning

The 'community' approach to tourism has been heralded as a way of empowering communities and affording them opportunities to break free of the destructive influences of mass tourism (Timothy, 2002: 149). More recently it has been referred to as 'community-based tourism'. Regardless of the terminology, it is a ground-up approach that can provide the following benefits:

♦ Tourism development that is acceptable to local residents

♦ Local involvement which is seen as one way of controlling the pace of development, integrating tourism with other activities and producing more individual-istic products

♦ Provision of an ongoing forum for the sharing of ideas, communicating positive examples and reinforcing behaviour of operators, businesses and agencies in an area; and

♦ Facilitation of the preparation of codes of conduct for specific groupings of businesses/operators, governments, community members and visitors.

Local participation in tourism planning that focuses on processes of policy making and decision making of various stakeholders is necessary to maintain both the local resources and the economic benefits of tourism. Local involvement can help to forge business linkages between tourism activity and other, formal and informal, activity in the community. As development proceeds and external interests become involved, the local community may lose control of the nature, level and rate of development of tourism, unless, very early, tourism planners have established a system of regulatory controls upon development (Butler, 1993).

Local participation in planning processes will not in itself ensure an equitable or 'fair' distribution of the costs and benefits of tourism development. However, it can provide a monitoring system of the numerous interrelationships and identify any concerns about a particular type of development early in the process.

The planning process

There are many forms of tourism planning. However tourism planning is about determining 'what should be as well as what is' (Newsome *et al.*, 2002: 150). This requires value judgements of visitors, managers, community and stakeholders and the scoping of projects to identify the most suitable. Thus the following steps are recommended for the sustainable tourism planning process:

♦ Scoping

♦ Profiling (audit)

♦ Visioning

♦ Goal setting

♦ Potential project identification

♦ Implementation

♦ Monitoring, evaluation and feedback.

Scoping

Tourism planning takes place on many levels and within a hierarchy of controls – site, destination, region, national, international. Planning is carried out by different agencies, organisations and businesses for different purposes and at different scales, possibly with the aid of external consultants. The responsibilities at each level of control must be clearly identified and a process of accountability must be implemented.

Composition of planning team

Because tourism is interdisciplinary, a steering committee will be required to lead the sustainable tourism planning process. The steering committee should be broad-based and contain representatives from all stakeholder groups – government, private sector, non-profit sector, community and other organisations (i.e. regional tourism organisations).

Members should have:

♦ Complementary skills

♦ A capacity to influence behaviour

♦ Community respect

♦ Leadership and initiative; and

♦ A commitment to long-term outcomes.

Expert advice is also needed in the areas of economics and finance, marketing, culture and heritage, environmental science, human resources development and management, infrastructure, new product development and strategic planning. Consultants who have specialist knowledge and experience in such areas as urban and regional planning, land use planning, site design, attraction planning, the environment and socio-cultural issues can provide effective assistance (Gunn, 2002).

Profiling

The tourism audit covers the supply side (tourism products and supporting factors and resources), the demand side (tourist preferences) and community attitudes to tourism development. This type of audit is necessary to determine, in the light of market trends, the strengths and weaknesses of the present state of the industry and highlight opportunities for tourism development as well as the challenges that must be met for the destination and its component firms to achieve and maintain its attractiveness.

Supply side

Activities which need to be undertaken to provide information about the supply side of the existing tourism products and services include:

♦ Inventory and evaluation of all types of cultural, natural and other tourist attractions and related activities, and identification of the relative importance of the attractions, with recommendations made on conservation of the attractions and their development with visitor facilities

♦ A survey and evaluation of existing tourist facilities and services, including assessment of the capacity of the community's supporting infrastructure – water, sewerage, safety, health and transportation systems, etc. – to support tourism growth

♦ Assessment of the present use of human resources and identification of problems and needs. Issues addressed may include deficient skills, insufficient training, under supply of senior managers, high turnover

♦ Evaluation of existing training programmes, hotel schools, universities, polytechnics, etc.

◆ Assessment of future human resource needs and formulation of education and training requirements of the tourism plan

◆ Assessment of the capacity of tourism suppliers to undertake sustainable innovations.

◆ Review of the organisational structures and laws and regulations relating to tourism including recommendations for improvements

◆ Review of the present tourism plans and investment policies and programmes with special reference to tourism investment

◆ Identification of codes of ethics or codes of conduct for tourists and tourism firms and the extent to which they are adhered to by stakeholders.

Demand side

Analysis of the demand side is required to:

◆ Identify the fit between market forces and the area's assets and resources

◆ Identify the role tourism currently plays in the local economy and in comparison with other industry sectors

◆ Identify trends in both domestic and international tourism

◆ Profile current tourists

◆ Quantify the number of tourists currently visiting the community and its attractions each year

◆ Identify the potential 'customers' for the destination's tourism products along with any major product gaps.

The level of analysis will depend upon availability of existing data.

Community profiling

Sustainable tourism planning must reflect local factors to avoid generalisation and inappropriate development. Community profiling assists tourism planners to integrate tourism development into the social, economic and environmental life of the community. This step establishes the current social condition of those areas and people in the community likely to be affected by the proposed development or its alternatives. In building a community profile, tourism planners can determine:

◆ How to involve people – general meetings, individuals, sectoral groups

◆ How best to communicate information – medium? languages?

◆ How to promote the plan – relating the plan to issues of importance to the community.

Profiling should identify the various community groups and the type and strength of links between them, establishing the current trends and concerns within the community. A profile of residents provides key information on such questions as:

◆ How local people feel about tourism growth

◆ Whether there are groups within the community that are less supportive of tourism

◆ Specific issues or concerns residents have that must be taken into consideration

- Which resident groups perceive that they benefit personally from tourism; and
- Which specific places or events residents do not want promoted to tourists.

Community workshops and consultative processes can be especially helpful in identifying:

- Primary values – what is it that residents and visitors value about the destination?
- Aspirations – what role do residents wish tourism to play in the economic and social development of the community?
- Fears – what concerns do residents have about the impact of tourism on the community?
- Possibilities – what are the special characteristics of the area that locals wish to share with visitors?
- Warts – what are the things that detract from the area being a desirable place to visit?

(Tourism South Australia, 1991; Hall, 2008)

Community profiling will also help determine how ready the community is to take on a new or growing tourism industry, which requires certain supporting facilities and public services. Methods for involving the community range from formal authority over, or membership of, a steering committee, to more informal involvement through:

- Surveys of community attitudes to tourism
- Public meetings
- Information booths
- Personal contact
- Focus groups
- Press releases
- Brochures
- The Internet.

Armed with an understanding of the community, tourism planners can identify an appropriate sustainable planning partnership, i.e.:

- Driven by community and resourced by local authority
- Process-driven by local authority with strategic involvement of community; or
- Equal involvement of community and local authority.

Understanding the community is essential to the long-term sustainability of destinations and is a process that will need to be undertaken routinely following six criteria:

- Allow 'lots' of time – community groups and individuals operate on different schedules
- Get personal – an effective method of communication
- Be sensitive to consultation times
- Go in with an open mind – consultation involves negotiation

- ◆ Don't have inflexible ideas about indigenous culture
- ◆ Avoid over consulting – identify the right contacts.

Visioning

According to Newsome et al. (2002: 147) the task of planning 'is to visualise the area, that is the product, as visitors and managers wish it to be in the future'. Visioning is an important step in formulating a tourism plan. In visioning, community members attempt to look into the future and imagine what they would like their community to be.

The community should develop a vision of where they would like to see their community in the future and how tourism fits into that vision. The process of defining a destination vision consists of three stages (Ritchie, 1993):

- ◆ Envisioning an image of a desired future organisational state
- ◆ When effectively communicated to followers
- ◆ Serves to empower those followers so they can enact the vision.

Visioning requires the community to identify what is really valued or desired and including those elements in the shared image of the community. The image can help a community become responsible stewards and to decide among alternatives how much of any type of development will fit within its vision and determine what levels of change are acceptable.

Goals

Specific goals of tourism planning will differ between communities and for different tourism projects. The community should have input into the goal setting process to help them work toward realisation of their vision. Without goals, the community will not be able to monitor whether its efforts are successful or not. Nor will it know when to stop further efforts. And without clear goals it is difficult to select between alternative development projects.

Once goals have been agreed upon, tourism planners can formulate an action agenda to achieve them, develop time lines and assign responsibilities to ensure the goals are met.

Goal setting will establish a target level for tourism development. Different plans may emphasise different goals but these specific goals should conform to the principles of sustainability and reflect the long run community vision.

Role of international organisations in formulating sustainable tourism plans

An important role of international organisations has been the development of codes of sustainable practice in tourism. These codes of conduct, relevant to all tourism stakeholders, articulate types of behaviour that support planning for sustainable tourism.

Codes of practice

Several industry codes of practice exist. Green Globe is a worldwide benchmarking and certification programme which facilitates sustainable travel and tourism for consumers, companies and communities. The WTO formulated the Global Code

of Ethics for Tourism. It draws inspiration from many similar declarations and industry codes that have come before. The code includes nine articles outlining the 'rules of the game' for destinations, governments, tour operators, developers, travel agents, workers and travellers themselves. The tenth article involves the redress of grievances and marks the first time that a code of this type will have a mechanism for enforcement.
(http://www.unwto.org/code_ethics/pdf/languages/Codigo%20Etico%20Ing.pdf)

Tourism planners should disseminate this information to the relevant stakeholders so that they can incorporate it into their tourism plans.

Potential project identification

Tourism planners need to identify priority short- and long-term projects as part of the tourism development plan. Relevant evaluation criteria are:

◆ Value to the tourist

◆ Value to the community

◆ Assessment of what projects can build the attractiveness of the destination and meet the needs of tourists.

This step involves developing a basic description of each of the priority projects, including projected revenues and costs (construction, operation and maintenance), employment and infrastructure needs, and determining whether the proposed projects fit within existing local and state plans and regulations. This stage includes the preparation of a financial plan for the tourism development strategy with recommended sources of funding for facilities development.

Impact assessment

Impact analysis is conducted to predict the likely economic, social and environmental effects of alternative tourism plans. The analysis will suggest who and what may be positively and adversely impacted by the proposed developments, including the trade-offs, and help the community decide which, if any, of alternative plans should be adopted.

Tourism planners need to undertake three types of impact assessment studies to determine the likely impacts of tourism development. These are: environmental, social and economic.

A broad definition of the environmental impact analysis (EIA) is:

> A process which attempts to identify and predict impacts of legislative proposals, policies, programmes, projects and operational procedures on the biophysical environment and on human health and well-being. It also attempts to interpret and communicate information about those impacts and investigates and proposes means for their management.
>
> (Canadian Environmental Assessment Research Council, 1988: 1)

Social impact assessment (SIA) refers to 'the systematic advance appraisal of the impacts on the day-to-day quality of life of persons and communities when the environment is affected by development or a policy change' (Burdge, 1999: 41).

EIA and SIA, taken in isolation or combined, have two basic objectives (Thomas, 2001). The first is to anticipate the likely future impacts associated with a proposed development. The second objective is to help develop policies that will guide proposals so that positive impacts are emphasised, and negative impacts are minimised, if not completely avoided (Barrow, 2000; Thomas, 2001). These techniques encourage rational decision making by determining the range of impacts of a range of alternative proposals, from which decision makers can select the most appropriate proposal for implementation (Burdge, 1999).

The economic impact analysis quantifies economic variables of the type listed in Table 2.5. In undertaking economic impact analysis, planners need to be able to model an economy, as far as is possible, as it really is, recognising other sectors and markets and capturing feedback effects. The effects of tourism growth cannot be anticipated a priori. The increased output of the tourism industry may be more than offset by contractions in output elsewhere in the economy. The preferred model for economic impact estimation is computable general equilibrium (CGE) modelling, in contrast to input–output models which have very restrictive assumptions and which give exaggerated results of the projected impacts of tourism development (Ennew, 2003; Dwyer et al., 2004).

To determine the net benefits from tourism development, tourism planners must go beyond financial analysis and economic impact analysis to undertake cost–benefit analysis which attempts to measure all of the costs (including environmental and socio-cultural) and all of the benefits of tourism development to all residents (Archer and Cooper, 2005). Economic impacts are different from economic benefits. The 'net benefits' of tourism development are a measure of the gain in economic activity less the costs of enabling this extra activity. The real costs of allocating resources to tourism is the value of the output which could have been obtained from their use in other sectors of the economy. Judging the costs and benefits of the proposed plan includes assessment of distribution effects (who gains and who loses).

The decision

The end result of the formulation stage is that tourism planners can decide on a specific set of recommendations for tourism development. This stage involves the development of an action plan to implement the chosen development option which will outline what needs to be accomplished, by whom, and by what date, together with measures to mitigate the adverse impacts.

Implementation

After the plan is written it is desirable that it be broadly circulated and discussed in the community to ensure that it is widely understood and accepted. Following this, the various elements of the plan are implemented by the organisations responsible for the action agenda.

Implementing a tourism plan requires the co-operation and combined resources of many individuals, agencies and organisations. At the implementation stage of a tourism plan, government, industry, the community and tourists can play important supporting roles (Economic and Social Commission for Asia and the Pacific, 1995).

Role of government in the implementation of tourism plans

Governments at all levels have at least five tasks to fulfil to provide a supporting context for the implementation of sustainable tourism planning. These are: promoting cooperation and coordination, enacting legislation, policy setting, education and training, and monitoring.

Promoting cooperation and coordination

◆ Possibly require various government agencies to formally 'sign off' on a tourism plan by assuming responsibilities for undertaking action to facilitate the action agenda.

◆ Design and implement public consultation techniques and processes in order to involve all stakeholders in making tourism-related decisions.

◆ Ensure coordination and cooperation between the different agencies, authorities and organisations concerned at all levels and that, where such institutions exist, their jurisdictions and responsibilities are clearly defined and complement each other.

◆ Ensure that tourism and the environment are mutually supportive at a regional level through cooperation and coordination between regions, to establish common approaches to incentives, environmental policies and integrated tourism development planning.

◆ Raise awareness of sustainable tourism and its implementation by promoting exchange of information between governments and all stakeholders.
(UNEP 2003)

Legislation

◆ Create the appropriate institutional, legal, economic, social and environmental framework by developing and applying a mix of instruments, as appropriate, such as integrated land-use planning and coastal zone management, economic instruments, and social and environmental impact assessment for tourist facilities.

◆ Support implementation of sustainable tourism through an effective legislative framework that establishes standards for land use, tourism facilities and management and investment in tourism.

◆ Enforce legislation against illegal trade in historic objects and crafts and desecration of sacred sites.

◆ Enforce legislation to promote ethical business behaviour with penalties for non-compliance.

◆ Take strong and appropriate action, through specific legislation/measures, against any kind of illegal, abusive or exploitative tourist activity, including sexual exploitation/abuse, in recognition of the fact that such activities have particularly adverse impacts and pose significant social, health and cultural threats.

Set policies

◆ Protect the environment by setting clear ambient environmental quality standards, and regulating inappropriate activities that damage ecosystems, from al sectors, including tourism and by preventing development in areas where it would be inappropriate.

♦ Ensure compliance with development plans, planning conditions, standards and targets for sustainable tourism by providing incentives, monitoring compliance, and enforcement activities where necessary.

♦ Promote a favourable framework for small and medium-sized enterprises, by reducing administrative burdens and facilitating their access to capital in recognition of the employment potential of sustainable tourism development.

♦ Develop quality assurance and occupational health and safety procedures for business conduct.

♦ Develop standards and regulations for economic, social and environmental impact assessments, monitoring and auditing of existing and proposed tourism developments

Education/Training

♦ Governments need to ensure that:
   ◊ local labour is employed and trained for more senior management posts
   ◊ gender bias is avoided
   ◊ international minimum labour standards are applied
   ◊ there is support for public education programmes which encourage ethical trade and ethical consumption in tourism.

♦ Design and implement educational and awareness programmes, which will sensitise people to the issues of sustainable tourism development.

♦ Improve institutional capabilities of the government, private sector and academic institutions to innovate, manage, operate and teach tourism.

♦ Ensure effective implementation of sustainable tourism and these principles, through capacity building programmes to develop and strengthen human resources and institutional capacities in government at national through to local communities (UNEP, 2003).

♦ Educate tourists about environmental and socio-cultural characteristics of the destination to encourage sensitivity and responsible behaviour.

♦ Disseminate information to the community about the complexity of tourism and about the objectives and criteria of sustainable tourism.

♦ Undertake capacity-building work with indigenous and local communities to facilitate their active participation at all levels of the tourism development process and to create awareness of the social, economic and environmental costs and benefits of tourism development.

Monitoring

Ensure consistent monitoring and review of tourism activities to detect problems at an early stage and to enable action to prevent the possibility of more serious damage.

Role of industry in implementation of tourism plans

Industry can undertake action programmes to guide the implementation of tourism development strategies. Four major activities involve environmental protection, marketing, education and training, and using locally sourced inputs in the production of tourism goods and services.

Environmental protection activities

Environmental protection activities take steps to implement eco-efficiency approaches, in order to reduce environmental impacts associated with travel and tourism activities. These activities may include:

♦ Minimising and eliminating pollution particularly carbon emissions
♦ Ensuring sustainable use of land and water
♦ Better waste management
♦ Adopting energy efficient practices
♦ Minimising environmental and health risks; and
♦ Replacing or restoring degraded environments and compensating groups or individuals for adverse effects.

(Tourism Stream Action Strategy Committee of Globe '90 Conference)

Marketing strategies

Consumer interest in the natural and socio-cultural environments will continue to increase, placing greater pressures on fragile systems. Reviewing Chapter 4 in this volume 'Marketing for Sustainable Tourism' will provide clear guidance on the contribution that marketing can make to sustainable tourism development.

Education and training

The private sector has an important role to play in providing in-house training to staff to promote skills development and awareness of the principles and practice of sustainable tourism, and the importance of ethical business practice in tourism operations.

Local sourcing of inputs

Using local goods and services, materials, local expertise and local design can help to reduce 'leakages' of tourism expenditure and maximise economic impacts of tourism to the destination. Additionally, forging links between local providers of goods and services helps to reinforce the importance of tourism in economic development of the local community.

Role of community in supporting implementation of tourism plans

The perceived hospitality of residents is a major social factor forming part of the macro-environment (Machlis and Burch, 1983; Canestrelli and Costa, 1991). The community plays an important role in ensuring successful implementation of tourism plans. Hospitality includes: warmth of reception by local population; ease of communication; willingness of residents to provide information to tourists; and attitudes towards tourists and tourism industry.

Other critical determinants of the sustainability of tourism developments are providing informative tourist guidance and information, good signage and safety and security. These elements are important to visitors feeling 'valued' by residents of a destination.

Role of tourists in promoting sustainable tourism

Many tourism impacts result from tourists' lack of information about the impacts they may have on the physical and socio-cultural environment. The successful implementation of a tourism plan can communicate to tourism enterprises the importance of management practices that lead to visitors acting in a sustainable manner. Government and industry both have an important role to play in educating tourists to act 'responsibly'. Tourism plans should include strategies to promote tourist education so that tourists:

♦ Learn about and respect the human and natural heritage of the host communities, including the geography, history, customs and current local concerns

♦ Act responsibly through respect for national laws, cultural values, social norms and traditions and following environmental regulations in natural and cultural heritage areas

♦ Travel in a culturally and environmentally responsible manner

♦ Choose operators who are ethical and environmentally sensitive, who refrain from behaviour that negatively affects the host community or degrade the natural environment

♦ Refrain from purchasing or using those products, services and transportation that endanger the local ecology, society or culture.

Barriers to planning implementation

Extensive barriers must be overcome to implement a successful community oriented approach to tourism planning (Woodley 1993; Timothy 2002). These barriers may include:

♦ A lack of overall vision for the community and the region

♦ A lack of interest or awareness of tourism on the part of local residents

♦ Power bases that preclude grassroots participation in tourism

♦ A lack of investment capital

♦ A lack of trained human resources to ensure local economic benefit from tourism

♦ Cultural barriers between hosts and guests that lead to low satisfaction levels and lower visitation

♦ Differing time requirements for local planning and political commitments of government

♦ Lack of cooperation, innovation and communication between stakeholders.

Planning frameworks such as the one set out here can assist in avoiding these barriers or provide the mechanism for developing strategies to overcome them.

Monitoring, evaluation and feedback

Many tourism plans fail because their implementation was not monitored and they were not properly evaluated when the planning timeframe had elapsed. In this step, the focus is on preparing a strategy for monitoring the tourism plan in the future. The purpose of monitoring is to compare a tourism plan's projected impacts against actual impacts; monitoring is also a long-term process of making sure the mitigation procedures are being carried out.

Specific organisations must be given clear responsibility for the evaluation and monitoring of tourism plans. This is especially true of the different government agencies that have responsibility to support plan implementation. Effective monitoring will require the identification and measurement of indices of change (Wall, 1993). There is a need to identify measurable indices for each of the sustainable development criteria so that the sustainability of developments can be monitored and assessed. The economic effects of tourism development are perhaps easier to monitor than the other impacts.

Criteria for monitoring tourism development

Tourism plans can be evaluated against various sustainability criteria to determine the extent to which they continue to promote sustainability (Wall, 1993). Key criteria must relate to the specific goals of the tourism plan within the overall goals of sustainable tourism development. Key criteria will include: ecological integrity; social integrity; cultural integrity; economic contribution; equity; community participation; and visitor satisfaction.

Environmental integrity

Are the environmental impacts of the tourism development the same as those projected at the plan formulation stage? Are these positive and negative impacts the same in type and scale as projected at the planning stage? How is each stakeholder group performing in respect of activities that foster environmental goals such as the maintenance of life-support systems (land, water, air and vegetation), the preservation of genetic diversity, and perpetuation of species and ecosystems, adoption of resource/energy/waste management practices, etc.

Social integrity

Are the social impacts of the tourism development the same as those projected at the plan formulation stage? Are these positive and negative impacts the same in type and scale as projected at the planning stage? How is each stakeholder group performing in respect of activities that foster social goals?

Cultural integrity

Are the cultural impacts of the tourism development the same as those projected at the plan formulation stage? Are these positive and negative impacts the same in type and scale as projected at the planning stage? How is each stakeholder group performing in respect of activities that foster cultural goals?

Economic contribution

Are the economic impacts of the tourism development the same as those projected at the plan formulation stage? Are these positive and negative impacts the same in type and scale as projected at the planning stage? How is each stakeholder group performing in respect of activities that foster economic goals? Have targets been achieved both in visitor numbers and revenue estimates? Is there consistent industry profitability that delivers increased local investment and employment? Is there a lower rate of business failure resulting from implementation of the tourism plan? Is the marketing system attracting high yield markets? Which industries have gained and which have lost from the tourism development?

Community participation

Is the extent of community participation in the tourism plan the same as that projected at the plan formulation stage? Is the participation of the same type and scale as projected at the planning stage? How is each stakeholder group performing in respect of activities that foster community involvement in tourism development?

Visitor satisfaction

Are visitor satisfaction levels the same as those projected at the plan formulation stage? How is each stakeholder group performing in respect of activities that provide visitor satisfaction? Is the tourism plan meeting customer needs and enabling satisfactory tourism experiences? Is there increased repeat visitation?

To address many of the issues relevant to these key criteria, attitude surveys must be developed and distributed to major groups of tourism stakeholders – industry, the community and visitors – to gauge their perceptions.

Addressing future challenges/ issues

While well-designed and collaborative partnerships can build sustainable tourism development, these partnerships are complex. The increasing movements of people will add to this complexity and call for new types of leadership along with innovative ways of disseminating and sharing information.

Tourism planning frameworks will continue to evolve and organisations will increase their adoption of codes of practice and certification. It is hoped that simple, rapid and cost-effective methods of evaluation and monitoring will assist planners in making the transition to sustainability at the destination level. There are a number of auditing tools that can assist in this task such as can be found at EC3 Global http://www.ec3global.com/, UNEP and WTO.

Review

There have been many improvements to tourism planning and development. This chapter encompasses those new directions in sustainable tourism planning. A major consideration is the importance of the community's role in the planning process. This role must be a cooperative one based on vision and dedication. Without these, the best tourism plans, objectives and projects will not be realised. Planning is one aspect of maintaining sustainable tourism development but it must be accompanied by sustainable practices in transport, human resources, marketing and operations to truly realise sustainable tourism destinations of the future.

Review questions

1   What are the possible impacts if tourism development were to proceed without appropriate planning?

2   What kinds of local participatory mechanisms could be successful to ensure the involvement of all stakeholder groups in tourism planning processes? What possible difficulties might occur and how should they be resolved during these processes?

3   How can tourism be developed as a tool for community development? Give some examples of planning implementation in tourism development practices.

4   What role do governments (at all levels) play in tourism development planning? What suggestions would you offer to government representatives?

5   Should the public be able to review/have an input into national tourism development plans? If so, (1) how does/doesn't it work? and (2) at what stage of the planning processes would such input be appropriate?

6   How do different tourism impacts overlap in development planning processes e.g. socio-economic/socio-cultural impacts or any environmental politics involved in tourism? Any examples?

7   List and discuss the barriers which prevent the successful implementation of a tourism plan. Are there others you can think of?

8   Discuss why monitoring is an important step in the tourism planning process.

9   Is any monitoring mechanism more important than any other? Substantiate your argument.

Useful websites

BEST EN   http://www.besteducationnetwork.org

BEST EN Wiki   http://www.fjconcepts.com/besten/wiki/index.php/Main_Page

Centre for Responsible and Sustainable Tourism Development   http://www.cenort.org.yu

Global Development Research Center (GDRC) – also the Sustainable Tourism Gateway
http://www.gdrc.org/sustdev/index.html
http://www.gdrc.org/uem/eco-tour/eco-tour.html

Global Partnership for Sustainable Tourism Criteria (GSTC Partnership)
http://www.sustainabletourismcriteria.org/

GREEN GLOBE   http://www.greenglobeint.com/

International Tourism Partnership   http://www.tourismpartnership.org

United Nations Environment Programme   http://www.unep.org/

United Nations World Tourism Organization   http://www.unwto.org/

References

Archer, B. and Cooper, C. (2005) 'The positive and negative impacts of tourism', in W. Theobald (ed.), *Global Tourism: The Next Decade*, 3d edn, Oxford: Butterworth-Heinemann, pp. 79-102.

Barrow, C.J. (2000) Social Impact Assessment: An Introduction, London: Arnold Publishers.

Burdge, R.J. (1999) *A Community Guide to Social Impact Assessment*, revised edn, WI: Social Ecology Press.

Bushell, R. and Staiff, R. (eds) (2003) *Sustainable Tourism in Context*, St Leonards, Australia: Allen and Unwin.

Butler, R. (1993) 'Tourism – an evolutionary perspective', in J.G. Nelson, R. Butler and G. Wall (eds) *Tourism and Sustainable Development: Monitoring, Planning, Managing*, Heritage Resources Centre, Joint Publication Number 2, Geography Publication Series # 52, Waterloo: University of Waterloo.

Canadian Environmental Assessment Research Council (1988) 'Evaluating Environmental Impact Assessment: An Action Prospectus', Catalogue No. En 106-1 1/ 1988. Minister of Supply and Services Canada: Canadian Government Publishing — PWGSC.

Canestrelli, E. and Costa, P. (1991) 'Tourist CC: a fuzzy approach', *Annals of Tourism Research*, **18** (2), 295-335.

Dwyer, L. and Forsyth, P. (2008) 'Economic measures of tourism yield: what markets to target?' *International Journal of Tourism Research*, **10**, 155-168.

Dwyer, L., Forsyth, P. and Spurr, R. (2004) 'Evaluating tourism's economic effects: new and old approaches', *Tourism Management*, **25**, 307-317.

Economic and Social Commission for Asia and the Pacific (1995) *Guidelines on Environmentally Sound Development of Coastal Tourism*, New York: United Nations.

Ennew, C. (2003) 'Understanding the economic impact of tourism' Discussion Paper 2003/5, Tourism and Travel Research Institute (www.nottingham.ac.uk/ttri/).

Gunn, C.A. (2002) *Tourism Planning: Basics, Concept and Cases*, 3rd edn, Philadelphia, PA: Taylor and Francis.

Hall, C.M. (2008). *Tourism Planning: Policies, Processes and Relationships*, London: Longman.

Machlis, G. and Burch, W. (1983) 'Relations among strangers: cycles of structuring and meaning in the tourist system', *Sociological Review*, **31**, 666-689.

Mathieson, A. and Wall, G. (1982) *Tourism: Economic, Physical and Social Impacts*, London: Longman.

Morra-Imas, L.G. and Rist, R.C. (2009). *Road to Results: Designing and Conducting Effective Development Evaluations*, Herndon, VA: World Bank.

Newsome, D., Moore, S.A. and Dowling, R.K. (2002) *Natural Area Tourism: Ecology, Impacts and Management*, Mona Vale, Australia: Footprint Books.

O'Reilly, T. (1986) 'Tourism CC: concepts and issues', *Tourism Management*, **8** (2), 254-258.

Ritchie, J.R.B. (1993) 'Crafting a destination image: putting the concept of resident-responsive tourism into practice', *Tourism Management*, **14** (5), 379-389.

Smith, V. (ed). (1989) *Hosts and Guests: The Anthropology of Tourism*, Philadelphia: University of Pennsylvania Press.

Thomas, I. (2001) *Environmental Impact Assessment in Australia: Theory and Practice*, 3rd edn, Sydney: Federation Press.

Timothy, D.J. (2002) 'Tourism and community development issues, in R. Sharpley and D. Telfer (eds), *Tourism and Development: Concepts and Issues*, Clevedon: Channel View Publications.

Tourism South Australia (1991) *Making South Australia Special: South Australian Tourism Plan 1991-1993*, Adelaide: Tourism South Australia.

UNEP (United Nations Environment Programme) (2003) *Tourism and Local Agenda 21: The Role of Local Authorities in Sustainable Tourism*, available at http://www.unep.org/ accessed 30 November 2009.

Wall, G. (1993) 'Towards a tourism typology' in J.G. Nelson, R. Butler and G. Wall (eds) (1993) *Tourism and Sustainable Development: Monitoring, Planning, Managing Heritage Resources*, Centre Joint Publication Number 1, Waterloo: University of Waterloo, pp. 45-58.

Woodley, A. (1993) 'Tourism and sustainable development: the community perspective', in J.G. Nelson, R. Butler and G. Wall (eds), *Tourism and Sustainable Development: Monitoring, Planning, Managing Heritage Resources*, Centre Joint Publication Number 1, Waterloo: University of Waterloo, pp. 135-148.

3 Sustainable Operations Management

Rajka Presbury and Deborah Edwards

Rationale

Unlike many business sectors, tourism is an amalgamation of various industries offering products and services ranging from airline and cruise ship travel and accommodation to restaurant meals, entertainment, souvenirs and gifts, park services, recreational vehicles, resort development, safaris, leisure and recreational opportunities.

There is growing recognition that established management practices have led to undesirable social and environmental impacts, some of which, in turn, threaten the sustainability of tourism operations. It is consequently the management of tourism operations, at the local and individual level, that has major implications for sustainability. It is essential that forces of change begin with company policy and actions at the organisational level.

The aim of this chapter is to introduce, discuss and analyse sustainable tourism as applied to real tourism operations. This chapter will introduce students to the principles of sustainable operations, will explore the ways in which tourism operations can progress to limit their negative impact and play a more responsible part in tourism sustainability.

Learning objectives

After reading this chapter, students should be able to:

- Understand key sustainability principles as they apply to operations management in tourism
- Identify the potential socio-cultural, environmental and economic impacts of tourism businesses
- Identify strategies to balance environmental and socio-cultural sustainability with economic viability
- Implement key sustainability practices in tourism operations; and
- Evaluate performance in achieving sustainable practice in tourism operations.

Identification

International agencies such as the United Nations World Tourism Organization (UNWTO) and the United Nations Environment Programme (UNEP) have called upon the tourism industry to develop environmentally, socially and culturally compatible forms of tourism. They are also seeking to continue the development and implementation of voluntary initiatives in support of sustainable tourism development, such that forms of tourism and initiatives meet, or preferably exceed, relevant local, national, regional or international standards.

Sustainable businesses have interdependent economic, environmental and social objectives and understand that long-term viability depends on integrating all three objectives in decision making. Rather than regarding social and environmental objectives as costs, a sustainable enterprise seeks opportunities for profit in achieving these goals by adopting business strategies and activities that meet the needs of the enterprise and its stakeholders today while protecting and enhancing the human and natural resources that will be needed in the future (Dyllick and Hockerts, 2002). A sustainable business incorporates profit, people and the planet into the culture, strategy and operations of companies (Kleindorfer et al., 2005: 482). This philosophy moves operations management from a concentration on cost to an increasing connectedness with sustainability.

Operations management

Operations management is concerned with 'the design, operation, and improvement of the systems that create and deliver the firm's primary products and services' (Chase et al., 2006: 9). It is managing a particular operation on a day-to-day basis and marshalling the physical equipment, the human resources and the service activities to ensure long-term sustainability. Operations management in tourism and hospitality is a complex web of process, design, capacity planning, inventory control, servicescape, productivity, quality and innovation. It is complicated by the fact that there are many types of operations, which have different bundles of customers, materials and information processing designed to provide products and services to different market segments (Wood and Brotherton, 2008).

Operations manager

Thus the role of an *operations manager* has far-reaching responsibilities, which impact on sustainability. Elliott (2001: 16) points to:

♦ **Product**: responsibility for the design of the operation in order to incorporate safety features, the minimisation of emissions, noise, dust migration, radioactivity, the collection and handling of waste;

♦ **Plant:** responsibility for site selection for output of the goods and services and the processes chosen to deliver that output, whilst always being mindful of staff, customer and community safety;

♦ **Process:** responsibility for the systems and procedures of the operation, particularly in choosing: an appropriate staff skills mix, materials, logistics, operating costs, quality, speed, flexibility and safety;

♦ **People**: responsibility for the operational, administrative and service staff levels, ensuring high productivity with the lowest negative impacts;

♦ **Programmes**: responsibility for the schedules and plans under which operations occur.

Kleindorfer *et al.* (2005: 485) suggest that in facing the call for sustainability, operations managers can use the following.

♦ **Internal strategies** to improve internal operations with continuous process improvements related to sustainability: including investing in capabilities to recover pollution-causing chemicals during production, develop substitutes for non-renewable inputs, and to redesign products and services in an effort to reduce consumption of energy;

♦ **External strategies** to improve extended supply chains and make the necessary trade-offs in the choice of materials and processes in line with sustainable principles. This includes developing core capabilities in products, processes and supply chains for long-term sustainability.

Impacts of tourism operations

Small and medium-sized enterprises (SMEs) make up the majority of the travel and tourism sector. These businesses are located in both built and natural environments where they are often the focus of intense visitation and impact, such as a resort, camping ground, picnic area, visitor information centre or car park (Newsome et al., 2002). Yet the protection of assets, for many operations, is not a high priority. Managers often concentrate on creating wealth and saving costs, a short-term approach that results in the exploitation of:

♦ **Environments**, through the misuse of resources

♦ Local **community** and **suppliers**, through inappropriate purchasing practices

♦ **Staff**, through poor management practices and lack of leadership

♦ **Customers**, through inappropriate pricing structure; and

♦ **Government** through misuse of resources and infrastructure.

The way an operation is managed on a day-to-day basis has a direct impact on its surroundings. Impacts occur when operations cause changes in the environment or in the value systems of the communities with which they interact. The ability of a tourism operation to sustain itself and the environment depends on the ability to understand the type of impacts that it may have. Impacts that may arise from activities can be grouped into five broad areas: environment, economy, community, staff, customers and governance.

Environmental impacts

Most aspects of tourism operations have implications for the environment. In order to provide customers with the expected facilities and services, tourism operators use important resources such as energy and water. In particular, hotels, resorts, golf courses, and food and beverage outlets generate large quantities of waste through grounds maintenance and food and beverage and housekeeping operations. This solid waste includes packaging, bottles, kitchen and garden waste, ill-considered use of pesticides, pollutant causing chemicals and outmoded equipment and furniture that places added pressure on existing community waste disposal systems.

A hotel can consume between 60 cu.m and 220 cu.m of water per guest room per year, depending on the facilities provided and whether water conservation practices in place are sound (Presbury and Edwards, 2004). These businesses are also significant users of energy in the form of heat and power. As heat and power often directly involve burning fossil fuels and the emission of greenhouse gases, they are contributing to global warming (UNEP, 2009).

Moore and Dowling (2002:101) state that 'accommodation and shelter provide continuous focal points of activity which range from simple overnight huts, camp-sites and caravan parks to resort and hotel development'. The situating of these facilities can lead to environmental disturbances and visual pollution through modified landscapes, land clearance, development of transport corridors, dredging and reclamation, which put views, specialised features like mangrove systems, shorelines and natural areas at risk of degradation (Moore and Dowling).

The extent of negative impacts will depend on:

♦ Where developments and facilities are located
♦ Building design
♦ Adaptation to existing natural conditions
♦ Waste management treatment systems; and
♦ Recycling and pattern of resource consumption.

As the costs of energy, water and garbage disposal have increased and public awareness is heightened by environmental pressure groups, it is important for operators to re-evaluate their operations and act more responsibly with respect to:

♦ Carbon dioxide (CO_2) emissions
♦ Chlorofluorocarbon (CFC) emissions
♦ Noise, smoke and smells
♦ Waste energy and water
♦ Waste food
♦ Garbage generation
♦ Fragile locations
♦ Soil erosion and contamination
♦ Land clearance
♦ Overuse of resources
♦ Misuse of resources.

Economic impacts

In both developing and developed countries, tourism can contribute to gross domestic output, and the revenues constitute an important part of the local and national economy (Convention on Biological Diversity, 2009). This contribution is via four major areas: *profits* earned and distributed to owners; *taxes* paid on sales; *wages* for jobs created; and *purchases* of supplies and materials.

Businesses provide a multiple taxing opportunity and can be viewed as contributing economically to local communities. However, it is worth noting that a positive relationship between business and government tends to exist in communities and countries that are well regulated and policy-driven. It is more important, then, in countries where regulations are not in place or enforced, for firms to act responsibly and undertake sustainable operations management activities.

The tourism industry creates jobs, yet it is renowned for its high turnover, anti-social working hours, low pay, seasonal employment, instability and low job status (Convention on Biological Diversity, 2009). However, SMEs can employ a significant proportion of women, minorities and young people and, due to the nature of tourism employment, enable low skill-level entry into the workforce for these groups in developing countries.

Impacts on the community

Impacts on host communities occur when tourism brings cumulative changes in value systems and behaviour through interaction with tourists and tourism firms. Impacts can be both positive and negative, but it is often the case that social impacts are value-laden and therefore perceived differently by different stakeholder groups. For example, one group may perceive job opportunities presented by an operation as overriding its environmental impact. Another group may place higher value on the environment and nothing may compensate for the negative impacts of the operation. The effects are not always obvious, and are often indirect; thus measurement is difficult and requires qualitative assessment.

Negative consequences occur when enterprises homogenise their products, voiding them of local content. This occurs because tourists desire the new and unfamiliar but not 'too' new. Few tourists actually look for completely new things. So enterprises adapt to satisfy visitor tastes in order to make money. Tourists who look for recognisable facilities in an unfamiliar environment – fast food restaurants, hotel chains, swimming pools, palm trees – compound this problem. This leads to a number of community impacts:

♦ Sacred sites and objects may not be respected when perceived by tourists as goods for sale.

♦ Loss of authenticity may occur as cultural expression is adapted to tourists' tastes.

♦ Local culture and customs may be exploited in order to satisfy visitor needs.

♦ Poorly paid staff may supplement their income by stealing and selling artefacts to tourists.

♦ Activities at hotels, clubs and entertainment venues such as discos can lead to noise pollution.

♦ The concentration of visitors at tourism operations can result in crowding and traffic congestion both at venues and the gateways leading to and from venues.

♦ The presence of comparatively wealthy tourists close to poor communities may foster criminal behaviour, resulting in car theft, stealing and mugging.

Staff and customer impacts

Managers have a responsibility to the 'health and safety of their employees and customers' (Jones and Merrilks, 1999: 145). Litter and the disposal of human waste, in particular, can bear negatively on the social, health and wildlife of a destination (Newsome *et al.*, 2002: 105). The systems used by firms to manage their solid and liquid waste should be those that avoid the spread of disease and do not put staff at risk.

Through the advances of technology and particularly television, public awareness of global environmental damage has risen. Therefore customers are more aware of and attracted to businesses that are showing responsibility and awareness for the environment of the communities in which they operate.

Just one example of this shift can be illustrated by an internal survey conducted by the Novotel and Ibis Hotels at the Sydney Olympic Park in Australia. The survey found that 90% of guests polled preferred to stay in a hotel that cared for the environment and 83% chose to use soap dispensers rather than individual soap cakes. They also found that at home or work, 91% of respondents said they recycle, 82% said they reuse plastic bags, and 46% make their own compost (International Environment Initiative).

There is a growing understanding that social responsibility goes hand in hand with risk minimisation, and that customers view the operator's 'duty of care' to extend to environment and the global community.

Governance

As governments make commitments to climate change and global warming initiatives, they set expectations for the industries that operate in their countries. Governments may then set policies, targets and legislation to regulate how operations need to be managed. Examples of these are the Earth Summit 1992; the Kyoto Protocol 1997; the Intergovernmental Panel on Climate Change 2006; and the various climate change bills currently being introduced in many countries. Incorporating these requirements into their operations will assist tourism businesses to avoid large penalties and fines.

Guiding principles of sustainable tourism operations

The United Nations Environment Programme (UNEP, 2000) has identified several guiding principles that underpin sustainable operations management. These include: monitoring, resource use, compliance, stakeholder involvement and raising stakeholder awareness.

Ensure consistent monitoring

All businesses are responsible for the ongoing review of their activities in order to detect problems at an early stage and to enable action to prevent more serious damage.

Minimise resource use

All businesses must take responsibility for efficient resource use and minimise the generation of wastes by using environmentally sound technologies (ESTs).

Industry insight: American Airlines

The airline has committed to a 30% reduction in its greenhouse gas intensity ratio by 2025.

To achieve this goal they have initiated a number of programmes to reduce greenhouse gas emissions which include the replacement of older MD-80 aircraft with Boeing 737-800 jets that have the potential to reduce emissions by 35% per seat mile; introducing the Fuel Smart initiative which has reduced fuel consumption across its fleet by 111 million gallons annually; and a number of ground energy efficiency measures.

(http://www.greenaironline.com/).

Ensure compliance

Businesses are responsible for complying with operational development plans, planning conditions, standards and targets for sustainable tourism by providing incentives, monitoring compliance and enforcement activities where necessary.

Involve all primary stakeholders

There are five main stakeholder groups with whom businesses interact:

♦ **Government authorities** – with responsibility for regulating and coordinating the tourism industry

♦ **Local business community** – who derive an indirect income from the operation of commercial enterprises that support the tourism industry

♦ **Non-tourism industry sectors** – such as manufacturing, mining and agriculture that operate alongside the tourism industry

♦ **Local community** – who share their area with each other

♦ **Visitors** – who make tourism possible.

Raise awareness

Tourism businesses have a responsibility to raise awareness of the principles of best practice in sustainable tourism by promoting the exchange of information between stakeholders. This strategy can play an important role in establishing networks for dialogue on implementation of these principles and promote broad understanding and awareness that helps strengthen attitudes, values and actions that are compatible with sustainable tourism operations.

They are principles that extend the operation beyond narrow economic measures to the establishment of sustainable management practices.

Benefits of sustainable tourism operations

The establishment of sustainable management practices can and does result in an improvement of relations with the community and local authorities. Also, many tourists feel good knowing that they have had a low-impact holiday and used the services of environmentally and socially responsible operators (UNEP, 2009).

Government authorities and the public at large are much more likely to support organisations that can show they care for their environment and community and are sensitive to the impact they have. The fact that an operator has policies and systems in place and shows due diligence in their operation may also make it easier for that operator to obtain operational permits or licences for future projects.

The application of sustainable tourism operations results in significant business benefits for tourism operators including:

♦ Saving money by cutting running costs – through careful planning of energy consumption and waste reduction

♦ Giving the business a quality image and competitive market position

♦ Appealing to a new and growing market – visitors from the UK and other European markets are becoming more environmentally aware and this is influencing their holiday choice

♦ Encouraging existing customers to return

♦ Helping conserve the immediate environment making it more attractive

♦ Bringing good local publicity

♦ Confirming the business as a respected and valued partner of the local community and economy

♦ Generating staff loyalty and enthusiasm to act as a team in the achievements of programmes to serve the community.

Ultimately structuring a tourism operation that conforms to green initiatives is healthier for occupants, and less expensive to operate. As Butler (2008: 234) recognises, 'green or sustainable development will be the new norm – and a norm is something enduring'.

The following sections of this chapter will discuss how businesses can realise sustainable tourism operations.

Understanding the operations function

Operations management is critical to achieving the objectives of all areas within businesses. It is the operations function within the organisation that is responsible for the arrangement of resources in order to effectively produce the goods and services. Therefore it is vital that managers have a sound understanding of the initiatives and approaches for operating sustainable tourism businesses. In this way they can develop sound operational strategies that realise company goals while being sensitive to the broader issues within which they operate.

The survival of the organisation for the long term and ultimately its competitive advantage over rivals is dependent on the operations function. This section discusses factors that should be considered when analysing the operation, and defines the role of an environmental audit from an operational perspective.

Each new project or facility has the potential to improve sustainability, with the benefits being not only environmental and social but also economic. There are five main forces for change within organisations: legislative and fiscal requirements, consumer attitude, public opinion, professionalism and leadership, and knowledge.

Legislative and fiscal requirements

Operators must show due diligence, that is reasonable care taken to control or prevent economic, environmental, social and cultural harm in the way that they operate their business. This is achieved through abiding by national and regional legislation, industry-specific codes of conduct, projects and procedures, the imposition of fines, and public and private partnerships for sustainability.

Additionally tourism businesses can take advantage of government policies that favour sustainable development and various incentive programmes which are rewarding green projects.

Consumer attitude

Community awareness of environmental and social issues is rising (Worboy and DeLacy, 2003). Tourism operators have the opportunity to be a positive force for change, through influencing the behaviour of their guests. Sustainable practices in water management, energy consumption and social responsibility can be communicated to the customer through the marketing activities of the tourism business.

Public opinion

A company's image or reputation is one of those intangible yet priceless assets that contribute to the operation's sustainability. Negative public opinion of an operator can destroy a business. 'As an industry tourism needs to be able to demonstrate to the community that it is contributing responsibly to the environment' (Worboy and DeLacy, 2003: 14).

Professionalism and leadership

Enlightened businesses are aware that rules, regulations and codes do not have to be a negative restraint, and can offer many opportunities to gain competitive advantage. The challenge for tourism operations managers is to recognise the full range of issues that must be addressed to execute sound sustainable activities whilst at the same time ensuring the highest standards in operations.

This kind of 'management is a complex task which requires professional knowledge and understanding of the environment' (Worboy and DeLacy, 2003: 15). As a result there has been a rise in the number of organisations, including government organisations, not-for-profit organisations and non-government organisations that have attempted to address the issues of best practice pertaining to the environment in particular. PATA Green Leaf and Green Globe combined in 2008 to become Green Globe earthcheck. It is a certification programme that provides a sustainable operational standard for organisations within the travel and tourism industry.

Sustainability requires managers to have a strategic mindset to lead their organisations into the future. For example in the hotel sector the major players such as Marriott, Hilton, Fairmont, Starwood and W are busy launching environmentally friendly initiatives and programmes to stay ahead of their competitors and reap the benefits as soon as possible (Butler, 2008).

According to US Department of Resources Recycling and Recovery (CalRecycle) (http://www.calrecycle.ca.gov/) there are savings to be made in areas such as energy, waste and water costs and environmental and emissions costs, as well as overall maintenance and operations costs. Additionally, the report notes improvements in health and productivity of people working in green buildings, resulting in reduced illness and reduced absenteeism, as well as improvements in attracting, recruiting and retaining staff.

Implementation

Implementing sustainable strategies depends on sound operational strategies. Operational strategies are concerned with managing the frontline organisational activities of the business. The systems and procedures put in place to manage operations will allow for identifying and correcting problems internally before they escalate. Proper checking and maintenance of equipment and facilities as well as periodical reporting will ensure that equipment and facilities are running well. These activities will prolong the life of the organisation's equipment and facilities and ultimately save money, as well as ensure the safety of employees using the equipment and customers using the services and facilities.

This section will consider operational strategies and systems that can assist businesses to operate in an environmentally, economically and socially acceptable way.

A framework for sustainability practices

A framework for enabling operations to incorporate sustainability practices into their operations is that of the '10 Rs' (Middleton, 1998). The 10 Rs can be introduced and implemented separately for an SME or integrated within it, as is often the case with large organisations. This is often followed by introducing an operations manual and/or training programmes, to initiate and motivate sustainable practices within the operation.

1 **Recognising** the issues, the problems, and the opportunities surrounding the principles of sustainability. Unless we have a full understanding of the issues and problems, we have no basis for evaluating and monitoring results.

2 **Refusing** to participate in activities that are deemed to be damaging to the sustainability of the operation: for example, not engaging in the illegal dumping or hazardous chemicals or a decision not to expand accommodation due to already congested roads and traffic.

3 **Reducing** the usage of energy and waste: for example, by placing presence sensors in rooms to control air-conditioning, using low-pressure sprinkler systems

and using portion control in coffee shops or restaurants to reduce the amount of food waste.

4   **Replacing** supplies and processes that may be deemed environmentally unfriendly: for example, replacing energy-inefficient incandescent lights with energy-efficient compact fluorescent bulbs, and installing timers on outdoor lighting circuits to ensure that lights remain on no longer than is necessary.

5   **Reusing** supplies in order to be more economically efficient: for example, recycling paper by using it on both sides for memos and scrap pads; reusing envelopes, with adhesive labels where possible, for internal and external communications.

6   **Recycling** those materials that the tourism operation can no longer use, by passing them on to other organisations to use as raw materials: for example, old guest towels can be given to charities or recycled for use as cleaning rags.

7   **Re-engineering** traditional corporate management structures and operations to achieve further growth and better competitiveness: for example, appointing a member of staff to develop programmes to reduce waste and increase recycling, which could be in the form of a 'green team' or a network of 'environmental champions' for larger properties or a group for smaller properties; writing a company environmental policy statement.

8   **Retraining** staff: for example, developing training programmes for top management to temporary employees about environmental issues in the workplace, including the environmental benefits of saving energy; involving staff in industry seminars and industry training sessions.

9   **Rewarding** groups and individuals within the operation for initiatives and implementation of sustainable practices: for example, developing energy conservation programmes for the workplace, with recognition or rewards given to those people who make special efforts and innovations towards the programmes or foster community relations, etc.

10   **Re-educating** customers: for example, incorporating best practice behaviour into information and promotional kits; training staff to communicate best practice behaviour to customers and visitors.

Table 3.1: Examples of best practice using the 10Rs

Environmentally friendly	Socio-culturally friendly	Economically viable
Developing recycling systems for paper, bottles and organic waste	Purchasing practices that source supplies from local communities	Encouragement of tourists to visit local tourism businesses
Reusing recycled supplies (e.g. paper bags)	Practising good neighbour principles by minimising noise and litter	Sourcing goods and services locally to distribute economic benefits
Installing water-saving devices in showers, toilets, and kitchens	Practising equal opportunity, in terms of pay levels and working conditions for locals	Engaging in cost-saving measures of energy waste and water management
Using low-energy light bulbs	Sourcing employees from local communities	Maximising revenue through yield management
Using technology to assist in energy conservation in areas that are not in use (e.g. room sensors)	Educating visitors on local customs and practices	Empowering staff to participate in the day-to-day decision making of the operation
Reducing the use of detergents and chemicals for cleaning and substituting with naturally made products such as vinegar	Training and 'mentoring' the small businesses that supply hotels	Setting up purchasing cooperatives with other tourism operators to gain economies of scale and reduce the number of vehicles coming into the area
Purchasing energy-efficient equipment, which is clearly labelled as such	Ensuring community services are employed in building and construction	Adhering to environmentally friendly operations management to reduce costs
Cutting down or trying to avoid the use of plastics, particularly portioned items	Encouraging staff and local schools to experience being socially conscious and part of the community	Undertaking business planning that incorporates forecasting, budgeting, cost control and expenditure analysis
Ensuring that washing machines and dishwashers are loaded to maximum capacity and, wherever possible, use cold water	Promoting community products and services	
Putting a procedure in place to cut off unnecessary appliances, lighting etc. at non-operating times	Donating items such as partially used soap, shampoos and wine corks to community charities for recycling	
Controlling the consumption, supply and storage of hazardous materials.	Cooperating with and participating in community clean-ups	
Collaborating with and participating in environmental conservation programmes	Working with educational institutions to develop sustainable operating practices	
Limiting the number of visitors in protected areas	Encourage guests to leave items they no longer require for distribution to other visitors and the local community	
Educating and informing staff and visitors of environmental issues		

Systems for sustainable performance

It is necessary for tourism operations to put in place systems that assist an organisation to fulfil its sustainable objectives. Many tourism operations, particularly medium to large operators, are now developing environmental management systems (EMSs) aimed at controlling all the environmental issues and concerns of the site. An EMS is that aspect of an organisation's overall management structure that addresses the immediate and long-term impact that its products, services and operations have on the natural and social environment.

By implementing an EMS, an operation is more likely to anticipate and meet growing environmental expectations and ensure ongoing compliance with national and international requirements. An EMS informs the operation as to how to comply with the corporate policy, objectives and legislation requirements. It does so by identifying environmental issues, relevant legislation, training requirements, personnel environmental responsibilities of the facility and environmental reporting requirements.

An EMS is an integrated system which incorporates ISO 1400 and ISO 14001. It includes and relates to other management systems such as the quality management system (QMS), occupational health and safety (OHS) and operational procedures. The EMS prescribes how the operation will comply with the corporate policy and objectives and with legislative requirements. It does this by identifying environmental issues, relevant legislation, training requirements, environmental reporting requirements and the environmental responsibilities of the operation. From this information an environmental action plan is formulated, which gives specific action items that need to be performed in order to attain regulatory compliance or environmental best practice.

Principles of an environmental management system

Within the EMS, every operation should have a policy statement which should make a commitment to the ideals of sustainability and which is framed to the culture of the operation. Without a policy, there is no mandate for employees, management or the public to undertake improvement plans or manage benchmarks in respect of sustainability issues. An EMS provides a mechanism through which the operation can comply with its policy and objectives. The policy should be developed by a committee, a working group or problem-solving group.

The policy, like all areas of an EMS, should be documented and communicated to all relevant people including clients, management, employees, suppliers, distributors, advertisers, public relations companies and retailers of the service or product. Furthermore, the committee should help build commitment, provide support to ensure its implementation and recognise the efforts of those who support it by celebrating successes. There are a number of principles that should underpin any operations policy statement including:

♦ Recognise that environmental management is among the highest corporate priorities

♦ Establish and maintain communications with internal and external stakeholders

- ♦ Determine the legislative requirements and environmental impacts associated with the organisation's activities services, and products
- ♦ Develop management and employee commitment to the protection of the environment, with clear assignment of accountability and responsibility
- ♦ Encourage environmental planning throughout the services and process lifecycle
- ♦ Establish a disciplined management process for achieving targeted performance levels
- ♦ Provide appropriate and sufficient resources, including training, to achieve targeted performance levels on an ongoing basis
- ♦ Evaluate environmental performance against appropriate policies, objectives and targets, and seek improvement where appropriate
- ♦ Establish a management process to review and audit the EMS and to identify opportunities for improvement of the system and resulting environmental performance
- ♦ Encourage contractors and suppliers to establish an EMS.

Essential to the EMS is the education of all personnel within the company about the company's environmental policy to ensure conformity with its objectives and targets. As the EMS forms only a part of the total management framework for the operation, it should be reviewed in conjunction with a quality management system, OHS system and additional requirements as set out by the needs of a constant review of the system.

Awards for best practice

Awards can be especially effective instruments for organisations and associations whose members do not have much chance to improve the environmental quality of their products individually. A number of private sector travel and tourism companies and industry associations present annual awards to recognise the outstanding actions of businesses on behalf of the environment. On the island of Tenerife, an annual prize has been created by the local hotel association, which is awarded for the environmental quality of the accommodation sector. Additionally, the association itself has drawn up a manual of best practices and criteria for hotel management.

Industry insight: Accor

For many years, Accor has been committed to sustainable development and has received a number of awards for its activities, such as an award for the best environmental information tools in support of sustainable development in December 2000. Accor's sustainable policy is incorporated in every level of its businesses. Actions taken under this policy include:

Cooperation with destinations:

- $1 per reserved room at Accor's Homebush Bay Novotel and Ibis hotels (Sydney) goes to support WWF.
- Financial support for five restoration projects of UNESCO program 'Memories of the future'.
- Financial support to develop small and micro enterprises in developing countries. These projects are carried out by the ONG Groupe Développement.

Customer awareness

- A leaflet for guests staying in its Red Sea hotels provides information on precautions that should be taken to preserve the coastal and marine environment.
- A comic book for children raises awareness of environmental issues.
- Support of ECPAT (End Child Prostitution, Child Pornography And Trafficing of children for sexual purposes)campaign against sexual tourism involving children.

Internal management:

- The charter is supported by an environmental guide for hotel managers to use as a training tool for hotel staff.
- Through the Academy Accor, all employees are trained on Accor's environmental policy by a six-minute video and a poster campaign.
- Development of a training guide on the rational use of electricity, water and gas for the hotels staff. The aim is that they reproduce best practices actions at home. 'A l'hôtel comme à la maison'.

Supply chain management:

- Accor has developed an Environmental Hotel Charter to be implemented in all its property hotels. The charter includes 15 actions to improve practices in waste management and recycling, technical controls, architecture and landscape, as well as awareness raising and training.
- For the Olympic Games in Sydney, Accor opened a 327-room hotel complex on the Olympic site in Homebush Bay. Its environmental features included the recycling of most of the rainwater and wastewater and 250 sq. m of solar panels on the rooftops, which produce 60% of hot water required for hotel bathrooms.
- Development of the use of renewable energies in many hotels.

Accor works in close collaboration with Groupe Développement, an international solidarity organisation set up in 1973 at the initiative of Air France, which is working towards sustainable development through microeconomics. Accor gave financial support to five projects on the development of small and micro enterprises in developing countries to fight against poverty. The projects are located in Egypt, Mali, Senegal, Chad, Colombia and Romania

(Tour Operators Initiative for Sustainable Tourism Development, 2010)

Codes of conduct

'A code is a set of expectations, behaviours or rules written by industry members, (often interchangeably) with an emphasis on accreditation of operators' (Newsome et al., 2002: 223–230). Examples include:

♦ Code of Ethics and Guidelines for Sustainable Tourism (Tourism Industry Association of Canada)

♦ Code of Sustainable Pratique (Tourism Council Australia)

♦ Environmental Codes of Conduct for Tourism (United Nations Environment Programme)

♦ Sustainable Tourism Principles (Worldwide Fund for Nature and Tourism Concern)

♦ Code for Sustainable Tourism (Pacific Asia Travel Association)

♦ APEC/PATA Code for Sustainable Tourism

♦ Declaration of Earth Friendly Travelers (Japanese Travel Association)

♦ Agenda 21 for the Tourist and Travel Industry (promoted by the World Tourism Organization, the Earth Council and the World Travel and Tourism Council).

Globally, many tourism industry sectors have responded to sustainable development through the establishment of voluntary initiatives. Historically, adoption of sustainable initiatives by industry has been slow for a number of reasons:

♦ Many SMEs, especially in developing countries, are simply not aware that such codes of practice exist.

♦ The documents do not find their way to the desks of small business operators.

♦ The language used in the documentation is intimidating for small business.

♦ The size of many SMEs restricts their ability to implement recommended guidelines and initiatives.

♦ SMEs, already too burdened with their day-to-day operations, have little time for locating and familiarising themselves with the relevant codes of practice.

♦ The codes often provide only generic principles, and businesses find it difficult to translate them to an operational level.

Certification, education and awareness programmes

For many years, management of the environment and natural resources in tourist areas has been ad hoc or based on a legislative approach through the issuing of compulsory regulations. This method alone, however, has often proved to be inefficient. Certification is just one in a wide range of tools that seek to encourage sustainable business performance.

Synergy (2000) found that tourism certification programmes generally provide a logo to those companies that exceed (or claim to exceed) a baseline standard. A recognisable logo primarily allows businesses or destinations to demonstrate their environmental credentials directly to consumers and offers potential competitive advantage to those businesses that display it. Unfortunately, certification programmes tend to encourage tourism businesses to focus on operational areas (e.g. energy conservation and water management) before addressing conservation initiatives.

To date, certification programmes have focused predominantly on the development of criteria for the accommodation sector and, to a lesser extent, tour operators and visitor attractions. Transport operations, which some critics would consider to have the largest ecological footprint, have not been addressed by many certification initiatives (Synergy, 2000).

Regrettably, there has been a proliferation of eco-labels with different standards, scope and cover which has led to confusion for tourists in their holiday choices. However, these programmes are a powerful form of moral persuasion, and scrutiny may be directed at businesses that do not consciously pursue sustainability.

Monitoring and evaluation

Monitoring is an essential component of any planning or management system and 'is the process of repetitive observation of one or more elements or indicators according to prearranged schedules in time and/or place' (Newsome et al., 2002: 259).

Monitoring and evaluation are undertaken in order to assess the major activities of an operation and determine cost-effectiveness; economic, social and environmental impacts; and visitor satisfaction levels.

This section focuses on the monitoring and evaluation of an operation in particular monitoring systems and methods of assessment.

Baseline information is necessary to enable informed decisions to be taken on any issue. In general, baselines are established to provide a measurement of significant change over time or between spatial areas at a given time. However, this depends on there being a baseline against which change can be measured. An evaluation of the impacts is often hampered by a country's or a community's lack of historic data and by the natural variability of a country's conditions.

Monitoring and evaluating an operation

Monitoring is an often-neglected activity in operations management, but it is essential where operations are required to report on the outcomes of their activities. Monitoring specifically aids in:

♦ The evaluation of an operation's effectiveness

♦ Providing information for management to assist with accountability and transparency

♦ Providing information for successful marketing and interpretation

♦ Avoiding unforeseen negative impacts arising from an operation's actions

♦ Incorporating changes that may occur in an operation's external environment.

'While management experience is an important element of decision-making, the results of systematic monitoring provide a more defensible basis for management actions' (Eagles et al., 2002: 151). Specifically, Eagles et al. identify four areas managers should focus on when monitoring their operations.

1   Areas where problems are most acute and/or where staff or visitors have indicated concerns. These are likely to include places where: conditions are at the limit or violate existing standards; specific and important values are threatened, conditions are changing rapidly.

2   Areas where new management actions are taking place (e.g. if the management plan introduces a wilderness zone with the aim of reducing visitor numbers or modifying visitor behaviour, managers should consider monitoring in that area to determine how the policy is working).

3   Areas where the effects of management are unknown (e.g. how recreation variables influence soil, vegetation and camp-site conditions).

4   Areas where information is lacking, and a monitoring programme will provide data on tourism and social and environmental conditions and trends (Eagles et al., 2002: 151).

A monitoring programme should be established at the outset of an operation's development and it is critical that baseline information be developed on initial conditions. This will ensure that subsequent monitoring will observe changes compared to baseline data and allow for early warning of future changes (Eagles et al., 2002). A monitoring programme should involve management and staff, visitors, suppliers and the community and should be undertaken in an organised and systematic manner.

It has been argued that the most comprehensive approach to achieving sustainable operations (i.e. to integrate economic, environmental and social thinking into core business activities) is the Triple Bottom Line (TBL) approach (Dwyer, 2005; Dwyer and Faux, this volume). TBL is a planning and reporting mechanism and decision-making framework used to achieve sustainable development of the organisation – an internal management tool as well as an external reporting framework.

Environmental audits

An environmental audit is a management tool comprising a systematic, documented periodic and objective evaluation of how well an organisation is performing, with the aim of helping to safeguard the environment (European Commission, 1999). Such an audit is undertaken to identify a company's environmentally sensitive activities, services and products and to evaluate compliance with environmental legislation. Environmental audits should review the progress of the organisation's initial plan and analyse if the series of projects initiated in their environmental policy have been fruitful.

Establishment of baseline information can be particularly useful for an operation to analyse the impacts of its activities on the environment. The analysis stage can identify and describe:

♦   The key attributes of a site from the tourists' perspective

♦   Locals' attitudes towards those key attributes

♦   The nature of attributes according to season, as locals and holidaymakers may value the same attribute differently at different times of the year

♦ The status of air, water, soil and biodiversity at the proposed site

♦ The range of tourist activities that can be sustainably undertaken at the site.

A year-on-year appraisal is an excellent way of measuring performance, which can then be compared to national data. For example, the Australian Institute of Hotel Engineering has established benchmarks to assist hotel operations to assess their hotel property compared to the average. Furthermore, hotels can make comparisons with other hotels of the same class, size and facilities to measure their own performance. The Australian Hotels Association (AHA) in 1992 introduced the Environmental and Energy Awards to promote environmental awareness and enable hotels to compare their results, and to reward excellence.

An operation may choose to hire external consultants to advise on management of environmental issues, set up an environmental management system and conduct periodical audits. This may be useful if the operation lacks the necessary internal expertise or manpower. Alternatively, audits can be conducted internally. This will usually be done by the engineering/maintenance department. These audits may vary from extensive quantitative measures to more qualitative assessments.

The monitoring system should:

♦ **Contain meaningful variables** that are useful in identifying changes in activity;

♦ **Be a reliable system** that draws on accurate results to form reliable conclusions;

♦ **Be affordable** – in that the operation must be able to resource and carry out recommended procedures

♦ **Be easy to implement** – making sure that procedures are in line with the nature of the operation

♦ **Be appropriate to management capability** – and implementable within the operation's capacity.

Future challenges and issues

It seems certain that economic, environmental and socio-cultural pressures will lead to increasingly stringent legislation and taxation designed to encourage people to act more considerately towards the environment (refer to Dwyer and Edwards, Chapter 3 of this volume). Therefore, the best businesses will anticipate such action and minimise their impacts well in advance. Self-management practices will increase through the adoption of codes of practice and certification schemes. It will also minimise compliance costs.

The significance of planning for sustainable tourism operations through management practices cannot be overemphasised. The monitoring of management practices against performance indicators and baseline measures will be an increasingly influential component of tourism operations. Operators will need to identify their own indicators and set them within the context of their broader environments, working in partnership with their communities and matching their business objectives with community objectives.

As explained at the beginning of this chapter, operations impact cumulatively on their environment, so there is a need for tourism operations to see themselves as part of a larger sustainable development system, where every element affects other elements. A number of gains have been made in the accommodation, tour operators and visitor attractions sectors but it is time for accreditation programmes and codes of conduct to broaden their scope to include conservation and socially aligned activities. This is why tourism operations of the future must become more interested in broader sustainable development issues.

Review questions

1   Identify the ways in which cost reduction measures are compatible and incompatible with the ideals of sustainable tourism operations.

2   Explore how improved environmental performance can contribute to successful business operations.

3   Evaluate how a hotel, tour operator, resort and tour guiding operation could implement the 10 Rs. Give examples where possible.

Useful websites

Centre for Environmentally Responsible Tourism   http://www.c-e-r-t.org/
Convention on Biological Diversity   http://www.cbd.int/tourism/
CRC for Sustainable Tourism   http://www.crctourism.com.au
Department of Resources Recycling and Recovery   http://www.calrecycle.ca.gov/
Global Reporting Initiative   http://www.globalreporting.org/
Green Globe   http://www.greenglobeint.com/

Greenhotelier   www.greenhotelier.org

Institute for Sustainable Development   http://www.iisd.org/
International Tourism Partnership   http://www.tourismpartnership.org/
Tour Operators Initiative for Sustainable Tourism Development http://www.toinitiative.org/
United Nations Environment Programme   http://www.unep.org/
World Tourism Organization   http://www.world-tourism.org/
World Tourism and Travel Council   http://www.wttc.org/

References

Butler, J. (2008) 'The compelling hard case for green hotel development', *Cornell Hospitality Quarterly*, **49**, 234-244.

Chase, R., Jacobs, R. and Aquilano, N. (2006), Operations Management for Competitive Advantage, 11th edn, New York: Irwin/McGraw-Hill.

Convention on Biological Diversity (2009) Biodiversity and Tourism, accessed 10 January 2010 at http://www.cdb.int/tourism

Dwyer, L. (2005) 'Relevance of triple bottom line reporting to achievement of sustainable tourism: a scoping study', *Tourism Review International*, 9 (1), 79-94.

Dyllick, T. and Hockerts, K. (2002) 'Beyond the business case for corporate sustainability', *Business Strategy and the Environment*, **11**, 130–141.

Eagles, P F.J., McCool, S.F. and Haynes, C.D. (2002) *Sustainable Tourism in Protected Areas: Guidelines for Planning and Management*, Cambridge: IUCN.

Elliott, B. (2001) 'Operations management: a key player in achieving a sustainable future', *Management Services*, **45** (7), 14-21.

Enz, C.A. and Siguaw, J.A. (1999 'Best hotel environmental practices', *Cornell Hotel and Restaurant Administration Quarterly*, **40** (5), 72-77.

European Commission (1999) *Integrating Environmental Concerns into Development and Economic Cooperation*, glossary of terms, available at Brussels website http://glossary.eea.eu.int, accessed 30 April 2004.

Farsari, Y., Butler, R. and Prastacos, P. (2007) 'Sustainable tourism policy for Mediterranean destinations: issues and interrelationships', *International Journal of Tourism Policy*, **1** (1), 58-78.

Faulkner, B., Moscardo, G. and Laws, E. (2000) *Tourism in the 21st Century: Lessons from Experience*, London: Continuum.

Harris, R. and Leiper, N. (1995) *Sustainable Tourism: An Australian Perspective*, Chatswood, Australia: Butterworth Heinemann.

International Council of Cruise Lines, International Federation of Tour Operators, International Hotel and Restaurant Association, World Travel and Tourism Council (2002) *Industry as Partner for Sustainable Development: Tourism* [Facilitator UNEP], Boston, MA: Beacon Press.

International Environment Initiative, www. ihei.org, accessed 22 March 2001.

Jones, C. and Jowett, V. (1998) *Managing Facilities*, Oxford: Butterworth Heinemann.

Jones, P. and Merrilks, P. (1999) *The Management of Food Service Operations*, London: Cassell.

Kirk, D. (1996) *Environmental Management for Hotels: A Student Handbook*, Oxford: Butterworth Heinemann.

Kleindorfer, P., Singhal, K. and Van Wassenhove, L.N. (2005) 'Sustainable operations management', *Production and Operations Management Journal*, **14** (5), 482-492.

Middleton, V.T.C. (1998) *Sustainable Tourism: A Marketing Perspective*, Oxford: Butterworth Heinemann.

Nelson, P. (1997) 'Waste energy and management at Conrad Jupiters', *Australian Journal of Hospitality Management*, **4** (1), 33-42.

Newsome, D., Moore, S.A. and Dowling, R.K. (2002) *Natural Area Tourism: Ecology, Impacts and Management*, Mona Vale, Australia: Footprint Books.

Newson, M. (2000) *Plan and Develop Ecologically Sustainable Tourism Operations*, Warnambool, Australia: South-West Sydney Institute of TAFE.

Olsen, M.D., West, J.J., and Tse, E.C. (2008) *Strategic Management in the Hospitality Industry*, 3rd edn, New York: Prentice Hall.

Presbury, R. and Edwards, D. (2004) 'Teaching Module: Sustainable Operations Management'. Business Enterprise for Sustainable Travel Education Network: University of Western Sydney, Australia.

Slack, N., Chambers, S., Harland, C., Harrison, A. and Johnston, R. (1998) *Operations Management*, London: Pitman Publishing UK.

Stabler, M.J. (1997) *Tourism Sustainability: Principles and Practice*, Wallingford: CAB International.

Stipanuk, D. M. (2001) 'Energy management in 2001 and beyond', *Cornell Hotel and Restaurant Quarterly*, **42** (3), 57-71.

Swarbrooke, J. (2002) *The Development and Management of Visitor Attractions*, Oxford: Butterworth-Heinemann.

Synergy (2000) *Tourism Certification: An Analysis of Green Globe 21 and Other Tourism Certification Programme*, London: World Wildlife Fund.

Tour Operators Initiative for Sustainable Tourism Development (2010) http://www.toinitiative.org/, accessed 29 January 2010.

UNEP (United Nations Environment Programme) (2001) *Ecotourism and Sustainability, Industry and Environment*, 24 (3–4), available at: World Heritage Publications website http://whc.unesco.org/pubs.htm#debut, accessed 27 February 2003.

UNEP (2002) 'Biological diversity and tourism: international guidelines for sustainable tourism', http://www.biodiv.org/programmemes/socio-eco/tourism/guidelines.asp, accessed 29 January 2010.

UNEP (2009) Green Meeting Guide. Roll out the green carpet for your participants, accessed on 10 January 2010 at: http://www.unep.org/pdf/GreenMeetingGuide.pdf

Wahab, S. and Cooper, C. (2001) *Tourism in the Age of Globalisation*, Abingdon: Routledge.

Wall, G. (1993) 'Towards a tourism typology', in J.G. Nelson, R. Butler and G. Wall (eds), *Tourism and Sustainable Development: Monitoring, Planning, Managing*, Heritage Resources Centre Joint Publication Number 1, Waterloo: University of Waterloo, pp. 45-58.

Weaver, D. and Lawton, L. (2002) *Tourism Management*, 2nd edn, Milton, Australia: John Wiley and Sons.

Webster, K. (2000) *Environmental Management in the Hospitality Industry: A Guide to Students and Managers*, London: Cassell.

Wood, R.C. and Brotherton, B. (2008) *The Sage Handbook of Hospitality Management*, London: Sage Publications.

Worboy, G. and DeLacy, T. (2003) 'Tourism and the environment: it's time!', paper presented to the 2003 Ecotourism Australia 11th National Conference, Adelaide, Australia.

World Tourism Organisation (WTO) (1996) *What Tourism Managers need to Know: A Practical Guide to the Development and Use of Indicators*, Madrid: WTO

4 Marketing for Sustainable Tourism

Tracey Firth

Rationale

The aim of this chapter is to introduce and discuss sustainable tourism as applied to tourism and hospitality marketing. Students will explore the ways in which tourism and hospitality marketing can play a more responsible part in tourism sustainability. 'Marketing is a social and managerial process by which individuals and groups obtain what they need and want through creating and exchanging products and value with others' (Kotler et al., 2005: 13). It is concerned with determining consumer needs and preferences, creating appropriate products, communicating information about products to consumers and advertising their benefits, in a sustainable manner. The knowledge, ethics and attitudes of stakeholders can have a major effect on the achievement of sustainable tourism objectives within individual businesses and within the broader tourism destination.

For tourism development to have sustainable outcomes, business operations must be sustainable. Sustainable development for business means 'adopting business strategies and activities that meet the needs of the enterprise and its stakeholders today while protecting, sustaining, and enhancing the human and natural resources that will be needed in the future' (IISD (Institute for Sustainable Development), 1994: 4). This chapter identifies how tourism marketing activities can contribute to the development of sustainable tourism.

Learning outcomes

After the completion of this chapter the student should be able to:

+ Apply the principles of sustainable tourism to the marketing of tourism
+ Identify sustainable tourism marketing practices from the destination management organisation perspective
+ Identify sustainable tourism marketing practices from the tourism business perspective
+ Understand how the principles of sustainable tourism can be incorporated into the Strategic Marketing Systems model
+ Understand how market intelligence and market research can be used to monitor and evaluate destination and enterprise performance in progressing towards the achievement of sustainable tourism marketing objectives.

The role of marketing in sustainable tourism

The overriding goal of tourism marketing within the context of sustainable tourism development is to achieve an appropriate balance between supply and demand. This involves:

♦ Managing tourism demand (the type and number of tourists targeted and their associated activities and timing of visits, duration of stay); and

♦ Managing tourism supply (the provision of quality tourism products, services, experiences and infrastructure within the resource capacity of the tourist destination).

The appropriate management of these variables should lead to the maximisation of tourism development benefits for the relevant stakeholders including tourism industry operators, government organisations, tourists and the host community while minimising the negative impacts on the socio-cultural and natural environments in which tourism operates. What constitutes an appropriate balance will vary from one destination to another and will be dependent on the goals of the local community and the unique characteristics of individual destinations.

Organisations responsible for tourism marketing

Marketing a destination is the responsibility of organisations at two levels. The first level is concerned with the destination as a whole and is the largely the responsibility of destination marketing organisations (DMOs). A destination marketing organisation is 'any organization at any level which is responsible for the marketing of an identifiable destination excluding separate government departments that are responsible for planning and policy' (Pike, 2004: 14). Examples of public DMOs are the national tourism organisation (NTO), state tourism organisation (STO) and regional tourism organisation (RTO). NTOs are the entities with overall responsibility for marketing a country as a tourism destination, while state tourism organisations market individual states and regional tourism organisations market smaller regional geographic areas.

The second level concerns the marketing activity of private sector operators promoting individual tourism products at the destination, the obvious tourism firms being the accommodation providers, transport carriers, tour operators and attractions.

The role of destination marketing organisations

The main purpose of any DMO is to foster sustained destination competitiveness (Pike, 2004). For many countries this means developing a coordinated public/private sector tourism strategy. Competitive advantage can be achieved by identifying and capitalising on a destination's strengths which often include natural resources (scenery, climate), cultural resources (history, cuisine, language), and human resources (skills and available workforce), which must be underpinned by mutual respect and stewardship.

DMOs contribute to destination marketing and destination competitiveness through the following activities:

♦ Research to establish and communicate to its industry partners' promotional priorities for targeted market and segments and to define destination images and branding

♦ Liaising with and influencing private sector partners to achieve priorities

♦ Coordinating elements of tourism products not provided by the private sector such as tourist information and destination web sites

♦ Providing investment and marketing support for new and growth products relevant to policy goals

♦ Creating appropriate and responsible marketing campaigns in conjunction with the private tourism operators

♦ Providing advice and leadership based on information sources.

(Middleton and Clarke, 2001: 335)

National and regional tourism organisations

National tourism organisations (NTOs) and regional tourism organisations (RTOs) have an essential role to perform for their destination in choosing messages and symbols that serve to identify and position or brand their destinations in the minds of prospective visitors and differentiate them from all others. As such, the images and messages chosen by these organisations can greatly influence potential visitors' perceptions of the destination including the tourist activities, services and facilities available and ideas concerning appropriate tourist behaviour.

Despite the significant promotional role of NTOs, especially in developed nations, a large proportion of leisure visits to developed nations will still continue to be made without DMO expenditure because visitors are also influenced by previous visits, recommendations of friends and the private sector marketing efforts of the tourism industry as a whole (Middleton and Clarke, 2001). This needs to be considered when outlining the role of DMOs in contributing to sustainable tourism objectives. Since destination marketing is commonly funded and carried out jointly as a partnership activity between the public and private sector working to agreed goals, it is essential that DMOs and individual tourism firms are clear on what the agreed goals are in terms of the sustainable development of tourism.

Marketing by tourism operators

The capacities and characteristics of travel and tourism businesses clearly influence tourist demand at a destination. Traditional approaches to business firm marketing have been concentrated around the narrow ideas of profit maximisation and treating the customer as 'king'. This commercial orientation of tourism organisations does not take account of environmental issues and destination resources. Instead it is about giving customers what they are prepared to pay for today, without concern for the long-term impacts of such consumption practices, in order to maximise short-term profits. Marketing towards sustainability in tourism is not just about being customer- or client-oriented. The process is not narrowly identified with commercial objectives and profit motives but also stresses the modern need for balance between company profits and consumer satisfaction as well as the overall goal of society's wellbeing (Luger, 2001).

Pressures for change from current practices toward sustainable tourism practices come from various sources including consumer choice, local government authorities, destination marketing organisations, initiatives by the travel and tourism industry, national and international regulations, pressure from local communities at the destination, resource shortages and increased competition.

How the marketing activities of tourism organisations impact on tourism sustainability

The marketing management practices of tourism organisations can influence progress towards the attainment of sustainable tourism objectives in a number of ways. The traditional 4Ps of **product**, **price**, **place**, **promotion**, also known as **the** 'marketing mix', are the tools marketers use to target their chosen markets. Marketing is a powerful influence on tourist behaviour through the products and services produced and distributed, the pricing strategies employed, and the images and messages conveyed through advertising and promotion. The marketing mix is often manipulated by management so as to target the greatest number of visitors and associated spending, with little regard given to the wider socio-cultural and environmental impacts on the host community.

While the continued growth of tourism is inevitable as international tourist numbers continue to increase, a better alternative for all nations where the lifestyle culture and natural environment are felt to be under threat may to be focus on quality rather than quantity. This could be achieved by providing high-quality tourism facilities and experiences aimed at attracting high spending tourists (Griffin, 2003).

Product

Tourism products and services are often designed only after considering the needs and wants of the visitors and the key competencies of the business, with little consideration being given to the overall goals, values and wishes of the host community. In many cases this has resulted in tourism businesses inevitably destroying the very resources that attracted tourists in the first place. The leisure tourism product is generally considered to be a luxury item, which has traditionally involved a high level of consumption and has been associated with a short-term focus on tourists having a good time with little respect for impact on the environment of the places they visit. For example, visitors may holiday at a destination known to have a fragile ecosystem, yet still demand the comforts of home irrespective of the negative impacts that supplying such resources might be having on the local environment.

Pricing

Pricing structures have often been based on maximising visitor numbers to an area and associated revenue without factoring in the cost of protecting and maintaining a high-quality environment and without consideration of the carrying capacity of the destination. This practice can result in overcrowding, place pressure on the natural and cultural resources in the host community and in some cases can result in resentment from the local residents who begin to experience more of the negative social and cultural impacts of tourism.

Place

Place includes the location of the business and the distribution channels used by the business to get the product to the customer. An emphasis on securing the most attractive location for the business often means tourism operators seek out pristine fragile environments with obvious appeal to tourists such as beachfront and alpine locations, further addressed in Chapter 1 in the context of ethics. However, it is these sites that are often more susceptible to negative environmental impacts that come with tourism development such as the destruction of flora and fauna.

Promotion

The promotion of many traditional tourism products has resulted in the degradation of the cultural and physical environment at the destination and the economic sustainability of the destination as it loses its appeal to tourists. Tourism advertising and promotion are often aimed at conveying a certain type of image to relevant target segments so as to maximise visitor numbers rather than portraying an accurate image of a destination. This promotion is a key influence in establishing consumer perceptions of a destination and indicating acceptable types of behaviour. Portraying unsustainable activities in advertisements, such as luxury tourism in national parks, may lead to such behaviour becoming the norm by visitors once at the destination.

People

Tourism marketers often include a fifth 'P' in their marketing mix: 'People'. Tourism and hospitality is a people industry and involves relationships among a range of stakeholders, including the tourism operators, the tourists, the public sector and the host community. Traditionally there has been a lack of cooperation and partnerships among tourism organisations and a lack of liaison and cooperation with local communities to ensure that their goals and the goals of individual tourism operators are compatible. This practice goes against a guiding principle of sustainable tourism, which suggests that all tourism stakeholders including the local community should be actively involved in working towards sustainable tourism, as discussed in Chapter 2

The benefits for tourism organisations undertaking sustainable marketing practices

If businesses do not accept a moral responsibility to promote sustainability then the business case for sustainable tourism development has to be made clear (Miller and Twining-Ward, 2005). There are three categories of benefits for tourism firms who change their practices to become more sustainable. They include:

Financial benefits

♦ Reducing operational costs through efficiencies and staff awareness

♦ Cost savings associated with following the 10R principle

♦ Supporting the local economy.

Survival benefits

- Benefits the environment by conserving resources
- Maintaining an attractive destination image through the management and maintenance of an attractive, healthy destination environment and quality of life
- Compliance with the law, if governments introduce compulsory requirements for business to become more environmentally responsible and to reduce their carbon footprint
- Compliance with business-to-business procurement policies
- Avoiding negative public relations and maintaining a positive public image
- Maintaining good neighbour relations and fostering local community support.

Catalytic benefits

- Product differentiation and competitive advantage through co-creation and innovation (see Chapter 8) which may include the development of environmentally friendly products and meeting membership criteria of green accreditation schemes like Green Globe
- Appealing to new and additional target markets of consumers who are more conscious of their impact on the environment and who are willing to pay more for 'green products and services'
- Meeting the growing expectations and demands of consumers who are more concerned about the impact of their purchase decisions
- Offering business customers green certified suppliers (Leiper and Harris, 1995).

For organisations to capitalise on these benefits they must first understand how to formulate and implement a marketing strategy aimed at making progress towards sustainable tourism.

Sustainable tourism marketing strategies for DMOs

Developing a sustainable destination vision

The first step in formulating a destination marketing strategy is to develop a destination vision. The destination vision drives the marketing strategy and all promotional activities undertaken by the DMO. A vision should be developed by the DMO in cooperation with other key stakeholders at the local level.

Stakeholders include:

- Local residents
- Community groups
- Environmental groups
- Business operators
- Government agencies
- Regional governments.

An increasing number of DMOs are recognising the importance of incorporating the principles of sustainable tourism development into the guiding vision for the destination. In doing so, DMOs communicate to other tourism stakeholders the stewardship principles of sustainable tourism and the goals they are working towards. For example, the tourism vision for South Australia as outlined in the South Australian Tourism Plan 2009–2014 is that 'by 2020 South Australia will have capitalised on its massive tourism potential and will be a world's best destination supporting a sustainable and profitable industry' (South Australian Tourism Commission, 2009: 16).

The concept of sustainable tourism has been at the heart of tourism plans for South Australia since 2003 as demonstrated by the 12 guiding principles of sustainability by which their tourism plan is bound (South Australian Tourism Commission). The provision of such knowledge is central to the leadership role of many DMOs at the destination level to support the professionalism and competence development of private tourism operators.

The role of a DMO promotional strategy

DMOs can take a leadership role and contribute to sustainable tourism through various actions depending on whether their focus is a promotional or facilitation strategy. For a little-known destination, the role of DMOs is mainly a leading promotional role. At these destinations, DMOs could attempt to increase the awareness of potential tourists of the sustainable tourism products on offer and of acceptable behaviour. The types of potential tourists attracted is an important consideration, as specific markets can be targeted to foster sustainability while others that are not in line with the principles of sustainability can be ignored.

A DMO's promotional strategy is concerned with devising and implementing promotional programmes to communicate destination messages to targeted segments of potential visitors. Such strategies can be used to facilitate sustainable tourism through various marketing activities aimed at creating awareness of sustainable tourism products, and encouraging potential visitors to seek out information about the destination via the Internet, product brochures or travel agents.

Each target market has its own information requirements encompassing not just the type of information needed but also the manner in which that information is communicated (Whiteman, 1999). If a DMO is focusing on implementing a promotional strategy, then the tools of the promotional mix should be used as the key tools to target the desired market segments and ensure that potential visitors have the information and knowledge regarding the sustainable tourism products provided.

These tools include:

♦ Advertising

♦ Public relations

♦ Films

♦ Promotional literature

♦ Websites/destination management systems.

However, as most DMOs only influence a small proportion of prospective visitors, individual tourism firms have a significant role to play in influencing tourist demand for more sustainable products and destinations, hence the importance of private and public sector partnerships. Arguably, printed promotional literature should be kept to a minimum.

The role of a DMO facilitation strategy

A facilitation strategy is aimed at creating marketing collaboration bridges between DMOs and individual travel and tourism firms and between the umbrella campaigns organised by the DMOs and industry marketing expenditure (Middleton and Clarke, 2001). Such a strategy requires extensive cooperation, mutual respect and joint decision making with private sector partners regarding the allotment of adequate budgets for competing market priorities.

For a more established destination, the role of the DMO is one of support, facilitation, image definition and branding. This requires DMOs to obtain detailed information about – or conduct research into – a destination's intrinsic attractiveness to visitors, before developing the destination's image. Destination images need to be based on genuine product values, attributes that can be delivered, are authentic and are consistent with community ethics and values.

A DMO's facilitation strategy can include market research and gathering and disseminating relevant data related to sustainability issues for travel and tourism firms. To undertake these functions, DMOs would need to:

♦ Collaborate with travel and tourism industry operators

♦ Use market research data to develop more sustainable tourism products; and

♦ Identify potential tourist market segments whose needs and wants are most compatible with the destination's products and sustainable development principles.

If a DMO has chosen to pursue a facilitation strategy, then the tools of the marketing facilitation mix can be used to develop the desired images, messages and information concerning the sustainable tourism products on offer in conjunction with key tourism firms at the destination. The key elements of the marketing facilitation mix include:

♦ Business-to-business (B2B) Internet services

♦ Travel workshops

♦ Joint campaigns

♦ Tradeshows

♦ Journalists' visits

♦ Familiarisation trips

♦ Reservation systems

♦ Representation abroad

♦ Tourist information services

◆ Support for new products

◆ Destination management systems.

Each of these tools can be used to disseminate knowledge on market trends to individual travel and tourism businesses, to assist them in making more informed marketing decisions regarding sustainable tourism opportunities. Such knowledge may identify potential target markets, new product development, and promotion and pricing activities that are more likely to contribute to the goals of sustainable tourism at the destination in which they operate.

Industry insight – Tourism Australia Sustainability Toolkit and Resources

Tourism Australia is Australia's National Tourism Organisation responsible for marketing Australia overseas and providing information and resources to industry operators to enhance their effectiveness in attracting tourists. Through their corporate website Tourism Australia provides a range of tools, resources and messages that tourism operators can use to incorporate greener practices into their businesses. The fact sheets provided in their sustainability toolkit are a good starting point for business operators wanting to get tips on how to make their business operation more sustainable.

(http://www.tourism.australia.com)

Monitoring and evaluation by DMOs

A critical component of implementing strategies aimed at achieving sustainable tourism is developing and implementing monitoring processes that provide credible measures of how well those strategies are doing.

> To assess progress towards more sustainable forms of tourism there is a need for relevant monitoring systems. Ideally these systems should focus on assessing the extent to which existing business practices in tourism are aligned with and help to achieve core sustainability goals.
>
> (Waldron and Williams, 2002: 181)

Marketing managers must measure the progress of the organisation and destination towards the goals of sustainability. In order for this to happen, businesses, in conjunction with DMOs, need to measure their existing practices against various sustainability indicators to gauge their progress. When tracked over time, this can also help to identify market trends. This will involve measuring and monitoring the consumption patterns of existing market segments being targeted by the firm, as well as the design and carrying capacity of existing operator activities (World Travel and Tourism Council, 2002). It is also necessary to identify the existing sustainable tourism policies and objectives of the organisation in relation to its marketing activities and set targets for operating performance.

Indicators used for assessing progress in the area of sustainable development should:

♦ Be selected on the basis of input received from a broad base of stakeholders

♦ Be designed to meet the varying informational needs of these different audiences

♦ Include objective measurements (e.g. biophysical measurements such as water quality parameters)

♦ Include subjective measurements (e.g. stakeholder perceptions and attitudes)

♦ Signal where necessary the need for comprehensive studies of more complex relationships.

(Maclaren, 1996)

Both DMOs and individual firms should work together in conjunction with other relevant stakeholders in the community to develop appropriate sustainability indicators for their destination. This will involve monitoring customer perceptions of the destination image, changes in consumer demand, and community perceptions of the impacts associated with the local tourism industry.

Some potential indicators that can be used by DMOs to measure a destination's progress in the area of facilitation include:

♦ Measures aimed at determining the effectiveness of advertising and promotional media in reaching the desired sustainable tourist markets

♦ Obtaining data on visitation and expenditure of tourist markets on sustainable product alternatives

♦ Monitoring market trends so as to identify opportunities and threats in terms of the sustainability of tourism at the destination so the DMO and individual tourism operators can change their marketing strategies accordingly

♦ Measuring local residents' perceptions of the destination image conveyed in DMO promotional material in various markets.

The data collected in relation to these indicators can then be disseminated to individual tourism operators through annual reports, seminars, workshops and public meetings with key stakeholders who can then make more informed marketing decisions in relation to sustainable tourism.

Sustainable marketing strategies for tourism firms

Before individual tourism firms can attempt to incorporate the principles of sustainable tourism into their marketing management practices, they must first develop a sustainable tourism marketing strategy. According to Lewis *et al.* (1995: 65), 'Strategic marketing includes all the decisions and actions used to formulate and implement strategies designed to achieve the marketing objectives of an organization or a destination'. Whereas marketing management involves developing and implementing the marketing mix, strategic marketing involves allocating resources and setting objectives after defining the market. If the principles of sustainable tourism are to be incorporated into the long-term marketing strategy of an organisation then strategy must precede management.

Incorporating the principles of sustainable tourism into the Strategic Marketing Systems model

The Strategic Marketing Systems (SMS) model in Figure 4.1 can be utilised to demonstrate how the principles of sustainable tourism can be incorporated into each aspect of the Strategic Marketing System. This model highlights the importance of developing a detailed strategic plan including a company mission statement, and undertaking a detailed situational analysis before developing the long-range marketing objectives and marketing plan for the firm (Shoemaker *et al.*, 2007).

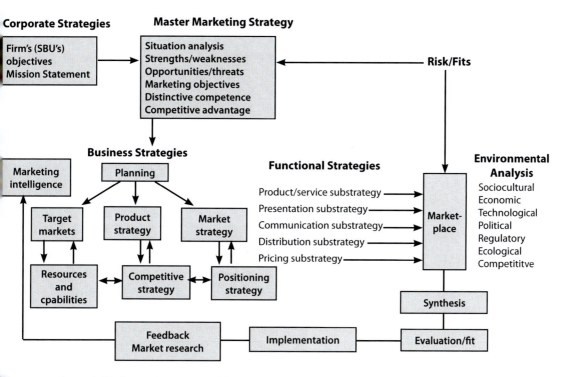

Figure 4.1: Strategic Marketing Systems model

The mission statement

The first step in incorporating the principles of sustainable tourism into the strategic marketing system is to ensure that the firm's management has included aspects of environmental and social responsibility into its overriding objectives and mission statement. This is important, as financial, corporate, competitive and consumer goals have tended to take priority with little regard for the natural, social and cultural environments. Unless the objectives of sustainability are included, there is little chance of their recognition by key stakeholders as important goals of the organisation. By defining short- and long-term goals in conjunction with other stakeholders in the community, tourism businesses can gain a better understanding of how their operation fits into the overall destination vision.

Industry insight: Intrepid Tours

Intrepid Tours is a Brunei-based tour operator providing activities, accommodation, travel, tours and packages in North-West Borneo – Brunei, Sabah and Sarawak.

Our Mission Statement reflects our extensive experience in North-West Borneo, our commitment to quality travel experiences, local education and development, our strong business ethics, and the area's potential as a unique, attractive and exciting destination.

- ◆ To operate visitor experiences that are fun, intriguing, educational, challenging, relaxing engaging and intellectually stimulating.
- ◆ To provide the highest standards of operational safety, programme quality and service reliability.
- ◆ To design and operate travel experiences that suit the specific needs of small groups, families, schools, couples, special interest and activity-oriented clients.
- ◆ To creatively integrate our fifteen years' experience with venues, transport options, accommodation services, guides, communities, activities and people in North-West Borneo into rewarding holiday experiences.
- ◆ To educate visitors in the cultural, religious and environmental uniqueness of Borneo so they may become more informed members of the international community.
- ◆ To promote environmental preservation on Borneo through operating standards, programme content, business associations and directing visitor income to the local people who actually do the work.
- ◆ To promote the traditional cultures and lifestyles of Borneo by supporting and developing community-based visitor operations and directing the income to these people.
- ◆ To operate with high standards of business ethics in our relationships with our clients, staff, agents and suppliers.
- ◆ To provide income for local partners and communities to facilitate staff training, visitor safety and programme quality, and to reduce the need for local communities to rely on illegal logging, wildlife hunting and other environmentally destructive practices.
- ◆ To build mutually beneficial business relationships with operators, suppliers and agents who share our values.

(http://www.bruneibay.net/intrepidtours/mission.htm)

Master marketing strategy

The next stage in the strategic marketing system is to develop a master marketing strategy. This strategy can be useful in identifying answers to the questions 'Where are we now?' (according to how the organisation is contributing to sustainable tourism) and 'Where do we want to be?' (goals relating to sustainable tourism) The master strategy is an important tool in sustainable tourism development as it is designed to be a long-term plan which is necessary when discussing sustainability as opposed to the short-term perspective adopted in the marketing plan.

The master strategy can enable a destination or business to articulate desirable, sustainable futures. It involves undertaking a situational analysis in order to identify factors in a firm's internal and external environments that could impact on its sustainable tourism goals and objectives.

External environmental analysis

Success or failure in progress towards sustainable tourism is the outcome of a network of forces. According to Middleton and Hawkins (1998), some of the key factors include:

♦ The development of new technologies

♦ Changes in distribution channel structure

♦ Competitors' actions

♦ Political, social and environmental attitudes

♦ Legal and regulatory frameworks

♦ Market determinations/consumer motivations.

Analysis of these areas can reveal opportunities for the business, such as new markets of environmentally responsible travellers, or threats, such as a degraded destination environment and the associated negative perceptions and lack of mutual respect, which could impact on the long-term sustainability of the products, organisation or destination. This information will influence marketing decisions as to which market segments to target, and is important in guiding the operational marketing strategies of the organisation.

Internal environmental analysis

A situational analysis of the overall resources of the firm can also enable a business to identify its strengths and weaknesses in terms of environmental performance and sustainability. Factors to investigate during this analysis include:

♦ Financial resources (available credit, cash flow, start-up capital, investors)

♦ Personnel (the expertise and skills of your staff)

♦ Operations management

♦ Corporate image and branding

♦ Location

♦ Buildings, sites, equipment and production capacity.

(Middleton and Hawkins, 1998)

Strengths

Anything that the organisation does well, in terms of contributing to sustainability. This can lead to the identification of a distinctive competency in terms of the products and services offered, target markets served, technology and equipment used, location, skills and the knowledge and expertise of employees.

Weaknesses

The situational analysis can also allude to any weaknesses of the organisation in its progress towards sustainable tourism principles. It can describe factors in one or more of the functional areas of the firm that might be detracting from a firm's image, such as the quality of the product on offer, insufficient or inappropriate advertising and promotional messages, inefficient distribution channels or an inappropriate pricing strategy.

Feedback, market research, marketing intelligence

Market research and intelligence in the form of feedback are essential elements of the strategic marketing system, as it is essential that businesses remain alert to changes in the external environment that could require the firm to change its current strategy. Marketing activities should consider customers' demands for sustainable products and ethical consumption. This will require changes to the organisation's market research efforts. This feedback can affect the way products are designed, produced, packaged, marketed and promoted. In some cases new markets may be added or existing markets redefined (IISD, 1994).

Sustainable operational marketing strategies

After undertaking the situational analysis and identifying potential opportunities, threats, strengths and weaknesses, operational strategies are used by marketing managers to implement actions that will move an organisation from its current position to where it wants to be. Such strategies allow the organisation to match its products and services to the relevant target markets, to the goals of sustainable tourism, and to allocate resources to generate consumer demand for such products.

Translating sustainable tourism goals and objectives into marketing terms is a major undertaking that will affect the entire organisation. This involves determining any modifications that should be made to the organisation's existing marketing activities and processes in order to ensure that day-to-day activities are performed in a manner consistent with sustainable tourism objectives.

The key operational marketing strategies used during the implementation stage include:

♦ Target market strategy
♦ Product strategy
♦ Competitive strategy
♦ Market strategy
♦ Positioning strategy.

The principles of sustainable tourism can be incorporated into each of these strategies in order to influence consumer behaviour to being more sustainable.

Target market strategy

Effective forms of visitor management commence by targeting appropriate and desirable market segments that exhibit characteristics compatible with the goals of sustainable tourism. Sustainability for tourism requires that the cumulative volume of visitor usage of a destination and the associated activities and impacts of servicing businesses should be managed below the threshold level at which the regenerative resources available locally become incapable of maintaining the environment

(Luger, 2001). This means that businesses must identify which segments are most appropriate based on their travel behaviour including the types of products and services they demand, the timing of their visit and the duration of their stay. These factors must correspond with the resources available at the destination.

Industry insight – The Green Passport Campaign

The Green Passport Campaign is an initiative of the International Task Force on Sustainable Tourism Development aimed at accelerating the global shift towards sustainable consumption and production. The Green Passport website introduces travellers to some of the things they can do to help make tourism a more sustainable activity.

(http://www.unep.fr/greenpassport/)

Product strategy

Product 'comprises the designed shape or form of a service offer, or product characteristics, that a business offers to targeted customers' (Middleton and Hawkins, 1998: 111). In travel and tourism, products have to be understood at two levels: first, the overall tourism product comprising all of the product/service elements a visitor consumes from the time they leave home to when they return; and second, specific, mainly commercial products, which are components of the overall tourism experience and which may include accommodation, transport, food and beverage, and attractions.

The essence of marketing is to design a product to fit the market. A product strategy is 'concerned with the offering of a range of different products and services to satisfy market needs' (Lewis *et al.*, 1995: 79). The growing number of green and ethical traveller websites suggests that there is a growing demand for quality tourism products that are sensitive to their surrounding cultural and physical environments. This in turn has led to the emergence of a variety of green tourism accreditation schemes for tour operators and accommodation providers such as Green Globe, the Green Tourism Business Scheme, Ecolabel and the Green Key programmes. These schemes aim to formally recognise those tourism organisations that are actively committed to the protection of the environment. Tourism organisations should consider how their product strategies can lead to the development of more sustainable tourism products that meet the criteria of these accreditation schemes so that they can achieve the benefits that come with a positive environmental image allowing them to capitalise on growing consumer demand for sustainable tourism products.

Industry insight: 'The Green Key' accreditation scheme

The Green Key is an international eco-label for leisure organisations. It originated in Denmark for the hotel industry but now exists in 13 countries and incorporates hotels, youth hostels, conference and holiday centres and campsites. Organisations awarded the Green Key fulfil technical criteria, management criteria and criteria on communication. Onsite checks are performed regularly on all Green Key owners. The Green Key is unique among tourism eco-labels as it also focuses on environmental education. The firm's staff, guests and suppliers all have a role to play in the achievement of the Green Key criteria. In each country a national steering group with representation from authorities, NGOs and business associations look after national Green Key activities and approves all applications from new Green Key businesses. Each business periodically receives a control visit from the national Green Key operator to ensure they are adhering to the accreditation criteria. Research suggests that Green Key businesses use up to 20% less electricity, 25% less energy for heating, and 27% less water per guest.

(http://www.kmvk.nl/greenkey/about.lp)

Competitive strategy

In developing a competitive strategy the firm chooses its competition including when and where it will compete. Based on objective situational analysis of where it is now, where it wants to be and how it can get there. In order to succeed, it is important to find a market where there is clear advantage and matching the product strengths with the chosen market (Lewis *et al.*, 1995).

In choosing where to compete, tourism firms should adopt a long-term view. There are numerous examples of firms that have opted for a short-term view, focusing on attracting the maximum number of visitors and associated expenditure in the shortest period of time. Such a short-term outlook has resulted in many firms contributing to the degradation of the attractions at the destination that appealed to tourists in the first place, leading to a decline in tourist visitation and revenue in the long term. Such an outlook is incompatible with sustainable tourism operations and sound destination stewardship.

Porter (1980) suggests that firms compete using one of three generic strategies cost leadership, differentiation, and focus or niche marketing. In marketing for sustainable tourism, firms need to consider how each of these strategies might impact upon the achievement of sustainable tourism objectives.

Cost leadership

Cost leadership is a strategy commonly used by tourism firms aimed at reducing operating costs and in turn product prices in an attempt to increase the volume of tourist visitation. To ensure that such a strategy is consistent with the sustainable tourism objectives of the business, managers should consider how their pricing strategy will impact not only on tourist demand for their products but also on the environments at the destination. Issues for consideration here include:

- The volume of tourist flow that is deemed appropriate
- The types of tourists being attracted
- The activities undertaken by such tourists
- The compatibility of these factors with the goals and quality of life of the local community.

Prices reflect commercial judgements of what the market will bear and they effectively determine the nature of the segments to be attracted and the volume or capacity to be offered. Cost leadership tactics enable a business to match its competitors' offers and are commonly used by tourism firms to address the issue of the perishability of their products, by selling any unsold capacity at the last minute. This process often dictates the price of products in the short term.

When formulating a pricing strategy, businesses should consider the various costs that need to be covered such as purchasing equipment, paying staff, training and overheads. The cost of environmental access, protection and management should also be factored into the costs that need to be covered by the product price, so that the environment is no longer treated as a free public good. Until this happens, environmental degradation and unsustainable practices will continue to take place.

Differentiation

Differentiation means differentiating a product or service from those of other firms in the entire potential market (Lewis *et al.*, 1995). If a business can distinguish its product or service from those of its competitors, then it is assumed that the customer will perceive greater utility, better price/value or better problem solution in the firm's product, and this will result in increased demand for the product.

Tourism firms can differentiate their product by offering a sustainable alternative to existing products on the market. Differentiation may be through attributes of the product itself such as environmentally friendly features, ethical purchasing or through advertising and promotion, which emphasise the benefits of using sustainable alternatives.

Focus/niche marketing

This strategy involves a business seeking out a unique market niche so as to avoid confrontation with other large competitors. Here the firm dedicates itself to serving one tourist market or focusing on one specific tourist activity so as to reduce the amount of overall direct competition. Ongoing market research can allude to emerging sustainable tourism markets and associated needs and demands upon which individual firms can choose to focus their marketing efforts so as to create new products or to market old products in new ways. For example while safari tourism operations in Kenya and Tanzania are not new, the approach to marketing and providing these products is. The new approach takes into account the need to impact as little as possible on the flora and fauna of the safari area. At the same time the economic value of the safari helps to preserve the product and this helps to attract tourists concerned about their impact on the environment (Edgell, 2006).

Market strategy

Market strategy is concerned with reaching the market with the product. This can be done by taking the product to the market or by getting the market to the product. A market strategy is important because if a business cannot reach the desired market even the best product and most well-defined strategy will fail (Lewis *et al.*, 1995).

Taking the product to the market

Incorporating sustainable tourism principles into this strategy means using the distribution system to take the sustainable tourism product to the market. Once appropriate markets have been identified, this strategy involves making the new more sustainable tourism products more accessible for these markets. This could involve a business forming new cooperative relationships with travel intermediaries to distribute the new products. In developing countries in particular, tour operators are a powerful influence over the type of tourist attracted, when they visit and the activities they undertake. Therefore it is important that the objectives of these tour operators are in accordance with the sustainable tourism objectives of the business.

This strategy may also involve using new or different types of distribution channels such as the Internet, which involves a reduced level of resource consumption and enables the business to be accessible to a greater number of potential tourists irrespective of where they are located.

Getting the market to the product

Promotion can be used to manage visitor demand by communicating certain messages about an organisation or destination's product offerings, which, in turn, influence the ideas, perceptions and expectations that potential visitors have of it.

This strategy would require that marketers choose appropriate tools from the promotional mix to reach potential tourist markets with relevant images, messages and information about sustainable tourism product alternatives. Increasingly this will involve taking advantage of new technologies such as the Internet and new social media, to increase the awareness of potential tourists of sustainable tourism products, allowing them to make online reservations, and to disseminate pre-trip information aimed at educating potential tourists about the benefits of choosing a more sustainable tourism product and about appropriate tourist behaviour. The use of these technologies will allow businesses to provide up-to-date information and reduce the number of hard-copy glossy brochures that are produced, reduce promotional costs and environmental waste.

Positioning strategy

Positioning is the act of designing the company's offer and image so that it occupies a distinct and valued place in the target customers' minds

(Kotler et al., 1996: 368).

It involves the company deciding how many differences and which differences to promote to the target customers. Many of the demand patterns in tourism reflect the unsustainable lifestyles of industrialised consumer societies. The overconsumption of resources by tourists and tourism infrastructure is incompatible with sustainable tourism development. Tourists often lack information and awareness about their impact in a different culture and environment, about their impacts on socio-economic and socio-cultural development and about the environmental costs of tourism. Tourism marketers have a role to play in educating the consumer about the impact of their travel behaviour and increasing their awareness of sustainable tourism principles. The media can be used to influence consumer travel decisions and tourist behaviour during all stages of the trip. Marketing managers can create and increase tourist awareness of responsible behaviour by promoting examples of best practice. Buyers tend to remember 'number one' messages or positions, such as 'best quality', 'best service' and 'lowest price'. At a time when there is increasing consumer concern for the environment, firms can also position themselves in the minds of their target customers by emphasising 'best environmental practice'. If a tourism firm continues to reinforce this position and convincingly delivers on it, it will probably be best known and recalled for this strength.

Monitoring and evaluation by tourism firms

Stakeholder analysis

Stakeholder involvement is an essential ingredient in the development of sustainable tourism strategies. There is a need to conduct evaluation to ensure that the goals and practices of individual tourism operators are in line with the goals and values of the host community. Stakeholder analysis is required early in the process, in order to identify all the parties that are directly or indirectly affected by the enterprise's operations. This should set out the issues, concerns and information needs of the stakeholders with respect to the organisation's sustainable tourism development activities. This in turn will lead to greater corporate accountability.

As tourism products and destinations face even greater competition, tourism operators who compete at the local level will be bound together in cooperative agreements such as joint marketing campaigns. Competition will be replaced by 'co-opetition', whereby local cooperation will allow tourism operators to meet competition more effectively regionally, nationally and internationally (Edgell, 2006).

External monitoring system

An effective external monitoring system is necessary for marketing managers to ensure that their marketing strategies, policies, objectives and management systems are appropriate for the rapidly changing external environment in which they operate. Information should be obtained on:

♦ New proposed legislation as it affects marketers

♦ Industry practices and standards as they relate to new product development, labelling, branding, packaging, pricing and advertising and promotion

♦ Competitor strategies

♦ Community and special interest group policies and activities

♦ Technical developments that could impact on the viability of existing products and provide opportunities for new developments in sustainable tourism;

♦ Impacts of the tourism activity on the community and environment (refer to Dwyer and Edwards, Chapter 3 of this volume).

The external monitoring system for individual travel and tourism businesses should also attempt to measure the following:

♦ Customer needs and visitor demand for sustainable tourism products (such feedback can affect the way products are designed, produced, packaged, marketed and promoted)

♦ Tourist perceptions of the prices of sustainable tourism products in comparison to their alternatives

♦ Tourist awareness of sustainable tourism products

♦ The effectiveness of promotional activities aimed at increasing potential visitor awareness of sustainable tourism products and the associated destination image;

♦ Progress towards reducing consumption of scarce resources

♦ Tourist and local resident perceptions of the accuracy of pre-trip product information

♦ Compliance of business marketing activities with sound environmental policy and practice, industry regulations, and marketing and sustainable tourism codes of conduct

♦ Local resident perceptions of business activities

♦ Collaborative arrangements between the business and other private and public sector organisations

♦ Tourist and local resident knowledge of the organisation's sustainable tourism products

♦ Effectiveness of advertising and promotional activities in generating demand for sustainable tourism products

♦ Performance of the business in comparison to competitors in terms of achieving sustainable tourism objectives; and

♦ Compliance of the business with the overall goals of the destination.

Internal monitoring processes

Performance monitoring is an important element of the marketing management process. Monitoring of marketing activities and outputs should be done on an ongoing basis. Internal monitoring may involve:

♦ Reviewing reports submitted by marketing managers

♦ Holding regular meetings with subordinates to review reports and to seek input on how procedures and reporting systems might be improved

♦ Conducting internal environmental audits to monitor the implementation of management policies for sustainable tourism in the area of marketing;

♦ Undertaking internal audits to monitor the marketing department's compliance with environmental policies and legislation.

(IISD, 2009)

Review

In today's rapidly changing business environment, it is imperative that businesses remain alert to emerging market trends and change their business practices accordingly, if they are to remain competitive. As tourists are becoming more educated and increasingly sophisticated in their consumption patterns and as they demand better quality tourism products and experiences, travel and tourism firms will need to respond with more creative marketing strategies based on better quality products and more informative and trustworthy advertising messages.

Those firms that are proactive in responding to this demand for quality tourism products will be more competitive than those firms that are reactive and only respond to environmental concerns when faced with regulatory pressure. Destination marketing organisations and individual travel and tourism firms can capitalise on this new wave of sophisticated travellers by formulating marketing strategies that are in accordance with the sustainable tourism goals of the destination in which they operate.

By implementing marketing strategies that are based on the issue of sustainability, and monitoring and evaluating their progress towards achieving these goals, operations can maximise their ability to remain competitive in the global market place. At the same time they can ensure that the integrity of the social, cultural and physical environments of the destination in which they operate is maintained for present and future generations.

Review questions

1   Think of a travel and tourism firm that you are familiar with. Discuss how each of the 5Ps in this business might be impacting on the sustainable tourism goals of the destination in which the firm operates.

2   Identify the key stakeholders that a marketing manager of a five-star hotel would need to consult with when developing an appropriate marketing strategy. Why is it important for the marketing manager to liaise with these stakeholder groups?

3   Explain why it is important that the marketing manager of this five-star hotel conducts an external environmental analysis when developing a master strategy that is in line with sustainable tourism principles. Identify one opportunity and one threat in each of the six external environments that could impact on sustainability at the destination.

References

Edgell, D. (2006) *Managing Sustainable Tourism: A Legacy for the Future*, New York: Haworth Hospitality Press.

South Australian Tourism Commission (2009) *South Australian Tourism Plan 2009–2014* at www.tourism.sa.gov.au/tourism/plan/Tourism_Plan_09-14.pdf, (2 March 2010).

Green Accreditation Scheme, at http://www.kmvk.nl/greenkey/about.lp, accessed 17 October 2009.

Green Passport Campaign, at http://www.unep.fr/greenpassport/, accessed 17 October 2009.

Griffin, T. (2003) 'An optimistic perspective on tourism's sustainability', in R. Harris, T. Griffin and P. Williams (eds), *Sustainable Tourism: A Global Perspective*, Burlington, MA: Elsevier Butterworth-Heinemann.

IISD (International Institute for Sustainable Development) at http://www.iisd.org, accessed 12 October 2009.

Intrepid Tours Mission Statement at http://www.bruneibay.net/intrepidtours/mission.htm, accessed 16 November 2009.

Kotler, P., Ang, S.H., Leong, S.M. and Tan, C.T. (1996) *Marketing Management: An Asian Perspective*, Singapore: Prentice Hall.

Kotler, P., Bowen, J. and Makens, J. (2005) *Marketing for Hospitality and Tourism*, 4th edn, Englewood Cliffs, NJ: Prentice Hall.

Leiper, N. and Harris, R. (1995) *Sustainable Tourism: An Australian Perspective*, Chatswood, Australia: Butterworth-Heinemann.

Lewis, R., Chambers, R. and Chacko, H. (1995) *Marketing Leadership in Hospitality: Foundations and Practices*, 2nd edn, New York: Van Nostrand Reinehold.

Luger, K. (2001) *Sustainability and Quality Tourism: Setting the Agenda for Another Marketing Perspective*, Salzburg: University of Salzburg.

Maclaren, V.W. (1996) *Developing Indicators for Urban Sustainability: A Focus on the Canadian Experience*, Toronto: Intergovernmental Committee on Urban and Regional Research (ICURR).

Middleton, V.T.C. and Clarke, J. (2001) *Marketing in Travel and Tourism*, 3rd edn, Oxford: Butterworth-Heinemann.

Middleton, V.T.C. and Hawkins, R. (1998) *Sustainable Tourism: A Marketing Perspective*, Oxford: Butterworth-Heinemann.

Miller, G. and Twining-Ward, L. (2005) *Monitoring for a Sustainable Transition: The Challenge of Developing and Using Indicators*, Wallingford: CABI Publishing.

Pike, S. (2004) *Destination Marketing Organisations*, Amsterdam: Elsevier.

Porter, M.E. (1980) *Competitive Strategy: Techniques for Analysing Industry and Competitors*, New York: Free Press.

Shoemaker, S., Lewis, R. and Yesawich, P. (2007) *Marketing Leadership in Hospitality and Tourism: Strategies and Tactics for Competitive Advantage*, 4th edn, Pearson Education.

South Australian Tourism Commission at http://www.tourism.sa.gov.au/tourism/publications.asp, accessed 17 October 2009.

Waldron, D. and Williams, P. (2002) 'Steps towards sustainability monitoring: the case of the resort municipality of Whistler', in R. Harris, T. Griffin and P. Williams (eds), *Sustainable Tourism A Global Perspective*, Oxford: Butterworth-Heinemann.

Whiteman, G. (1999) 'Sustainability for the planet: a marketing perspective', *Conservation Ecology* **3** (1),13, available at: http://www.consecol.org/vol3/iss1/art13, accessed on 16 March 2003.

World Travel and Tourism Council (2002) 'Agenda 21 for the travel and tourism industry towards environmentally sustainable development', at: http://www.wttc.org/promote/agenda21.htm, accessed 16 March 2003.

5 Sustainable Human Resource Management

Rajka Presbury

Rationale

The cornerstone of sustainable human resources is the recognition that it is the 'people' input that is of the greatest importance (Baum, 1995, 2006). This is because tourism is about people's experience as guests, and the delivery of the tourism product and service is evaluated by people's demands and expectations. The delivery of the product and service is also by people, and tourism and hospitality employees are part of the product which visitors pay for. Therefore investment in people should be a long-term commitment by which all actions are guided. Consequently tourism development must include sustainable practices in human resource management.

Unlike many business sectors, tourism is a blend of various industries and sectors offering products and services which range from airline and cruise ship travel and accommodation, to restaurant meals, entertainment, souvenirs and gifts, park services, recreational vehicles, resort development, safaris, leisure and recreational opportunities. Consequently it should be understood that small and medium-sized enterprises (SMEs) are a major part of the travel and tourism sector. Although the human resource management needs of small business are not of the same size or complexity as those of a large organisation, they face equally important human resource management issues. As Wager (1998) suggests, small firms are best advised to emulate successful large firms in managing their human resources.

The aim of this chapter is to introduce, discuss and analyse the main elements of human resource management that reflect sustainable tourism practices. The chapter emphasises the critical role of human resource management in promoting sustainable tourism, whether it be in a large organisation that has the full resources of an experienced and qualified human resource team or a small operation where the owner operator or manager has the responsibility for the management of human resources. Although this chapter focuses on large tourism operators, many of the policies regarding human resource issues can be documented and implemented by even the most modest of business enterprises. Furthermore this chapter emphasises the importance of evaluating performance in achieving sustainable practice in human resources and addresses future challenges/issues associated with the way human resource management can contribute to the sustainable development of tourism.

Learning objectives

After reading this chapter, the students will be able to:

 ♦ Understand that sustainable principles should be a part of corporate goals and organisation and the organisational structure should be appropriate to local culture
 ♦ Recognise that a local focus and equitable approach should be used in recruitment, and sensitivity to local cultures and local community needs is important
 ♦ Apply the principles of sustainable tourism to the traditional human resource activities: recruitment; selection; orientation; training and development; remuneration; and performance management
 ♦ Compile ethical, adaptable, negotiated performance standards that are appropriate to a local context and sustainable tourism principles
 ♦ Apply a sustainable tourism ethos to the workplace with critical elements that include employee-focused principles
 ♦ Develop policies that support employees during employment and post-employment, including opportunities for job growth, good quality of personal life (including family), appropriate separation benefits, and skills training to aid with future employment.

Human resource management

Human resource management practices and strategies are essential for long-term sustainability of organisations, because they carry the main responsibility for human capital. Sustainable human resource management is the pattern of planned or emerging human resource developments and activities that are intended to enable a balance of organisational goal achievement and reproduction of the human resource base over a long-lasting calendar time and also to control negative impact on the human resource base.

In SMEs, the human resources function is often managed by the principal of the company or a line manager. Many of these people have little knowledge of the human resources aspect of the business and often concentrate on creating wealth and saving costs. As these management practices are short term in nature, they frustrate long-term sustainability of the enterprise. This short-term gain often results in the exploitation of **staff**, through poor management practices and lack of leadership in human resource management (Timo and Davidson, 1999).

The main objectives of sustainable human resource managment according to Ehnert (2006) are:

 ♦ To balance the ambiguities and the duality of efficiency and sustainability over a long-lasting calendar time
 ♦ To sustain, develop and reproduce an organisation's human and social resource base
 ♦ To evaluate and assess the effects of human resource activities on the human resource base and on the sources of human resources.

The stakeholder perspective of sustainability proposed by Docherty *et al.* (2002) encompasses three levels: the individual; the organisational; and the societal. Arguing that sustainability at one level cannot be built on the exploitation of the others, they link the key stakeholders of an organisation (personnel, customers, owners and society) to these levels with the aim providing an even balance between the needs and goals of all stakeholders.

Role of human resources

The above-mentioned definition and objectives point to the role of human resources as being the management of people to meet the optimal needs of the company and the community of the present without compromising the ability to meet the needs of the future.

The responsibilities of the human resource **manager** in the organisational context, which have implications for sustainability, are wide-ranging, including the following.

Cooperation

Three major stakeholder groups are concerned with tourism within any destination including:

♦ Local community

♦ Local business community

♦ Government

Each of these stakeholder groups has different members with different values, aspirations and needs.

Recognition of the importance of broad community participation, of effective coordination and support between all involved parties, is crucial to development of sustainable tourism.

Recognition of the interdependence of different industries, into which a community's economic and social fabric are inextricably interwoven with tourism and other existing industries, is essential. Since all industries share responsibility for heritage and natural resources protection, cooperation between businesses, governments, residents, employees and visitors is vital to success in achieving responsible standards and goals for the tourism industry.

As Mariappanadar (2003: 912) argues, 'organisations do not exist in a vacuum'. Organisations interact with the government and the wider communities to utilise the human resources supply. Fundamentally, the argument is that the government provides the initial resources needed for communities to build their human resources supply. This supply is then taken up by organisations to achieve their organisational objectives, whilst at the same time the community has the opportunity to have a fulfilled and meaningful life through employment. The taxes which are collected by government through employees is then spent on building the infrastructure needed to enjoy both work and leisure activities.

Industry insight: Redturs Latin America

Redturs is a network of indigenous and rural communities, institutions and human resources devoted to supporting the sustainable development of tourism. The network is promoted by the International Labour Organization (ILO) and has bases in Peru, Bolivia and Ecuador, offering services for travellers, rural and indigenous communities, associations, corporations, cities and institutions. One of the project's objectives is to create opportunities for the employment for women and men who are often located in remote areas where development opportunities are scarce.

www.desti-nations.net/homepage/cases/redturs-network-of-community-based-sustainable

Commitment to local staff recruitment

Tourism plans should encompass appropriate training, to ensure that local people have access to the full range of jobs in the local tourism industry. This means that companies within tourism regions must demonstrate a faith in the capability of people in the community within which they locate and should invest in enabling these people to achieve their full potential (Baum, 1995).

Designing a sustainable organisational structure

Human resource management practices need to be focused at the individual, group and organisational level. A sustainable organisational structure would be characterised by formal employee participation, social activities to promote sustainable efforts in the community, and the use of bonuses and incentives to create both awareness and work toward the firm's sustainability objectives.

Create career paths

The tourism industry in any region depends on a stable pool of skilled employees who can progress in their careers to higher levels of employment. Sustainable tourism development involves the establishment of education and training programmes to improve understanding and enhance business and professional skills. The United Nations Environmental Programme (UNEP) encourages tourism plans to include capacity building programmes to develop and strengthen human resources and institutional capacities in government at national and local levels, and amongst local communities; and to integrate environmental and human ecological considerations at all levels (UNEP, 2000).

Businesses and communities must work together to inform, educate and inspire in everyone appreciation for our natural and cultural heritage, and its protection through responsible conduct.

Education in sustainable objectives

Organisations need to act quickly to re-skill their workforces in green skills, knowledge and work to achieve a more carbon-constrained future, and improve environmental performance. According to the ILO (2008), tourism is one industry which will be most affected by climate change and other environmental crises, therefore action to create new green jobs (that have low impact on the environment) in the most susceptible regions is a high priority. Accordingly business, supported by governments, needs to allocate resources to fund specialised job positions that attend to sustainable programmes and training. Creating positions like environmental officer and community relations officer allows for real commitment and expertise and training toward sustainable outcomes.

Creation of shared ownership arrangements

As the initiatives for assisting local communities to realise tourism opportunities grow, the sharing of ownership will evolve over time. The nature of activities usually ranges from small one-village initiatives for organising handicrafts production to building powerful networks of small accommodation providers, through to marketing networks, learning from experience and sharing knowledge. From these initiatives, effective multi-stakeholder processes evolve, followed by replication of successful ventures. However, support is required from the international community for creating space and human resources capacity to assist the players who have been active leaders of these processes (Earth Summit 2002, Economic Briefing No 4.).

Formulation of policy and governance

Both local and national governments have a large part to play in the promotion of sustainable tourism, through the development of policy, capacity building, guidelines for good practice, promotion of awareness and local involvement. Specifically, government authorities have a role in the following:

◆ Ratifying international human resource agreements and then supporting the infrastructure for sustainable tourism

◆ Assisting with management and development of human resource growth through cooperation and coordination between agencies

◆ Facilitating the involvement of the local community, with the aim of building their skills and knowledge to improve career opportunities in tourism.

Taking responsibility

In accordance with a stakeholder perspective, an organisation must take responsibility for its actions, both positive and negative, on all stakeholders and society in general, and in particular has a moral obligation to its employees. The proponents of sustainability argue that beyond this responsibility and obligation is the assumption that it is economically rational to act in a sustainable way when it is clear that the world's resources are scarce. Therefore the role of HR is to manage this balance of social responsibility whilst at the same time being economically rational.

Strategies for sustainable human resource management

Tourism firms cover a broad range of activities and businesses of different kinds, different sizes and different business philosophies, therefore requiring human resource managers to engage in sophisticated planning and administration. Tourism organisations are high pressure areas and need to be managed with skill and precision. In broad terms, the management of human resources can be divided into three main areas:

◆ Planning and analysing
◆ Organising, controlling and implementing
◆ Evaluating.

Whilst the balance and order of activities may change depending on the nature or purpose of the business, all stages need to be professionally managed.

Planning human resources

Because tourism is interdisciplinary, a steering committee may be required to lead the sustainable human resource planning process. The steering committee could be broadly based and contain representatives from a variety of stakeholder groups – government, private sector, non-profit sector, community and other organisations (e.g. regional tourism organisations). Members should have:

◆ Complementary skills
◆ A capacity to influence behaviour
◆ Community respect, and ability to manage the relationship with stakeholders
◆ Leadership and initiative in creating the change necessary
◆ A commitment to satisfactory long-term outcomes.

Analysing the operation

While the process of sustainable tourism involves the establishment and maintenance of harmonious relationships, the goal (desired outcome) is the creation of continued viability and development of tourism-related entities. Hence, proponents of sustainable tourism engage in a process of creating a mutually beneficial balance between the macro-environment (social, cultural and environmental) aspects and the micro-environment (internal workings of a specific organisation). The objective (goal) of this process is the institutionalisation of the tourism industry as a contributor to the socio-cultural welfare and development of each and every destination. In essence this goal seeks what might be called a 'triple-win' outcome.

External influences

In identifying influences that will impact on the organisation and the management of its human resources, a human resource manager needs to look both externally and internally.

Some of the major external influences according to Stone (2002) are:

◆ Political ideologies regarding sustainable practices, especially government regulation and political attitudes to sustainable principles
◆ Laws and regulations that may be applicable to sustainability
◆ Government and community concerns regarding energy conservation; environmental pollution; workplace health and safety

- ◆ Technological advancement to enhance the organisation's ability to work sustainably
- ◆ Capacity of community to work in tourism
- ◆ Cultural values and norms of the community with respect to sustainable practices
- ◆ Demographic of the human resources available to the organisation in terms of numbers, geographical distribution, gender, age and skill levels
- ◆ Changing social values concerning the environment and social practices generally within the community
- ◆ Business competition and size of the tourism and hospitality industry and their capability of supporting, planning and implementing sustainable human resource practices
- ◆ Economic activity and a country's economic resources that can be reasonably used to create sustainable practices.

Internal influences

Some of the major internal influences according to Stone (2002) are:

- ◆ Organisational culture in terms of the values, beliefs and symbols that define the business. These will tell the employees how things are done, what's important, and what kind of practice and behaviour will be rewarded.
- ◆ Organisational structure to ensure that its values and beliefs will drive the achievement of its strategic objectives.

Evaluating human resource management objectives, strategies and policies

Human resource management objectives, strategies and policies should be evaluated in terms of their contribution to achieving the organisation's strategic objectives. However, the organisation's strategic objectives must be kept in check, to meet the overall principles of sustainable tourism. Therefore the human resource manager's involvement at the top levels of the hierarchy is essential to ensure that appropriate compliance and energy resources are dedicated to sustainable practices and then communicated down the line through policy and procedure.

To minimise problems, policies should be established as early as possible, preferably at the start of the business venture, as they will become useful guides in all areas of the firm's human resource management. Over time the owner/operator and/or manager become more experienced and can build the resources needed to hire a human resource management consultant to assist.

Organising, controlling and implementing sustainable human resources

According to Thom and Zaugg (2004: 217), sustainable human resource management is concerned with 'those long-term orientated conceptual approaches and activities aimed at a socially responsible and economically appropriate recruitment and selection, development, deployment and release of employees'. Whilst there is no one single formula that connects sustainability and business success, nor is there a set of practices that can definitively produce the outcomes for best sustainable results, there are a number of proven strategies which have been used by companies.

Recruitment and selection

A positive human resource management outcome requires not simply hiring suitable employees but also fostering a strong sustainable service culture by focusing on training, developing and empowering employees. However, as a recent article by Ross (2006: 75) published in the *Business Review Weekly* explains, tourism and hospitality companies are faced with a dilemma. For example, 'Hoteliers around the globe are creating one-of-a-kind properties that promise exceptional hotel experiences. But these grand developments share the same problem: finding the right staff to keep finicky, grumpy, often jet-lagged business travellers happy'. So while hotel companies are increasing their spending on constructing niche hotels that cater to their customers' demands for pampering, the human resource managers are faced with the difficult task of trying to find adequately skilled people with the required attitude.

Companies can only succeed in the long term if they recruit and motivate people who are able to respond to and shape the challenges of the future, and thus can strive within a changing environment. Therefore:

♦ Recruitment should be based on careful analysis of the local community and its labour market.

♦ Recruitment of staff should be based on long-term human resource planning.

♦ Staff should be recruited on the basis of potential development.

♦ Staff should be recruited locally from schools/colleges/universities.

♦ Expatriate staff should only employed to meet short-term needs and to develop local staff.

♦ High staff turnover should be seen as problematic and undesirable.

♦ Active company policies should be designed to minimise staff turnover.

♦ An exit interview policy must be followed.

♦ Relatively low staff turnover is to be achieved.

It should be noted here that in a competitive labour market, applicants pre-assess the social and environmental performance of companies; research shows that potential employees do consider sustainable and ethical management as an important factor in their job search. For example a Globescan (2006) survey on corporate responsibility and sustainability identified that in North America 70% of people surveyed said that they would not apply for a job at a company exhibiting poor social responsibility. Results were also significantly high in other regions: Oceania 62%; Western Europe 56%; and Asia 46%. Additionally, research shows that being a responsible corporate organisation does transcend into employee motivation commitment and loyalty (Zappala, 2004). Thus an added incentive for sustainable tourism can transcend into good business practice.

Orientation

Orientation gives organisations the opportunity to embed sustainable principles in the minds of employees. In particular, the employer has the responsibility at this stage to set the scene and induct staff into cultural norms such as multicultural awareness and mutual respect, corporate culture, and a sense of community spirit and engagement. For example, it is increasingly popular for organisations to be involved in charitable community programmes and many establish internal workplace giving programmes based on employee preference, where they deduct moneys from an employee's payroll (Zappala, 2004).

Orientation is also a good forum to discuss the employees' own responsibility for themselves, their community, and other stakeholders within their work environment. Thom and Zaugg (2004) contend that employees have an equal responsibility for themselves and their careers. This responsibility extends to the employee participating in decisions, and guarding against the negative effects of human resource policy and practice that may transcend into community risk.

Training and development

The human resource department can play a key role in training staff to understand and respond to the changing needs of the environment, especially focusing on the staff development and learning required to link sustainable principles and the bottom line. As Baum (2006) postulates, in a globalised business such as tourism and hospitality the major challenge is to match employee skills with changing industry requirements. If organisations are to be serious about recruitment policies that promote local community employment, training and development becomes a serious endeavour.

Therefore a planned training and development policy and strategy is an important aspect of human resource management. The training needs to be fast and appropriate to the task. Training and development of staff can be considered as an investment for the whole industry rather than for individual firms. Despite the fact that work in this industry is transitory, tourism organisations need to think of industry sustainability as well their own individual organisations. Career mobility is to be embraced and recognised as a beneficial outcome for all industry partners, and training needs to be linked to both internal and external opportunities for pro-motion. Whist the responsibility for training and development of human capital is traditionally an human resource task, it should be recognised that supervisors and managers play the most active role, and that the senior executives up to the level of CEO must be committed to it.

Additionally, as education institutions around the globe make tourism and hospitality courses more available, partnership between industry and education is a course of action that makes great sense, provided that education programmes can be based on industry, research-identified needs and industry-developed skills can easily be recognised and certified by education, while allowing for those who are able and willing to participate in education/training courses to further develop and progress to more senior roles.

It is important that equal employment opportunities allow for those who do not have the life, education and training opportunities to enter the industry and be trained and developed rather than exploited and de-skilled.

Industry insight: Grameen Shakti (India)

Grameen Shakti is a social entrepreneur company that aims to reduce poverty, protect the environment and break down social inequalities to empower rural people in Bangladesh through access to green energy and income through the Grameen Technology Center (GTC) programme. The Center trains women on renewable energy technologies and helps them to set up their own businesses.

More than 1000 women technicians have been trained and around 300 of these women are working in some capacity. Some are marketing solar systems; others are promoting and constructing improved cooking stoves.

These women have set up their own businesses at home and marketplaces assembling and marketing solar accessories. Others are assembling solar accessories at GTCs and selling these to GS.

http://www.gshakti.org/green-women.html

Performance management

Traditionally tourism and hospitality careers have not commanded the competi-tive salaries, wages and hourly rates seen by other service sectors like banking and finance. In fact an ILO report published in 2001 concluded that on average tourism and hospitality workers earn 20% less than in these sectors. As a result employees often feel undervalued.

Thus it is extremely important to create incentives for exceptional performance through rewards that can motivate employees, such as:

Financial security through competitive rewards and benefits with employment conditions which are designed to balance the organisation's need for financial suc-cess and the employees' need for appropriate recognition whilst at the same time being mindful of local/individual circumstances and needs.

Bonus arrangements that will allow for everyone to prosper in the good times

This can the benefit of fostering a commitment and feeling of belonging among employees, and provide appropriate recognition for doing a good job.

Conditions that reflect flexibility, which are seen as employer–employee partnership with mutual benefits. Conditions that reflect the organisation's support for learning, family and community responsibilities are welcomed.

Monitoring the attitudes of staff through employee surveys, focus groups, or through exit interviews in order to ensure they consistently learn and improve.

Retention through nurturing of employees

Human resource management literature (such as the *International Journal of Human Resource Management* and the *Asia Pacific Journal of Human Resources*) has for the past 20 years focused on the need for employers (especially in the service industry) to recognise the competitive value of their human capital. To this end articles in HRM journals have advocated that:

♦ Staff should be seen as a key resource

♦ Staff should be perceived as an asset

♦ Democratic, participative management culture needs to be practised

♦ Responsibility should be delegated to all levels of staff – 'empowerment'

♦ Staff should be consulted and involved with decisions affecting their area of responsibility

♦ Corporate culture should respond and be flexible to local culture and needs

♦ Organisations need to be concerned for the health and safety of employees and the community within which they operate

♦ Organisations need to embrace and make provision for work/life balance.

Additionally, human resource industry bodies have advocated that 'employees are motivated by a complex mix of rewards ... ranging from financial security and bonuses to promotion and peer recognition, and from taking on new challenges to making a difference to the things they care about' (World Business Council for Sustainable Development, 2000).

Furthermore international research by MORI showed that 80% of employees working for large-sized companies felt greater motivation and loyalty towards their job and their company the more socially responsible their employers became (www.ipsos-mori.com, accessed April 2009).

Industry insight: KPMG (a large global professional services network)

A survey by KPMG looked at 1600 world companies and examined why they are committed to corporate responsibilities. The report articulated that:

By earning the trust of their employees, communities, trading partners and the capital markets companies with a culture of corporate responsibility are able to generate value where others cannot.

http://www.humanresourcesmagazine.com.au

Work intensity and work/life balance

Finally, another initiative which has been enhanced by sustainability proponents is that of quality of life. In recent years there has been an increase in reports that workloads have increased and that work has become more intense, with a quarter of the population working more than 50 hours per week; and with over 50% of those working overtime not being paid (cited in Goldie *et al.*, 2005). These intensive workloads make it increasingly difficult for people to maintain a reasonable work, life balance and thus contribute to negative outcomes for employees and for HR in general. As Docherty *et al.* (2002) explains, intensive work systems consume human resources physically, cognitively, socially and emotionally. Thus the proponents of sustainable work claim that the human resources that need to be fostered include skill, knowledge, cooperation, trust, motivation, constructive industrial relations and training, so as to regenerate and develop human resources, and keep employees motivated and loyal. Community health authorities around the world are pushing the idea that 'healthy bodies and minds, healthy business, healthy environment and healthy group relations' are what sustainability is about (Newport *et al.*, 2003)

Exit

Generally the goal of human resource managers is to minimise employee turnover. However, turnover in tourism and hospitality organisations are an industry norm and thus the human resource manager must become adept at providing professional exit procedures for those seperating from the organisations.

Individuals who choose to leave the organisation of their own free will are considered to be 'voluntary separations'. In most cultures it is appropriate for these people to give reasonable notice of the intent to leave their positions within the organisation. This gives the managers of the organisation time to replace the vacated position.

Involuntary exit takes place when individuals are asked to leave their positions with the hospitality organisation. While such a scenario is unpleasant for the exiting worker, human resource practitioners realise that these cases support the overall welfare of the organisation and those people who do perform in accordance with expectations.

One of the finalisation procedures for these exiting individuals is a formal meeting with a human resource representative to discuss the reasons for leaving the organisation, as well as to find out the perceptions of that person regarding the experiences of being employed with the organisation. The exit interview in these situations should include an opportunity for the seperated employee to share his or her impressions concerning the organisation prior to the incident which caused the separation, as well as to voice their impressions of the situation leading to the termination. The objective here is for the person to leave the organisation with a sense that he or she was listened to and that the organisation was fair in dealing with the situation. Where appropriate, the human resource practitioner may offer to assist with outplacement services in such cases. Immediately upon the completion of the exit interview, the human resource practitioner will record all observations

This information could be entered into a database for an analysis of trends that indicate the positive and negative perceptions of separating employees about their experiences with the organisation. Human resource practitioners will use the information to reinforce those positive impressions (strengths) and to correct negative perceptions (weaknesses), in an effort to improve the workplace environment.

An important element of a fair workplace is that organisations should uphold a policy of providing procedures to hear employee complaints and grievances. One of the questions that should be asked of employees with negative perceptions of their experience with the organisation is whether they pursued these procedures prior to deciding to leave the organisation.

Barriers

In a highly competitive environment, managers need to excel in information gathering, decision making and action taking; managers also need to have strong skills in, and be involved with planning, organising, staffing, leading and controlling (Shenhar and Renier, 1996). Managing tourism businesses is complex because the sector is 'reactive, fragmented, susceptible to interruptions, and involves large numbers of contacts' (Dann, 1990). This environment is often not conducive to operating in a sustainable way, and can be fraught with problems caused by a number of barriers, including a lack of overall vision of sustainable tourism, a lack of interest or awareness, a lack of trained human resources, cultural barriers, standardised practices and perception of high costs.

Lack of an overall vision of sustainable tourism

The strongest input to sustainable tourism is by the managers and supervisors who direct and lead tourism businesses. Managers have direct influence over the resources used and the roles that employees undertake, the design of the service delivery system and the organisational culture. It is the managers who are responsible for the service interactions and the behaviour of their employees, and consequent failure of a business to act responsibly. If the management lacks an overall vision to act sustainably, then it is unlikely that the firm will be able to make the change to sustainable principles.

A lack of interest or awareness

The opinions, values, beliefs and behaviour of staff members with respect to the environment, socio-cultural understanding, the service industry and work itself can all be impediments to sustainability. Finding the right people with the right attitude can be difficult, and inconsistencies with supervision and performance management of employees can further complicate the issue.

A lack of trained human resources to ensure local economic benefit from tourism

Lane (1992) declares that non-sustainable human resource management is one that includes 'no career structure' and 'employees imported', as compared with 'a career structure with employment according to local potential'. Without training, residents of host communities often will not be able to actively participate in the tourism industry and gain the related economic benefits. Without a trained local workforce, staff must be imported.

Additionally, Baum alleges that 'developing the people asset or human capital is frequently a short term expedient, designed to train staff to do their current job better' (2006: 287).

Along with technological changes to replace human capital, standardisation across the industry, job deskilling and calls for productivity increases, the exploitation of people working in the tourism industry is growing. All this leads to a lack of trained human resources to ensure local economic benefit from tourism.

Cultural barriers

It is increasingly recognised that the success of sustainable development initiatives depends on widespread public identification and support. Indeed, public participation has become a core component of the official discourse of sustainable development, particularly at local level (Macnaghten and Jacobs, 1997). However, the cultures of residents and visitors often differ, and therefore communication barriers are inevitable due to the barriers that stem from our society's historical, religious, scientific, technological, economic and political foundations and parameters. It is important for human resource managers to understand how culture is conceptualized and used in tourism (Liburd and Ren, 2009) to avoid hampering the sustainable growth of a tourism and hospitality operation.

Standardised practices

One practice that is common among centralised organisations is to establish and enforce consistent standards for performance for all tourism and hospitality locations. This may not be suitable for sustainability within a given locale.

Perception of high costs

Throughout this chapter the benefits of sustainable development have been outlined. However, there are those who believe the costs of being involved in sustainable practices are high and may yield little or no advantage over traditional human resouce practices. Nevertheless, the ultimate goal is to have human resouces as a strategic partner in the implementation of cultural change that will impact positively and drive the organisation to a model of sustainability.

In many cases, tourism operators, under pressure from corporate offices and shareholders, prefer short-term financial gains rather than endeavouring to grow in a sustainable way. It may be argued that the adherence to tight budgetary management leads managers to cut expenditure on training and development as well as those sustainable actions that in the short-term cost more. Such budgetary discipline is understandable in the short term, but it needs to be recognised that it takes time for the benefits of longer-term measures to become apparent.

Human resouce evaluation/monitoring

In most instances, evaluation and monitoring can occur through sharing information about an organisation's sustainability priorities, goals, initiatives and performance. This process should illustrate a commitment to good governance and transparency. It should also serve as an entry point for stakeholder engagement and is the main vehicle for disclosing information about the organisation's programmes as well as soliciting feedback on the company's performance.

As a part of the annual reporting process, organisations measure and evaluate their performance, and communicate their progress and challenges. Together, these activities help organisations continually improve their contributions toward addressing global sustainability challenges and advancing sustainability at the local level.

The commitment to sustainable development requires that management understands the immediate and longer-term interactions with, and impacts on people and the environment. It requires business decisions that enhance stakeholder trust, and build social and environmental capacity. This commitment can only be successful if organisations engage in the following practices:

♦ **Walking the talk.** An organisation cannot promote change in others if it is not striving to exemplify that change in its own organisational values and activities.

♦ **Keeping up to date.** As professionals, employees have a responsibility to keep learning and constantly informing themselves about the emerging science and practice of sustainability – both what is happening to the world, and what can be done about it.

♦ **Telling the truth about the trends, as you see it.** In a world of great media noise and confusion, where sustainability issues and global concerns must compete for attention, organisations have a responsibility to their clients to keep them informed. Be clear to clients about what the most important trends affecting the world and their future may be, and why.

♦ **Sharing information, and credit, with other professionals.** While client confidentiality must always be respected, it slows down progress in the field of change for sustainability if information is hoarded regarding new ideas, the development of new methods and relevant activity in the market. It also damages overall progress when the work of other people is used without appropriate permission or citation.

♦ **Prioritising cooperation over competition, and impact over income.** In the community of sustainability practice, seek first for opportunities to work with others and build on complementary strengths, rather than to compete for primacy; and weigh the chance to make change as more important than making money.

♦ **Make referrals to other professionals whenever appropriate.** If someone else, or a different methodology, would be significantly more effective in meeting a specific client's needs, make the client aware of that option.

♦ **Tithe to the volunteers**. Donate some fraction of your revenues to voluntary or non-profit initiatives that are advancing the practice of sustainability.

♦ **Explain your ethical choices.** Be transparent about the criteria used for structuring human resource practices and for choosing professional engagements.

♦ **Consider the systemic impacts of your advice and actions.** Human resource managers have a special obligation to think systemically, and to take into account the potential impacts of what they recommend or do, including impacts beyond the boundaries of the system they are operating in.

♦ **Seek to do no harm.** In working with clients and promoting change, seek to avoid actions and interventions that may cause lasting damage to people, nature, community and organisational health.

(Atkinson, 2008)

Sustainable policy

The sustainability challenge is about incorporating social, economic and environmental risks and benefits into business decision making. Whether exploring for new development, operating sites, interacting with communities or closing and rehabilitating depleted reserves, having a clear human resources policy communicates commitment to sustainability in every aspect of management. It is another step toward an integrated, real-time sustainability governance and decision-making process.

Such a policy can guide the organisation to an integrated approach, which balances the potential social, community, environmental and financial consequences of human resource strategies. As well, it sets high standards of environmental and safety performance which are accountable for achievements against these standards.

Government regulation

A commitment to human resources sustainability principles should be tied to state and federal laws which require records to be kept and maintained in relation to:

♦ Terms and conditions of engagement

♦ Leave entitlements (sick, annual, long service)

♦ Payroll and taxation

♦ Superannuation

♦ Workers' compensation

♦ Occupational safety and health

♦ Training.

Industry insight: Accor Hotels

Accor's sustainable policy is incorporated in every level of its businesses. Actions taken under this policy include: development of ecolabels; an environmental hotel charter; use of 'clean construction', energy saving measures and solar power at its hotels; dissemination of information to its clients; and awareness raising towards sustainability. The Group has an environment department, supported by a network of correspondents on all five continents. Accor developed its sustainable policy in partnership with major institutions such as ADEME (the French Environment and Energy Management Agency) and ICAEN (the Catalan Institute for the Environment).

http://www.accor.com/en/sustainable-development.html

Codes of conduct

A code of conduct defines the core principles that govern employee behaviour and the way the company conducts its business. The code of conduct reflects changes in industry practices and provides a user-friendly format, with supporting questions and answers, decision guides and lists of additional resources available to employees.

The code of conduct should set forth the ethical standards that apply to all those who work in and with the firm, with respect to:

♦ Health and safety

♦ People management

♦ Environmental management

♦ Socio-cultural management

♦ Business practice

♦ Conflict of interest.

With an offer of employment, potential employees should be provided with information on a company's code of conduct, and should be asked to confirm, at that time, that they agree to act in accordance with the code. Employees reaffirm their commitment to the code annually.

An advisory committee, chaired by a senior member of staff who has the authority to make decisions on behalf of the company, should be set up to support the code of conduct. Its primary role would be to support employees in resolving matters that arise in their day-to-day employment. The committee's membership should reflect the diverse range of employees.

Sustainable work systems

According to Forslin (2000b) a sustainable work system is a work system in which the quality of work (employees' health, wellbeing and personal development); the quality of the organisation (productivity, efficiency, the ability to meet the challenges of tomorrow's business); and the quality of connections with the environment (both natural and society) are constantly kept at the same high levels. Forslin (2000b) explains that a sustainable work system should reproduce resources in a reproduction cycle that allows for growth.

Sustainable work systems attend to four interrelated parts:

♦ Reproduction and development of human resources through skill, knowledge, cooperation and trust, motivation, employability and constructive industrial relations, as well training systems

♦ Paying attention to quality of working life and competitive performance by considering improvement to working conditions and organisational performance

♦ Sustainable change processes for renewal and learning, by building up internal capabilities to deal with the competitive pressures and ever-changing environments

♦ Improving local employment and employment levels by taking on unemployed people.

(Forslin, 2000a)

Industry insight: Starbucks

Starbucks' code of conduct framework articulates limiting child labour and supporting workers' access to safe housing and healthy workplaces. Starbucks' code states that 'we believe in the importance of progressive environmental practices and conservation efforts', '...wage and benefit levels should address the basic needs of workers and their families', and '...people have the right to freely associate with whichever organizations...they choose'.

http://www.starbucks.com

Future challenges/issues

The human resouce environment consists of many players: the government and local authorities; the communities within which a company operates; the customers, investors and shareholders; and the employees. Therefore human resouce managers need to deal with the commercial, political and social realities and the challenges of being understood and accepted by those who work in the company.

Ultimately this means that the human resouce strategies and tactics must reflect the aspirations of the company team through the alignment of organisation strategy, values and culture, in order to deliver sustainable returns to investors; help address customer needs; and respond to emerging societal trends and government regulations pertaining to sustainable development and management.

What is certain for human resource managers is that sustainability now belongs in the mainstream of business activity and therefore human resouce managers will in the future be required to act as agents of change to bring sustainable development activities into their organisation's agenda. This now becomes the new challenge.

Review questions

1   Is sustainable human resource management incompatible with good business practice? Why? Discuss your answer.

2   How are the potential implications of climate change to be incorporated in a human resource policy?

3   Discuss how the differences between east and west thinking may impact on tourism and hospitality organisations across the globe.

4   Suggest at least three ways that a centralised formal appraisal process could apply the principles of sustainability.

5   Identify a large metropolitan resort hotel in a developed country and one in a remote area of a developing country. Would the implementation of participative decision making (as discussed throughout this chapter) be the same within both these organisations? Why or why not?

6   Developing compensation strategies that are sustainable and equitable for a diverse employee market (for example expatriates versus local employees) is complex. Compensation strategies must be considered with a degree of sensitivity to the host community. Consider two or three ways in which you would remunerate the different employees and how these remuneration packages may impact the motivation of the different types of employees.

Useful websites

Australian Human Resource Institute   http://www.ahri.com.au

Chartered Institute of Personnel and Development   http://www.cipd.co.uk/

Globescan   www.sustainability.com

Human Resource Magazine   www.humanresourcesmagazine.com.au/

International Confederation of Free Trade Unions   http://www.icftu.org

International Labour Organization   http://www.ilo.org

International Monetary Fund   www.imf.org

Ispos MORI   http://www.ipsos-mori.com/

Transparency International   http://www.transparency.org

United Nations   www.un.org

World Bank   www.worldbank.org

World Business Council for Sustainable Development   http://www.wbcsd.org/

Journals

Asia Pacific Journal of Human Resources

Journal of Industrial Relations

International Journal of Human Resource Management

International Journal of Employment Studies

International Employment Relations Review

References

Accor Hotels http://www.accor.com/en/sustainable-development.html, accessed on 9 January 2010

Addo, M.K. (ed.) (1999) *Human Rights Standards and the Responsibility of Transnational Corporations*, Boston, MA: Kluwer Law International.

Albrecht, M. (2001) *International HRM: Managing Diversity in the Workplace*, Oxford: Blackwell. (Chapters in Part V: Employee Relations).

Atkinson, A. (2008) *The ISIS Agreement: How Sustainability Can Improve Organizational Performance and Transform the World*, London: Earthscan.

Baum, T. (1995) *Managing Human Resources: An International Perspective*, London: Chapman and Hall/Buckingham: University of Buckingham.

Baum, T. (2006) *Human Resource Management for Tourism Hospitality and Leisure: An International Perspective*, London: Thomson Learning.

Broussard, S.R. and Bliss, J.C. (2007) 'Institutional commitment to sustainability', *International Journal of Sustainability in Higher Education*, **8** (3), 272-284.

Bushell, R. 2003, 'Balancing conservation and visitation', in, Buckley, R., Pickering, C. and Weaver, D. (eds), *Nature-based Tourism, Environment and Land Management*, Wallingford and Cambridge, MA: CABI Press, pp. 197-208.

Dann, D. 1990. 'The nature of managerial work in the hospitality industry', *International Journal of Hospitality Management*, **9**, 319–333.

de Schutter, O., (2006) *Transnational Corporations and Human Rights*, New York: Palgrave-Macmillan.

Docherty, P., Forslin, J. and Shani, A.B. (2002) *Creating Sustainable Work Systems: Emerging Perspectives and Practice*, Routledge, London.

Drost, E.A. Frayne, C.A., Lowe, K.B. and Geringer, J.M. (2002) 'Benchmarking training and development practices: a multicountry comparative analysis', *Asia Pacific Journal of Human Resources*, **40** (1), 81-104.

Ehnert, I. (2006) 'Sustainability issues in human resource management', paper prepared for the 21st Workshop on SHRM, 30-31 March, Birmingham.

Elashmawi, F. (1999) *Multicultural Management 2000: Essential Cultural Insights for Global Business Success*, Houston, TX: Gulf Publishing.

Evans, P., Pucik, V. and Barsoux, J.-L. (2002) *The Global Challenge: Frameworks for International Human Resource Management*, Boston, MA: McGraw-Hill, 489-496.

Forslin, J. (2000a) 'Sources of work intensity', paper prepared for Stockholm: SALTSA/SWS Research Group, March.

Forslin, J. (2000b) 'Exploring the concept of sustainable works systems', in F.M.van Eijnatten, and A.B. Shani (eds), *From Intensive to Sustainable Work Systems: Beyond Time Limitations in the European Context*, Toronto Academy of Management Symposium.

Globescan (2006) www.sustainability.com, accessed on 12 February 2010.

Goldie, J., Douglas, B. and Furnass, B. (2005). *In Search of Sustainability*, Melbourne: CSIRO Publishing.

Grameen Shakti http://www.gsh,accessed on 14 February 2010.

Hampden-Turner, C. and Trompenaars, A. (2000) *Building Cross-cultural Competence: How to Create Wealth from Conflicting Values*, New Haven, CT: Yale University Press.

Harris, P.R., Moran, R.T. and Moran, S.V. (2004) *Managing Cultural Differences: Global Leadership Strategies for the 21st Century*, Amsterdam: Elsevier.

Hotel Mocking Bird, http://www.hotelmockingbirdhill.com/en-sustainability.shtml, accessed 21 January 2010.

International Labour Organization (ILO) (2001) *Human Resource Development, Employment and Globalization in the Hotel Catering and Tourism Sector*, Geneva: ILO.

ILO (2008) *Report of the Committee on Employment and Social Policy, Employment and Labour Market Implications of Climate Change*, Geneva: ILO.

KPMG http://www.humanresourcesmagazine.com.au, accessed on 11 January 2010.

Lane, C. (1992) *Management and Labour in Europe*, Aldershot: Edward Elgar.

Liburd, J.J. and Ren, C. (2009) 'Selling difference: Conceptualising culture in tourism education and managment', in M. Blasco and M. Zølner (eds), *Teaching Cultural Skills: Adding culture in higher education*, Copenhagen: Nyt fra Samfundslitteratur, 71–90.

Macnaghten, P. and Jacobs, M. (1997) 'Public identification with sustainable development: investigating cultural barriers to participation', *Global Environmental Change*, **7** (1), 5-24.

Mariappaandar, S. (2003) 'Sustainable human resource strategy', *International Journal of Social Economics*, **30** (8), 906-923.

Newport, D., Chesnes, T. and Lindner, A. (2003) 'The "environmental sustainability" problem: ensuring that sustainability stands on three legs', *International Journal of Sustainability in Higher Education*, **4** (4), 357-363.

Ross, E. (2006) 'Living well', *Business Review Weekly*, 9–15 February, pp. 23-24 and 74–85.

Schuler, R.S., Jackson, S.E. and Luo, Y. (2004) *Managing Human Resource in Cross-border Alliances*, London: Routledge.

Scullion, H. (2003) *Global Staffing*, London: Routledge.

Shenhar, A.J. and Renier, J. (1996) 'How to define management: a modular approach', *Management Development Review*, **9**, 25–31.

Sparrow, P. and Brewster, C. (2003) *Globalizing Human Resource Management*, London: Routledge.

Starbucks, 'Code of conduct', http://www.starbucks.com, accessed on 20 January 2010.

Stone, R.J. (2002) *Human Resource Management*, John Wiley and Sons Australia.

Spitzengruppenbefragung in europäischen Unternehmungen und Institutionen' in E.J. Schwarz (ed.), *Nachhaltiges Innovationsmanagement*, Wiesbaden: Gabler, pp. 217-245. (Cited in: Ehnert, I. (2006) 'Sustainability issues in human resource management', paper prepared for 21st Workshop on SHRM, 30-31 March, Birmingham.)

Timo, N. and Davison, M. (1999). *Flexible Labour and Human Resource Management Practice in Small to Medium Size Enterprises*. London: Cassell

Thom, N. and Zaugg, R. J. (2004) 'Nachhaltiges und innovatives Personalmanagement:

Towards Earth Summit (2002) Economic Briefing No.4 Sustainable Tourism Briefing Paper at www.stakeholderforum.org, *accessed 16 February 2005.*

Van Eijnatten, F.M. (2000) 'From intensive to sustainable work systems', paper presented at TUTB-SALTSA Conference, 25-27 September, Brussels.

Wager, T.H. (1998) 'Determinants of human resource management practice in small firms', *Journal of Small Business Management*, **36** (2), 13-23.

World Business Council for Sustainable Development (2000) *Corporate Social Responsibility: Making Good Business Sense*, Geneva: World Business Council for Sustainable Development.

Zappala, G. (2004) 'Corporate citizenship and human resource management: a new tool of or a missed opportunity?', *Asia Pacific Journal of Human Resources*, **42** (2), 185-201.

6 Corporate Social Responsibility in Tourism

Camelia Tepelus

Rationale

This chapter addresses the development of corporate social responsibility (CSR) as a paradigm supporting sustainable tourism development. It aims to provide students with an understanding of the theoretical fundamentals of the CSR concept, its evolution and applications to the tourism sector. After describing CSR origins and typologies, the chapter presents aspects of CSR integration in the enterprise's core operations, and reviews the manner in which CSR has been reflected in tourism development in recent decades.

The questions analysed in this chapter concern the boundaries between a tourism enterprise's legal responsibilities and the CSR commitments it may consider assuming voluntarily. Is it in a company's interest to go beyond legal requirements and obligations stemming from collective agreements in addressing other societal needs? If not, should the company address such needs as part of its operations anyway?

Learning outcomes

Upon completing this chapter, the student should be able to:

♦ Explain the meaning of CSR and in particular as it applies to sustainable tourism development

♦ Describe different theories supporting the introduction of CSR in business

♦ Discuss the roles of stakeholders in tourism CSR, and critically identify potential conflict of interest

♦ Explain the role of CSR and its potential from a tourism marketing perspective

♦ Identify stakeholders who can drive CSR towards sustainable tourism development.

Conceptualisation

CSR, also called corporate citizenship, has recently become the umbrella term describing the contribution of the business sector to sustainable development. Corporate social responsibility is the concept 'whereby companies integrate social and environmental concerns in their business operations and in their interactions with their stakeholders on a voluntary basis' (European Commission, 2006). Two of the defining characteristics of CSR are:

1   Comprehensive scope – linking economic performance of the enterprise with non-economic (social and environmental) concerns of its stakeholders

2   Voluntary nature – motivating the enterprise to voluntarily assume responsibilities moving beyond its strictly legal obligations.

CSR requires enterprises to act as good citizens within the communities they operate. Tourism CSR is concerned with tourism enterprises' practices supporting sustainable tourism development, assumed on a voluntary basis and going beyond legal obligations. CSR should not be seen as a substitute for regulation. CSR is merely the conceptual framework concerned specifically with the responsibility of the private sector in advancing sustainable tourism separately and complementing the responsibilities of other tourism stakeholders (tourists, governments and tourism authorities, destinations, etc.).

CSR origins and typologies

An early definition of CSR was provided by H.R. Bowen (1953) as the obligation of businessmen to pursue those politics, to make those decisions, or follow those lines of action which are desirable in terms of the objectives and values of the society. This definition raises the major question of what is desirable for the society. A potential answer to this question emerged with the expansion of the sustainable development framework in the 1990s. According to Zadek (2001), the articulation of the CSR paradigm developed initially as a reaction to business practices which abuse or violate human rights; inconsistent application of legal principles by trans-national corporations; contribute to environmental offences; downgrade labour standards; and entice host-governments to act for self-interested purposes and market favours. Garriga and Melé (2004) map out CSR theories under four categories: instrumental, political, integrative and ethical. Instrumental CSR theories focus on the economic return to the firm. Social investments are supported only to the extent they would provide returns to the firm. Political theories build on the acceptance of a social contract by the enterprise, making it use its power in society responsibly. Integrative CSR theories apply when an enterprise integrates societal demands into its strategies. Finally, ethical theories apply when managers place social impacts above all other CSR considerations.

Common dimensions these theories encompass are: ethical values, profits, social demands and community performance. These elements appear very similar to the values of mutuality, knowledge, ethics and professionalism identified by the Tourism Education Futures Initiative to ensure that underlying responsible stewardship and touriam leadership are incorporated.

As illustrated in Figure 6.1, Carroll (1991) sees CSR classifiable by the nature of responsibilities into four groups: economic (be profitable for shareholders, provide good jobs for employees, produce quality products for customers); legal (comply with laws and play by the rules of the game); ethical (conduct business morally, doing what is right, just and fair, and avoiding harm), and fourth, philanthropic responsibilities (make voluntary contributions to society, giving time and money to good works).

Figure 6.1: Carroll's pyramid of CSR (Carroll, 1991)

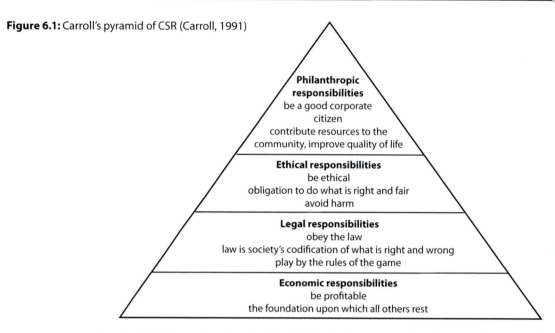

Lantos (2001) prefers to classify CSR into three moral, value-based categories: ethical (morally mandatory fulfilment of an enterprise's economic, legal and ethical responsibilities); altruistic (the fulfilment of an organisation's philanthropic responsibilities, going beyond preventing possible harm); and strategic CSR (the fulfilment of those philanthropic responsibilities which will benefit the enterprise through positive publicity and goodwill).

Van der Putten (2005) builds on the Garriga and Melé' classification to investigate the international aspects of CSR, which he considers to be often of greater complexity than domestic CSR studies. This is justified by the observation that an increasingly larger proportion of business and services in industrial countries involve suppliers from developing countries, either directly (through direct investment or trade) or indirectly (via extra-company supply chains). However this raises two issues. First applying CSR standards that originated in the West may be regarded as a form of 'cultural imperialism' in developing countries. Second, according to De George (1994) there is a risk in businesses inconsistently applying international labour or human rights norms, such as when Western firms automatically place local values and norms above international ones, acting in disregard of universal standards (Lewis and Unerman, 1999).

Tschopp (2005) observes differences in the pace and depth of developing CSR practices between the USA and Europe, with Europe appearing to be more progressive in embracing the CSR paradigm, while the USA has a more developed philanthropy industry (The Economist, 2004). Hopkins (2007) notes some academics still equate philanthropy with CSR, including well-known management scholars such as Michael Porter, who stated 'corporate philanthropy – or corporate social responsibility – is becoming an ever more important field for business. Today's companies ought to invest in CSR as part of their business strategy to become more competitive'.

Drivers, motivations and criticism of CSR

From a theoretical perspective, there are two opposite positions on CSR. One is the *shareholder theory* inspired by the classical view derived from neoclassical economic theory, which focuses on profit for shareholders. The best known proponent of this theory is Friedman (1970), joined by a number of contemporary adherents including Barry (2000), Coelho *et al.* (2003) and Henderson (2005), Van Oosterhout and Heugens (2006). In a classic 1970 *New York Times* article, Friedman argued that the only responsibility of managers is to increase shareholder value. His position was simplified as 'the only responsibility of business is business'. Friedman was objecting to expenditures that benefited 'society' and were not related to corporate policies that benefit shareholders. He nevertheless acknowledged the positive contribution of the company to 'community', referring to the community where the firm's employees reside. In agreement with Friedman's 1970 position, a 2005 survey by *The Economist* also argues that corporations act in the best interest of society when they act in their own best interest. Under the shareholder ideology it is the role of governments, not business, to decide questions of social, environmental and industrial policy.

Further support for shareholder theory argues that CSR refers to the increased vulnerability of a company that declares itself socially responsible: 'a firm that embarks on a plan of corporate social responsibility may be setting itself up for a worse, not a better reputation' (*The Economist*, 2004). Acting 'good' and advertising it may elicit charges of hypocrisy, leading other companies to decide that CSR might be more trouble than it's worth. In the view of The Economist the undemonstrated link between CSR and profits also raises an ethical question about a choice the enterprise has to make: if it implements profit-maximising CSR actions, it will be still criticised as self-interested; if it implements non profit-maximising CSR actions (philanthropy) it behaves unethically to its shareholders. With regard to the stakeholders' requests for transparency and accountability, critics of CSR point to the assumption of guilt made by activists, that enterprises are inherently immoral unless they demonstrate that they are the opposite – in effect, guilty before innocent (*The Economist*, 2002). Another CSR critic is David Henderson, former chief economist at the OECD and professor for the Institute of Economic Affairs in London, who characterises CSR as being merely 'global salvationism', a doctrine to accompany a gloomy perspective of global poverty and 'an apocalyptic pessimism' about the planet's environmental prospects. Henderson argues that in a competitive market economy, businesses should be free to take the path of CSR but also free to reject it (*The Economist*, 2001), and not to be forced in making a choice between profit-oriented and altruistic behaviour (Henderson, 2005). Castelo Branco and Lima Rodrigues (2007) note that this view is justified on the basis of neoclassical economic theory, being based on notions of free market, economic efficiency and profit maximisation. But even conservative think tanks agree that merely following the law would not exhaust a firm's ethical responsibilities, since some things that are legal are unethical, and many things required by ethics are not required by law (*The Economist*, 2005). In this regard, it is important to observe that making the 'business case' for CSR is a topic still ardently debated. Studies of the association between responsible corporate ethics and profitability indicate that often the two go together, however, a causal link has not been fully proven. A comprehensive study conducted by Orlitzky *et al.* (2003) as a meta-analysis of 52 other studies integrating 30 years of research shows that corporate virtue in the form of CSR and, to a lesser extent, environmental sustainability 'is likely' to pay off. Orlitzky et *et al.* al found a positive association between corporate social and financial performance across industries. Importantly, they also found that market forces do not penalise companies that are high in corporate social performance. They conclude that 'portraying managers' choices with respect to corporate social and financial performance as an either/or trade off is not justified in light of 30 years of empirical data'. Until the argument will be decided, the business case for CSR is likely to remain a question at the core of today's CSR research agenda across all economic sectors.

Opposed to the shareholder position is the *stakeholder theory*, which states that in addition to shareholders, there are several agents interested in the actions of the companies. Clarkson (1995) describes the stakeholder theory and argues that the company has a social responsibility requiring it to consider the interests of all parties affected by its actions, including local communities, suppliers, employees, creditors, the environment, and the society as such (Jacobs, 1997). Central to normative stakeholder theory developed in the 1980s and 1990s is what is desirable for the society and by the assumption that truth and freedom are best served by seeing business and ethics as connected (Freeman *et al.*, 2004).

A middle-ground research trend has recently emerged through analyses of CSR from a strategic corporate perspective. Representatives of this position are Porter and Kramer (2006) and McWilliams *et al.* (2006) who argue that CSR should be considered 'as a form of strategic investment', and otherwise treated as all investment decisions are treated. Porter and Kramer (2006) call today's CSR practices 'fragmented and disconnected'. They acknowledge four arguments for the CSR case: moral obligation, sustainability, licence to operate and reputation, and call for a strategic approach to CSR. Porter and Kramer (2006) propose a classification of the social issues a company faces into three categories: generic (important to society but irrelevant to the company's long-term competitiveness), value chain social issues (significantly affected by the company's ordinary activities within its value chain) and issues from the competitive context (factors in the external environment affecting competitiveness in places the company operates). Arguing that generic societal issues should be left to NGOs, Porter and Kramer call on companies to prioritise the value chain and strategic CSR practices. Once mapped, the social issues concerning a corporation should addressed in a competitiveness context.

CSR integration in core operations of business

The main reasons for tourism enterprises to adopt CSR practices include:

♦ Improving the environmental and social performance of the tourism product

♦ Supporting a corporate message about the values and ethical bases of the enterprise's operations and building a culture of 'doing the right thing'

♦ Generating customer and employee loyalty, including recruitment and retention of staff

♦ Positive contribution to the welfare of the local community where the enterprise operates

♦ Improved public relations and positive image for the business and its shareholders

♦ Brand differentiation and competitive advantage for an increasingly discerning public, particularly in the western tourism-generating markets which have seen ethical consumerism increasing over recent years

♦ Pre-empting regulation – through voluntary CSR measures tourism enterprises can show that issues of environmental pollution, diversity, health and safety, etc. are being taken seriously, being 'good citizens' with respect to already existing norms and laws.

The main reasons against tourism enterprises adopting CSR practices include:

♦ Added costs in non core-business programmes, including additional pressures on staff time and top management

♦ Vulnerability to criticism, public and media scrutiny.

♦ Strategies to integrate CSR with the core operations of the company require integration within company strategy, operations and policies. Such integration comes with advantages but also potential risks. The Boston College Center for Corporate Citizenship identified ten tactics that companies use to pursue CSR practices, and mapped the associated opportunities and risks (see Table 6.1).

Table 6.1: Strengths and weaknesses of different tactics to integrate corporate citizenship within the broader corporate strategy (Boston College Center for Corporate Citizenship, 2004)

The Ten Half-Truths of Integrating Corporate Citizenship

Yes...	Half-Truths	But...
Connects corporate citizenship to the business agenda and opens the door to more strategic discussions	**1** Make the business case	Can be overstated, underwhelming, and mask the real value of corporate citizenship as a core organizational element; can inhibit strategic thinking
Ties the company to the legitimacy of third-party objectives; provides a structure for measurement	**2** Adopt an external code or standard	Can lead to volumes of data to fulfill 'box-checking' compliance; may not translate into company-specific vision and actions that advance and deepen corporate citizenship
Provides a powerful motivator; leverages a well-established business concept	**3** Make risk mitigation a primary driver	Can put company in reactive mode; corporate citizenship can lose its orientation toward opportunity
Ensures priority status and is essential to securing resources	**4** Get buy-in from the top	Waiting for executive endorsement can delay progress and inhibit activities where approval is unnecessary; support at the top doe not secure support throughout organization.
Assigns an owner to foster alignment between corporate citizenship and company strategy	**5** Designate an owner of corporate citizenship	Can result in the perception of corporate citizenship as a unilateral responsibility and peripheral to the core business

Drives accountability, puts company on the public record; focuses internal attention on corporate citizenship	**6** Produce a social report	Can be a time-consuming bureaucratic exercise that distracts from progress; can become a substitute for actual corporate citizenship activity.
Creates a forum to share issues and knowledge across the company; produces new ideas, synergy and alignment	**7** Convene a cross-functional committee	Can be seen as a meeting-for meeting's sake; can create competition between staff and line.
Broadens buy-in and ensures corporate citizenship links with business strategy	**8** Engage the line organization	Can result in fragmented, inconsistent activity and commitment in the absence of an integrating mechanism
Increases comfort, reduces resistance; provides a 'tried-and-true' approach; jump-starts corporate citizenship	**9** Build on existing policies and systems	Can dampen innovation and energy over time
Builds deeper connections to stakeholders, leverages outside perspectives, and can build exciting programmes.	**10** Form cross-sectoral partnerships	Can diffuse the corporate citizenship agenda; doesn't replace internal commitment to stakeholder engagement

Institutionalisation of CSR

In Europe, CSR has been endorsed since the late 1990s. In 2001 the European Commission launched its own CSR strategy, through a 'Multi-stakeholder Forum on CSR', which operated between 2002 and 2004. Initially it focused on investigating the willingness of companies to implement social standards. In 2006, the Commission launched a 'European Alliance for CSR' as an open network acting as the EU political umbrella for CSR initiatives by large companies, SMEs and their stakeholders (European Commission, 2006).

At the global level, the United Nations is also playing an important role in promoting the CSR agenda through the Global Compact. It is a framework for businesses to align their operations and strategies within ten universally accepted principles of human rights, labour, environment and anti-corruption (UN Global Compact, 2007). The UN Global Compact is currently the largest and most recognized global CSR initiative, with over 7700 member companies in 130 countries. Illustrated in Table 6.2, the Global Compact asks companies to embrace, support and enact, within their sphere of influence, a set of core values in the areas of human rights, labour standards, the environment, and anti-corruption

Table 6.2: UN Global Compact Principles (UN, 2007).

Human Rights
Principle 1: Businesses should support and respect the protection of internationally proclaimed human rights; and
Principle 2: make sure that they are not complicit in human rights abuses.
Labour Standards
Principle 3: Businesses should uphold the freedom of association and the effective recognition of the right to collective bargaining
Principle 4: the elimination of all forms of forced and compulsory labour
Principle 5: the effective abolition of child labour; and
Principle 6: the elimination of discrimination in respect of employment and occupation.
Environment
Principle 7: Businesses should support a precautionary approach to environmental challenges
Principle 8: undertake initiatives to promote greater environmental responsibility; and
Principle 9: encourage the development and diffusion of environmentally friendly technologies.

Anti-Corruption

Principle 10: Businesses should work against corruption in all its forms, including extortion and bribery.

Utting (2002 and 2003) criticises the Global Compact for its weak compliance monitoring, for allowing companies to pick and chose which of the principles to address, and for diverting attention from malpractice. The Global Policy Forum Europe, a non-profit lobby group monitoring UN policy making also points to the risks of 'greenwash', 'bluewash', structural and other factors that encourage a 'business-as-usual' attitude in the way the UN Global Compact operates (Global Policy Forum Europe, 2007). The Global Compact acknowledges criticisms that while reporting on a CSR aspect, some of its members may simultaneously be accused of carrying out business involving negative and exploitative practices, engage in corruption, discrimination of labour violations. Even with these caveats, according to Ruggie (2002) the Global Compact maintains a strong position that the sustainability challenges should be addressed by business through an explicitly voluntary, non-regulatory, approach.

Application of CSR in sustainable tourism

Although still in its infancy, a body of knowledge explicitly linking CSR and tourism is developing. Despite a multitude of individual sustainability initiatives specifically focused on ecological issues, or operating within established regional boundaries, there are only a few examples of self-identified 'tourism CSR initiatives'.

The scarcity of self-described tourism CSR initiatives was initially pointed out by the NGO community (including tourism watchdogs, faith-based groups, trade unions and southern grassroots groups), and more recently acknowledged by international development agencies such as the World Bank and the International Finance Corporation (WB and IFC, 2003). Regarding the scope of existing CSR initiatives, Epler Wood and Leray (2005) point out that existing voluntary initiatives, guidelines and codes of conduct have so far addressed mostly questions of environmental management, almost completely ignoring all issues of human rights, governance and labour. This is particularly relevant as some activists characterise tourism as an industry 'rife with appalling working conditions, child labour and lacking concern for occupational health and safety standards' (KATE et al., 2004).

Tourism Concern, a UK non-governmental watchdog, wrote in 2002 one of the first reports setting out the scope of the role of CSR in tourism (Kalisch, 2002). The report builds on the concept of 'fair trade' in tourism, which many activists lobby for in relation to trade agreements such as the GATS and other market liberalisation processes. Among the first industry publications specifically addressing CSR and tourism is a 2002 report by the World Travel and Tourism Council (WTTC, 2002). WTTC is a high level forum of the presidents, chairs and CEOs of the world's foremost travel and tourism companies, and co-authors of the first Agenda 21 for Tourism in 1996. The report includes examples of corporate social leadership by top companies, and presents the business case for CSR to consist of: favouring by governments and communities prioritising sustainability; building brand value and the market share of socially conscious travellers; attracting socially conscious investors; enhancing ability for recruitment of highly skilled workforce; improved risk assessment and response capacity.

WTTC explicitly argues against regulation, stating that: 'a voluntary approach is crucial. To take advantage of what business has to offer – entrepreneurship, innovation, and management capability – companies must be free to choose how they respond to community needs as the competitive market dictates. Attempting to regulate social responsibility would not only be impractical, given the diverse needs of different communities, it would undermine the personal commitment and creativity that fuel it' (WTTC, 2002).

A 2006 PricewaterhouseCoopers survey of the leading 14 European hotel groups found that despite some recent progress, particularly in terms of implementing environmental policies, the tourism sector lags behind other European industries on CSR and 'faces a challenging agenda to catch up and respond effectively to the concerns of stakeholders' (PricewaterhouseCoopers, 2006). This seems to be confirmed by Palau (2006), who carried out a study of 24 hotel chains representing 60% of all the hospitality chains in the Catalonia region in Spain. Palau finds that most of these companies do not develop CSR strategies due to a lack of knowledge about existing international standards such as GRI, SA8000, etc. As one of the most visited regions in one of the most visited European countries, Palau (2006) finds a low level of relation and dialogue between the hospitality chains and their main stakeholders. Beyond the few activities promoted by NGO activists and international development agencies, academic investigation on tourism and CSR was characterised by Papaleo and Beeton (2006) and Henderson (2006) as scarce and underdeveloped.

CSR stakeholders in tourism

CSR stakeholders are primarily the tourism enterprise and its shareholders, the employees and the customers. Secondarily, CSR stakeholders include the local and national authorities, other civil society and public interest groups, international development agencies and other international tourism organisations (both governmental and international private-sector associations) interested in promoting sustainable tourism development, and an active engagement from the tourism private-sector. Tourism private-sector associations may also interfere in lobbying against norms and regulations, and are often advocates of CSR and deregulation mostly to pre-empt additional legal obligations.

Civil society groups have lobbied intensely calling for CSR development in tourism. Tourism NGOs are watchdogs which are quick to point out problems but often reluctant to engage directly in developing solutions collaboratively with the industry. However, as researchers in other fields point out (Schiller, 2005), civil society organizations have became much more 'business like', and interested in forging partnerships with the private sector. Although progress was made notably in the areas of conservation, community development natural resources management, prevention of child sex tourism, etc., dialogue between NGOs and tourism businesses on CSR issues is in general difficult, characterised by initial scepticism and suspicion on both sides. Furthermore, civil society organisations compete to earn the 'attention' of the same small pool of large tourism operators (hotels and tour operators), as well as for project funding from development agencies. Several large NGOs faced criticisms and lost credibility for making decisions perceived as 'compromises', and 'selling out' for endorsing the agendas of inter-governmental organisations or large tourism operators.

In addition to direct contact, the use of social networks and overt media campaigning, a recent avenue for the promotion of CSR in tourism, is shareholder activism. Influence over the managing boards of large, publicly listed tourism companies is exercised through a process called 'proxy voting' and via submission of shareholder resolutions. Resolutions put forward at annual shareholder meetings can request companies to adhere to environmental, social, or human rights standards. The main strength of this approach results from the legal obligation that the companies have to their shareholders. Consequently, companies are more inclined to engage in dialogue with those having a stake in the profitability of the company, rather than with NGOs perceived as external stakeholders. Based on this, the shareholders have an important position from which to encourage social responsibility (Hollenhorst and Johnson, 2007). A case of shareholder activism in tourism is that of Mariott hotels. Lobbied by a coalition of socially responsible investors from Europe and North America, Mariott implemented a corporate policy to protect children from sexual exploitation in tourism (Tepelus, 2008). Although the company agreed under pressure to develop policies and carry out internal trainings as requested by the investor groups, the results of these changes remain to be evaluated.

International development and technical cooperation agencies are other stakeholders showing interest in socially responsible tourism as an approach towards sustained economic development. Development agencies such as the Dutch SNV, German GTZ, and the Italian Development Cooperation (Cooperazione Italiana, part of the Ministry of Foreign Affairs) sponsor tourism development projects in poor countries and fund projects under the auspices of the UNWTO ST-EP initiative. USAID has also funded youth employment programmes in tourism in Brazil (USAID, 2005). However, large financial institutions, such as the World Bank, noted the absence of ethical bases and experience of socially responsible guidelines in tourism development projects. Of all industrial sectors that the World Bank Group CSR Practice reviewed in 2003, tourism was found to be the 'least developed in terms of codes of conduct and CSR initiatives' (WB and IFC, 2003).

Arguably, a critical role in the promotion of a globally accepted CSR framework in tourism rests with the UNWTO. Although an inter-governmental body having governments as members, the role of UNWTO as the international tourism policy-maker is central to any new concept and strategic development for sustainability in tourism.

Several structural weaknesses hamper UNWTO's ability to take progressive action: not having the USA, the UK and Scandinavian countries as members; and ambivalence on its responsibility with respect to the tourism private sector. Although UNWTO's influence manifests mostly onto its member governments, its body of Affiliate Members consisting of a Business Council, a Destination Council and an Education Council, good CSR practices have been profiled in the areas of climate change and energy efficiency, and environmental management. While it is true that tourism predominantly comprises of small and medium-sized enterprises many of whom having little knowledge of UNWTO and its directives, the larger enterprises and tourism universities are cognisant of the knowledge and recommendations generated by UNWTO, which in time, may trickle down to the small operators.

Environmental CSR in sustainable tourism

It is important to remember that tourism CSR is only a chapter within the wider domain of sustainable tourism development. While this assigns responsibilities to all tourism stakeholders (the private sector, clients, local communities, destinations and their management organisations, local and national authorities including their political leadership), tourism CSR is strictly concerned with the private sector, corporate good practices supporting sustainable tourism development.

Environmental management and impacts minimisation have received the most attention with respect to CSR activities in tourism. During the 1980s and 1990s, tourism CSR translated largely into development of voluntary performance schemes such as eco-labelling and codes of conduct, used by the tourism industry to transmit information on non-financial performance going beyond regulatory requirements. Although not always identified as CSR initiatives, codes of conduct are preferred and intensely promoted by the industry as alternatives to enforced regulation, and are often put forward in an effort to pre-empt regulation (UNEP, 1995). The main developers of codes of conduct for tourism are governments, industry associations, non-governmental organisations and multi-stakeholder groups. In 1995, the United Nations Environment Programme (UNEP) carried out an assessment of no less than 30 codes of conduct existing at that time. It was followed in 1998 by 28 other labelling schemes, finding the common elements of verification and monitoring as common weak points of all these initiatives. In Europe, for the Nordic countries alone, no less than 17 labelling programmes existed and another five were in progress in 1999 (RAMBØLL et al., 2000). Hammele (2002) observed that there were about 60 environmental certificates and awards in Europe alone by 2001, covering nearly all types of tourism suppliers, the majority of which (over 30) certified accommodation. Although such forms of environmental CSR are still common, some of the existing schemes were also criticised for poor organisation, precarious financial sustainability and vulnerability to commercial interests (Font, 2001).

Social and ethical CSR in tourism

While tourism's contribution to poverty alleviation has been extensively studied, in a globalisation context, poverty is associated and works in tandem with other social issues that may interfere with tourism development (USDOJ, 2007). These include gender discrimination, labour exploitation, labour migration and trafficking in human beings to serve tourism destinations, child sex tourism, etc. On gender and tourism, a mapping exercise by Sinclair (1997) found a complex spectrum of gender-related tourism issues, ranging from employment discrimination, limitation of women to jobs in to catering and accommodation, lack of participation in decision making, inequality in wages, extremes forms of exposure to personal and sexual abuses or prostitution. Only a handful of tourism CSR initiatives on social issues have been developed since 2000. Examples include: the UNWTO Task Force on the Protection of Children in Tourism (addressing trafficking, labour and sexual exploitation), the ECPAT Code of Conduct for the Protection of Children from Sexual Exploitation in Travel and Tourism (addressing child sex tourism), the Accor work against HIV and malaria, etc. Forthcoming research by UNWTO and UNIFEM will review the status of gender issues in tourism focusing on the role and treatment of women.

The most comprehensive reference document on the relationship between sustainable tourism and social CSR ethics is the UNWTO Global Code of Ethics in Tourism (GCET), developed by UNWTO in consultation with stakeholders in 1997, and ratified by the UN in 2001. GCET acts as a guide for tourism stakeholders in addressing environmental and social issues in tourism in a more integrative manner – through a set of ten principles setting the frame of reference for responsible and sustainable tourism. While GCET is not legally binding, one of its articles provides for a voluntary mechanism of dispute conciliation through a World Committee on Tourism Ethics (WCTE). The stakeholders may refer to this committee on matters concerning the application and interpretation of the GCET (UNWTO, 2007b).

Future developments on CSR in tourism

Following the launch of the Millennium Declaration signed by 189 countries in September 2000 and in correlation with the WTO transformation into a UN specialised agency in 2005, and its subsequent support for the UN Millennium Development Goals (MDGs), poverty alleviation became the top CSR priority (UN, 2007). Although the academic body of work underlying the importance of tourism for poverty alleviation has always been significant, poverty only became the central objective of the MDGs, after UNWTO launched the 'Sustainable Tourism – Eliminating Poverty' (ST-EP) initiative at the WSSD in September 2002. ST-EP aims to promote sustainable tourism as a force for economic growth and poverty reduction, particularly in Africa and developing countries (UNWTO, 2007a).

Why and how different tourism stakeholders should position themselves vis-à-vis the emergence of CSR for sustainable tourism will certainly evolve in relation to the anticipated elaboration of ISO standards on CSR. The ISO 26000 series 'Guidance on CSR' (IISD, 2004a) is a process currently under development, with guidelines expected for publication in 2010. The two countries leading the ISO technical working group on CSR standards are Sweden and Brazil. Publication of the ISO 26000 series standards is anticipated in the form of initial guidelines and not certification (IISD, 2004b).

It is worth noting that even existing CSR initiatives are largely focused on tourism impacts documented by research carried out in the 1970s and 1980s prior to observations of new phenomena that globalisation brought forward in relation to the neo-liberal trade and development agenda. The scope of future CSR initiatives is more likely to incorporate issues such as fair trade in tourism, pricing and labour practices, workforce migration, trafficking of human beings for labour or other exploitative purposes, all in the context of poverty alleviation as set by the MDGs and the UN Global Compact. Several tourism corporate leaders, mostly large companies have emerged in recent years as winners of CSR prizes on a variety of issues going beyond environmental management. These include Accor Hotels rewarded for their work on combating TB, malaria and prevention of HIV/AIDS, WTTC's Tourism for Tomorrow Awards, Air France-KLM topping the Dow Jones sustainability index for their work on CO_2 emission reduction and community engagement, Carlson Companies CEO Marilyn Carlson Nelson recognised for her work against human trafficking and sexual exploitation. Finally, it is worth observing that emergent CSR initiatives, notably the UN Global Compact, acknowledge the importance of supply chains and the interconnections between companies, an aspect often left outside the boundaries of previously existing voluntary performance programmes.

Review

CSR is the umbrella term describing the specific responsibility of the business sector to support societal transformation towards sustainable development. CSR is not only concerned with how the enterprise fulfils its legal obligations, but to what extent it assumes a responsibility to its stakeholders and to the community regarding social and environmental concerns going beyond the scope of legal requirements. The UN Millennium Development Goals, the UNWTO Global Code of Tourism Ethics and the UN Global Compact are initiatives that build on the CSR concept and call tourism companies to answer to their stakeholders and to society in general in a more holistic manner, going beyond 'being green'. CSR does not substitute laws and regulations. It is assumed that enterprises implementing CSR already comply with existing legal standards, voluntarily taking additional steps beyond the mandatory requirements, in the attempt to advance sustainable development and societal good.

CSR has not been addressed in tourism research until very recently. A number of guidance instruments aiming to support sustainable development in tourism have been developed in the form of voluntary performance certification programmes notably in the 1980s and 1990s, most addressing environmental management. Generally, such initiatives were not purposefully designed within a CSR theoretical framework at the time of their launch, but operated as voluntary tools for promoting incremental environmental improvements. The scope of CSR initiatives in tourism widened in relation to international initiatives such as the UN Global Compact and the UN Millennium Development Goals that address wider societal concerns including human rights and fair labour practices in business. Although examples of CSR good practices going beyond environmental aims are still scarce and mostly limited to large tourism companies, it is to be expected that CSR initiatives will continue developing, in a global environment of increased public awareness and scrutiny of the tourism sector, given its role and impacts for sustainable development.

Review questions

1 How can CSR drive sustainable tourism development?

2 Who are the stakeholders a tourism company has to consider when deciding to pursue a particular CSR programme? Is CSR always recommended? What factors may affect the decision to start a CSR programme for a tourism enterprise?

3 Review questions for the case study: CSR at British Airways includes a voluntary carbon offset scheme allowing the passengers to pay to offset the carbon emissions from their air travel. Should BA implement this scheme on a mandatory basis for all flights? If so, would BA be entitled to request tax incentives from the government for going beyond the legal requirements on CO_2 mitigation? Would such a measure be fair and acceptable for all stakeholders?

Case Study: CSR at British Airways

Dr Graham Miller, University of Surrey

British Airways (BA) is one of the world's largest airlines, carrying more than 33 million passengers in 2008/09 to more than 300 destinations, employing 40,629 full time equivalent members of staff, 245 aircraft and operating principally from London's Heathrow airport. BA reported revenue of nearly £9 bn in 2008/09.

BA first established its corporate environmental department in 1989, with an externally audited review of performance first completed in 1990 and published in 1991. Since then, an environmental report has been published annually showing a laudable commitment to setting targets, monitoring performance and publishing results. The aim of BA now is to become 'the world's most responsible airline', which it seeks to achieve by examining how it flies, what it flies and what it buys.

Environment

The 1992 Environmental report identifies global warming and the contribution of aviation in general, and BA specifically to that issue. Today, BA recognises climate change to be one of its principal challenges and has set itself a long-term challenge of reducing net CO2 emissions by 50% by 2050, with a 25% reduction by 2025 as an interim target (using 2005 as a base). This can be seen in context of the UK government targets to achieve 80% reduction by 2050 and 34% by 2020 (with 1990 as a base). One effect of BA's targets will be that it will be necessary for UK residents and industry to make greater cuts to their carbon emissions in order that BA can make reduced cuts to its own emissions. The reductions BA plans to make will need to come largely through its aim to fly more carbon-efficient planes. The aim has been to reduce CO2 emissions per passenger kilometre (gCO2/paxkm) by 25% from 111gCO2/paxkm in 2005 to 83gCO2/paxkm in 2025. In 2008, BA emitted 107gCO2/paxkm.

BA was the first airline to commit to emissions trading, and is now preparing for the European Emissions Trading Scheme, which will cover all airlines from 2012 with preparatory reporting from 2009. BA opposes the fact that the scheme will apply to all flights in and out of the EU, rather than just intra-European flights. The concern is that BA will be subject to regulation that non-European registered airlines will not be, and so be placed at an unfair disadvantage relative to its long-haul competitors. However, the concept of emissions trading is one that BA supports and sees as being the most effective economic instrument to control aviation emissions.

In addition to promoting carbon efficiency and emissions trading, BA offers a voluntary carbon offset scheme as a way to address climate change. BA acknowledges support for the scheme has been 'steady'. In 2008, 157,719 passengers voluntarily paid to offset 55,318 tonnes of CO_2 emissions. This needs to be seen in the context of BA's overall carbon footprint of 17.5 million tonnes of CO_2 in 2008. To achieve its climate change targets, BA identifies the development of alternative fuels as one of the main elements of its future work. However, in view of the need to make progress rapidly, such fuels will need to be compatible with the existing infrastructure of engines, airports and fuel supply systems and it is far from clear to what extent such a technology will become available.

In earlier environmental reports, there was a key focus on noise, waste and congestion, and while these are still relevant to the airline, their prominence seems to have diminished slightly. BA continues to replace older and noisier planes with quieter planes and this has helped to win the arguments for the expansion of London's Heathrow airport. Air quality remains important as the approval to build a third runway at Heathrow requires it to be operated within EU legislation on acceptable air quality standards, while the scale of BA's operations determines that waste will continue to demand attention. However, it is instructive to see how much space is devoted in corporate reports to climate change as an issue compared to other environmental issues.

Community

Following the development of the environment group, BA established a community department in the early 1990s, which then joined with the environment group to become the sustainable business unit, producing a joint social and environmental report. In 2008/09 BA supported over 120 community and conservation projects in the form of funding, bursaries, merchandising, offering cargo space and fundraising events in the destinations where it operates. The effect of these efforts was calculated to be worth £5.4m, with direct contributions of £440,000. Staff donations to charities in 2008/09 were £630,000. BA's commitment to conservation activities have allowed experts, trainees and freight to travel for free to destinations served by BA's network. The founder of this programme, Rod Hall, was recognised with an MBE by the Queen for his efforts.

Located close to its London offices, BA has developed a community learning centre that offers 'airline focused activities' relevant to the school curriculum for primary and secondary schoolchildren. Since 1999, over 50,000 children have participated in learning activities at this centre. Perhaps the most well-known of BA's activities is the 'Change for Good' programme that collects spare change from customers. Since its beginning in 1994 this programme has raised over £26 million, with £1.3 million in 2008/09. As an example of the kind of work this programme supports, in Nigeria 36,000 insecticidal nets have been purchased to combat the spread of malaria, while in China immunisation and education services are being provided to children of migrant workers in Beijing.

Conclusion

As a large, diverse and complex organisation, BA has an enormous task just to manage its core business. Problems with suppliers, unions and high levels of staff sick leave are illustrative of the challenges. However, climate change in particular has become central to the future success of the airline. BA will need considerable technological advances to be able to meet its stated targets, and then it will need to develop an argument to justify its targets being short of those that others will face. Much may depend on the extent to which mechanisms such as emissions trading are adopted internationally and allow airlines to purchase emissions from sectors of the economy where the cost of abatement is cheaper. Issues previously listed under the heading of corporate responsibility will shift to become issues to demonstrate corporate relevance in the face of the necessary transition to a green economy.

Sources: BA Corporate Responsibility Reports 1992-2009; Personal communication: Dr Hugh Somerville, former Head of Sustainable Business Unit, BA.

Useful websites

Accor Group, Sustainable Development:
   http://www.accor.com/en/sustainable-development.html
Air France – KLM, Sustainable Development:
   http://corporate.airfrance.com/en/sustainable-development/headline/
Carlson Wagonlit Travel, Corporate Social Responsibility:
   http://www.carlsonwagonlit.com/en/global/our_company/corporate_social_ responsibility
Code of Conduct for the Protection of Children from Sexual Exploitation in Travel and Tourism: www.thecode.org
UN Global Compact: http://www.unglobalcompact.org/AboutTheGC/TheTenPrinciples
UN Millennium Development Goals: http://www.un.org/millenniumgoals/
UN World Tourism Organization Global Code of Ethics for Tourism:
   http://www.unwto.org/code_ethics/eng/global.htm
UN World Tourism Organization Sustainable Tourism – Eliminating Poverty:
   http://www.unwto.org/step/index.php
UN World Tourism Organization Task Force on the Protection of Children in Tourism:
   http://www.unwto.org/protect_children/index.php?op=0
Voluntary Initiatives for Sustainable Tourism: http://www.visit21.net/

References

Azilah, K. (2006) 'The need for business environmental and social responsibility in the tourism industry', *International Journal of Hospitality and Tourism Administration*, **7** (1), 1-22.
Bowen, H. (1953) *Social Responsibilities of the Businessman*, New York: Harper.
Boston College Center for Corporate Citizenship (2004) *State of Corporate Citizenship: 2003-2004*, Boston, MA: Boston College Center for Corporate Citizenship.
Carroll, A.B. (1991) 'The pyramid of corporate social responsibility: toward the moral management of organizational stakeholders', *Business Horizons*, **34**, (4), 39-48.

Carroll, A.B. (1999) 'Corporate social responsibility: evolution of a definitional construct', *Business and Society*, **38** (3), 268-295.

Castelo Branco, M. and Lima Rodrigues, L. (2007) 'Positioning stakeholder theory within the debate on corporate social responsibility', *Electronic Journal of Business Ethics and Organization Studies*, **12** (1), 5-15.

Clarkson, Max, B.E. (1995) 'A stakeholder framework for analyzing and evaluating corporate social performance', *Academy of Management Review*, **20** (1), 92-117.

Coelho, P. R. P., McLure, J.E. and Spry, J.A. (2003) 'The social responsibility of corporate management: a classical critique', *Mid-American Journal of Business*, **18** (1), 15-24.

Barry, N.P. (2000) 'Controversy: Do corporations have any responsibility beyond making a profit?'', *Journal of Markets and Morality*, **3** (1), 100-107.

De George, R.T. (1994) 'International business ethics', *Business Ethics Quarterly*, **4** (1), 1-9.

Dubbink, W. (2005) 'Democracy and private discretion in business', *Business Ethics Quarterly*, **15** (1), 37-66.

Elkington, J. (1997) *Cannibals with Forks: the Triple Bottom Line of 21st Century Business*, Oxford: Capstone Publishing

Epler Wood, M. and Leray, T. (2005) *Corporate Responsibility and the Tourism Sector in Cambodia*, Washington, DC: World Bank Group.

European Commission (2002) 'Corporate social responsibility: A business contribution to sustainable development', COM (2002) 324 final of 2.7.2002, Commission of the European Communities, Brussels.

European Commission. (2006) 'Implementing the partnership for growth and jobs: making Europe a pole of excellence on CSR'. COM(2005) 136 final. Commission of the European Communities, Brussels. Accessed 17 September 2007, at http://ec.europa.eu/enterprise/csr/policy.htm.

Fennell, D.A. (1999) *Ecotourism. An Introduction*, London: Routledge.

Font, X. (2001) 'Regulating the green message: the players in ecolabelling' in X. Font and R.C. Buckley (eds), *Tourism Ecolabelling: Certification and Promotion*, Wallingford: CABI Publishing.

Freeman, E.R., Wicks, A.C. and Parmar, B. (2004) 'Stakeholder theory and "the corporate objective revisited"', *Organization Science*, **15** (3), 364-369.

Friedman, M. (1970) 'The social responsibility of business is to increase its profits', *New York Times Magazine*, 13 September, New York.

Garriga, E. and Melé, D. (2004) 'Corporate social responsibility theories: Mapping the territory', *Journal of Business Ethics*, **53**, 51-71.

Global Policy Forum Europe (ed.) (2007) 'Whose partnership for whose development? Corporate accountability in the UN system beyond the Global Compact' accessed on 17 September 2007, at http://www.globalpolicy.org/reform/business/2007/0801w hosepartnership.pdf. Global Policy Forum Europe.

Hammele, H. (2002) 'Eco-labels for tourism in Europe: moving the market towards more sustainable practices', in M. Honey (ed.), *Ecotourism and Certification: Setting Standard in Practice*, Island Press.

Henderson, D. (2005) 'The role of business in the world of today', *Journal of Corporate Citizenship*, **17**, 30-32.

Henderson, D. (2006) 'The role of business in the modern world', *Journal of Financial Planning*, August, 10-14.

Hollenhorst, T. and Johnson, C. (2007) 'Tools for corporate social responsibility', accessed on 25 July 2007, at http://sconnect.prod.ifpeople.net/resources/downloads/tools/sri-en.pdf.

Hopkins, M. (2007) *Corporate Social Responsibility and International Development. Is Business the Solution?*, London and Sterling, VA: Earthscan.

IISD (2004a) 'What should an ISO standard on social responsibility look like?', accessed on 28 September 2007 at http://www.iisd.org/standards/csr.asp.

IISD (2004b) 'Stakeholder engagement, ISO and corporate social responsibility', accessed on 28 September 2007, at http://www.iisd.org/standards/csr.asp.

IISD (2010). 'ISP 26000 (CSR Guidance)', accessed on 20 January 2010 at http://www.iisd.org/standards/csr.asp.

Jacobs, M. (1997) 'The environment as stakeholder', Business Strategy Review, 6 (2), 25-28.

Kalisch, A. (2002) *Corporate Futures. Consultation on Good Practice. Social Responsibility in the Tourism Industry*, London: Tourism Concern.

KATE, Tourism Watch and ACSUD (2004) 'Corporate social responsibility. Dialogue with the tourism industry', accessed on 11 August 2006, at http://turismovision.kate-stuttgart.org/aktuelles/download/1838/projectflyer.pdf. KATE.

Lantos, G.P. (2001) 'The boundaries of strategic corporate social responsibility', *Journal of Consumer Marketing*, **18** (7), 595-630.

Lewis, L. and Unerman, J. (1999) 'Ethical relativism: a reason for differences in corporate social reporting?'', *Critical Perspectives on Accounting*, **10** (4), 521–547.

Mason, P. (2003) *Tourism Impacts, Planning and Management*, Oxford and Burlington, MA: Butterworth Heinemann.

McWilliams, A., Siegel., D. and Wright, P.M. (2006) 'Corporate social responsibility: strategic implications', *Journal of Management Studies*, **43** (1), 1-18.

Orlitzky, M., Schmidt, F.L. and Rynes, S.L. (2003) 'Corporate social and financial performance: a meta-analysis', *Organization Studies*, **24** (3), 403-441.

Palau, R. (2006) 'Corporate social responsibility in the Catalan hospitality chains', *Best-EN Think Tank VI 'Corporate Social Responsibility for Sustainable Tourism'*, accessed on 20 January 2010 at http://www.besteducationnetwork.org/ttvi/ttvi_papers.php.

Papaleo, C. and Beeton, S. (2006) 'Exploring Clarkson's typical corporate and stakeholder issues model as an approach to understanding corporate social responsibility in tourism: the case of Lonely Planet', University of Southern Denmark, Best-EN Think Tank VI 'Corporate Social Responsibility for Sustainable Tourism'', 13 June 2006, University of Western Sidney, Sydney, pp. 1-17.

Porter, M.E. and Kramer, M.R. (2006) 'Strategy and society: the link between competitive advantage and corporate social responsibility', *Harvard Business Review*, December, 78-94.

PricewaterhouseCoopers (2006) 'Corporate responsibility in the hospitality sector: pain or gain?', *Hospitality Directions Europe Edition*, 13 March.

RAMBOLL, Helsinki School of Business Economics and Administration and IIIEE (2000) *Challenging Diversity. A Review of Environmental Recognition Schemes and other Sustainable Tourism Activities in the Nordic Countries*. RAMBOLL, Virum.

Ruggie, J.G. (2002) 'The theory and practice of learning networks. Corporate social responsibility and the Global Compact', *Journal of Corporate Citizenship*, **5**, 27-36.

Ryan, C. (2003) *Recreational Tourism. Demand and Impacts*, (Aspects of Tourism, 11) Clevedon: Channel View Publications.

Schiller, B. (2005). *Ethical Corporation Report. Business–NGO Partnerships*, London: Ethical Corporation.

Sinclair, T.M. (ed.) (1997) *Gender, Work and Tourism*, London: Routledge.

Swarbrooke, J. (1999) Sustainable *Tourism Management*, New York: CABI Publishing.

Tepelus, C. (2008) 'Destination unknown? The emergence of corporate social responsibility for sustainable development of tourism', doctoral dissertation, Lund University.

The Economist (2004) 'Doing well and doing good', 31 July 2004.

The Economist (2005) 'The good company. A survey of corporate social responsibility', 22 January 2005.

The Economist (2001) 'Curse of the ethical executive. Why '"corporate social responsibility"' is not a welcome fashion', 15 November 2001.

The Economist (2002) 'Irresponsible. The dangers of corporate social responsibility', 21 November 2002.

Tschopp, Daniel, J. (2005) 'Corporate social responsibility: a comparison between the United States and the European Union', *Corporate Social Responsibility and Environmental Management*, **12**, 55-59

UN Global Compact (2007) 'What is the UN Global Compact?', accessed on 17 September 2007, at http://www.unglobalcompact.org/AboutTheGC/index.html, UN Global Compact.

UN (2007) *The Millennium Development Goals Report 2007*, accessed on 14 September 2007 at http://mdgs.un.org/unsd/mdg/Resources/Static/Products/Progress2007/UNSD_MDG_Report_2007e.pdf, United Nations Department of Economic and Social Affairs, New York.

UNEP (1995) *Environmental Codes of Conduct for Tourism*, Paris: United Nations Environmental Programme, Industry and the Environment.

UNWTO (2007a) 'ST-EP. Poverty and Tourism', accessed on 14 September 2007 at http://www.unwto.org/step/index.php, UN World Tourism Organization, Madrid.

UNWTO (2007b) 'Ethics in tourism. Background', accessed on 14 September 2007 at http://www.unwto.org/code_ethics/eng/global.htm, UN World Tourism Organization, Madrid.

USAID (2005) 'USAID and sustainable tourism: meeting development objectives', accessed on 20 January 2010 at *pdf.usaid.gov/pdf_docs/PNADE710.pdf*, USAID, Washington, DC.

USDOJ (2007) 'Child sex tourism. Factors supporting the child sex trade', accessed on 14 September 2007 at http://www.usdoj.gov/criminal/ceos/sextour.html, United States Department of Justice, Washington, DC.

Utting, P. (2002) 'The Global Compact and civil society: averting a collision course', *Development in Practice*, **12** (5), 644-647.

Utting, P. (2003) 'The Global Compact: why all the fuss?', *UN Chronicle*, 1.

Van der Putten, F.P. (2005) A Research Agenda for International Corporate Social Responsibility, *Nyenrode Research Group Working Paper Series*, November 2005, no. 05-09, Nyerode Business Universiteit.

Van Oosterhout, J.H. and Heugens, P.M.A.R. (2006). 'Much ado about nothing. A conceptual critique of CSR', ERIM Report Series Research in Management, accessed on 17 September 2007, from https://ep.eur.nl/bitstream/1765/7894/1/ERS-2006-040-ORG.pdf. Erasmus Research Institute of Management (ERIM).

WB and IFC (2003) *Company Codes of Conduct and International Standards, an Analytic Comparison*, Washington, DC: World Bank and International Financial Corporation.

Wheeller, B. (1991) 'Tourism's troubled times: responsible tourism is not the answer', *Tourism Management*, 12 (2), 91-96.

WTTC (2002) *Corporate Social Leadership in Travel and Tourism*, London: World Travel and Tourism Council.

Zadek, S. (2001) *The Civil Corporation: The New Economy of Corporate Citizenship*, London: Earthscan.

7 Triple Bottom Line Reporting of Tourism Organisations to Support Sustainable Development

Larry Dwyer and Jeffrey Faux

Rationale

The purpose of this module is to provide the student with a detailed understanding of the principles and practices of the triple bottom line (TBL) approach to evaluating performance in the context of tourism and hospitality operations. This approach encompasses consideration of the financial, environmental and social outcomes of the enterprise and its stakeholders. The module identifies the key benefits of TBL performance such as efficiencies and improved stakeholder relationships. It also identifies the roles of internal stakeholders, government and industry associations. The module highlights the necessary changes in organisational attitudes and behaviour needed to underpin the implementation of the TBL approach. Through an understanding of the challenges of integrating TBL into company strategic planning processes, students will be able to identify effective outcomes and performance measurements for TBL reporting. Issues in this course include the transparency and accountability required to demonstrate corporate social responsibility to stakeholders and government. Students will be able to identify the key facilitators and inhibitors of TBL performance and will understand the measures and reporting requirements. After completing the subject the student will understand the importance of the TBL perspective in promoting sustainability in tourism operations.

Learning objectives

The learning objectives of the subject are to enable the student to:

♦ Define and understand the principles and practice of TBL
♦ Understand the benefits of a TBL approach to hospitality and tourism management
♦ Develop the attitudes and behaviour essential for a TBL commitment
♦ Understand how to overcome the challenges of integrating TBL into firm decision making
♦ Understand how to implement TBL collection and reporting
♦ Analyse the role of government in supporting TBL

♦ Analyse the role of industry and professional codes of conduct in supporting TBL; and

♦ Implement planning and management strategies to improve performance based on TBL evaluation and to promote sustainable tourism.

The principles and practice of TBL

The tourism industry shares with local residents, governments and community the obligation to protect and maintain the natural and cultural heritage resources of our planet, both to sustain economies and to be passed on unimpaired to future generations. The most comprehensive approach to achieving sustainable operations (i.e. to integrate economic, environmental and social thinking into core business activities) is the triple bottom line (TBL) approach. TBL is a planning and reporting mechanism and decision-making framework used to achieve sustainable development in both private and public sector organisations – an internal management tool as well as an external reporting framework.

Increasingly, organisations around the world are recognising the value of demonstrating transparency and accountability beyond the traditional domain of financial performance. This trend has come about through increased public expectations for organisations to take responsibility for their non-financial impacts, including impacts on the community and the environment. In response, business, government, academics and non-government organisations (NGOs) have begun developing frameworks addressing these concerns. The need for business change brought on by the looming environmental imperative and calls for greater social involvement by enterprises has seen the development of conceptual frameworks for the conduct of business and in particular the notion of the TBL. Change to business institutions brings with it a range of terms that reflect the transformation that is taking place, such as TBL, sustainable development and sustainability.

TBL is primarily about an entity adopting performance standards not only in regard to its economic activities but also to its social and environmental activities (Elkington, 1998). Simple explanations of the terms belie the deep philosophical change required of business and the expanded role, responsibility and accountability that change will embody. The dilemma facing businesses that wish to adopt the new philosophy is one of identifying, in the first instance, the accountable areas in the environmental and social 'bottom lines' and then indicators of performance.

The tourism industry operates throughout the world: in developing and developed economies; in countries with cultural diverse backgrounds; with entities from large multinational companies to very small owner-operated businesses; and in remote locations as well as cities and towns. This diversity, not reflected in other commercial sectors, presents tourism entities with an opportunity to provide leadership in the conduct of business and particularly in the adoption of the new philosophy that reflects not only the ideals of the societies in which they operate but also the international community. Part of the leadership role is the active engagement and reporting by the tourism sector of TBL performance.

Natural, social, financial capital

Three definitions are important for the discussion to follow:

Corporate economic sustainability

*'Economically sustainable companies guarantee at any time cash flow suf-
ficient to ensure liquidity while producing a persistent above average return to
their shareholders' (Dyllick and Hockerts, 2002: 132).*

Corporate ecological sustainability

*'Ecologically sustainable companies use only natural resources that are con-
sumed at a rate below the natural reproduction, or at a rate below the development
of substitutes. They do not cause emissions that accumulate in the environment
at a rate beyond the capacity of the natural system to absorb and assimilate these
emissions. Finally they do not engage in activity that degrades eco-system services' (Dyllick and Hockerts, 2002: 132).*

Corporate social sustainability

*'Social sustainable companies add value to the communities within which
they operate by increasing the human capital of individual partners as well as
furthering the societal capital of these communities. They manage social capital
in such a way that stakeholders can understand its motivations and can broadly
agree with the company's value system (Dyllick and Hockerts, 2002: 133).*

Importance of corporate social sustainability

The social sustainability of companies arises from their corporate social responsibility practices (see Chapter 6). Corporate social responsibility (CSR) is a concept
that has become more and more apparent in company reporting. 'Perhaps CSR's
biggest contribution has been to stimulate new thinking about the business–society
relationship' (Blowfield, 2005: 517).

CSR forces organisations to consider their responsibilities and self-interest,
making them more accountable and responsible to their stakeholders for the decisions that they make. Companies typically are very concerned about the potential
damage to their reputations that may accrue as a result of media exposure of corporate malpractice. 'Increasing numbers of trans-national organisations and large
domestic companies, supported by business and industry associations, are adopting
a variety of voluntary initiatives that aim to improve their social, environmental and
human rights record' (Utting, 2005: 380). TBL reporting is one of these initiatives.

Relevance of TBL to sustainability

TBL is a philosophy for business that emphasises economic, environmental and
social goals rather than the narrower financial bottom line. The notion of TBL stems
from the work of Elkington and is defined as:

*Focusing corporations not just on the economic value they add, but also on the
environmental and social value they add – and destroy. At its narrowest, TBL is
used as a framework for measuring and reporting corporate performance against
economic, social and environmental parameters. At its broadest, the term is used*

> *to capture the whole set of values, issues and processes that companies must ad-dress in order to minimise any harm resulting from their activities and to create economic, social and environmental values.* (1998: 32)

TBL is not merely about measuring and reporting performance but is also about the adoption of ideals that are reflected in the idea of sustainable development. This clearly identifies a broader level of accountability for companies. TBL is closely related to sustainable development defined in the Brundtland Report (1987) as the 'development that meets the needs of the present world without compromising the ability of future generations to meet their own needs'. Sustainable development operates at macro and micro levels.

The macro level is about the development of social and economic policies that enhance environmental protection, social wellbeing and economic justice. The macro level is usually reflected in government policy directions and activities.

The micro level is about balancing the environmental system, the economic system and the social system and includes the activities of companies and community interest groups. The way in which the terms 'TBL' and 'sustainable development' are used creates much confusion as individuals and organisations use the terms erroneously and interchangeably.

Figure 7.1: Triple bottom line issues

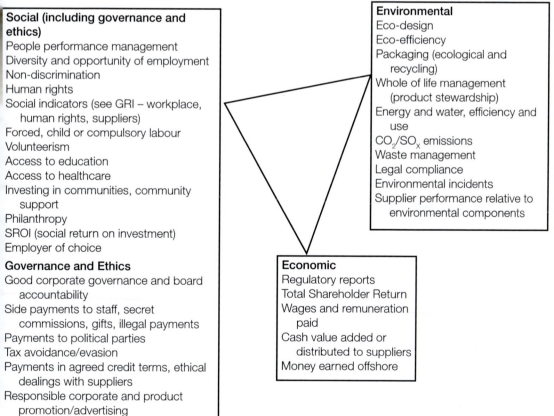

Social (including governance and ethics)
People performance management
Diversity and opportunity of employment
Non-discrimination
Human rights
Social indicators (see GRI – workplace, human rights, suppliers)
Forced, child or compulsory labour
Volunteerism
Access to education
Access to healthcare
Investing in communities, community support
Philanthropy
SROI (social return on investment)
Employer of choice

Governance and Ethics
Good corporate governance and board accountability
Side payments to staff, secret commissions, gifts, illegal payments
Payments to political parties
Tax avoidance/evasion
Payments in agreed credit terms, ethical dealings with suppliers
Responsible corporate and product promotion/advertising

Environmental
Eco-design
Eco-efficiency
Packaging (ecological and recycling)
Whole of life management (product stewardship)
Energy and water, efficiency and use
CO_2/SO_x emissions
Waste management
Legal compliance
Environmental incidents
Supplier performance relative to environmental components

Economic
Regulatory reports
Total Shareholder Return
Wages and remuneration paid
Cash value added or distributed to suppliers
Money earned offshore

TBL indicators

The ability of a tourism operation to sustain itself and the environment depends on its ability to understand the type of impacts that it may have. There is a substantial research literature on environmental and social indicators for tourism (Bossel, 1999; Manning, 1999; McCool *et al.*, 2001). Generally, the discussion has focused on indicators for sustainable development at a macro (destination) level, rather than at the micro level of the firm. Indicators are critical to the success of environmental monitoring and reporting as they provide the basis for objective performance assessment. Indicators function as a 'measuring stick', by which companies can evaluate how they are accomplishing explicit goals (Suggett and Goodsir, 2002).

A list of economic, social, environmental indicators appears in Figure 7.1. The issue list is based largely from GRI (Global Reporting Initiative) web sources but is further extended by a number of specific industry supplements such as the Tour Operators' Sector Supplement (GRI 2002).

Understanding the benefits of a TBL approach to hospitality and tourism management

Having three reporting considerations instead of one is inextricably linked to the financial bottom line. In other words, financial success itself is reliant upon not only economic sustainability but also social and environmental sustainability. TBL can be used as a process for integrating sustainability into the business environment, creating a new measure of corporate performance of balancing traditional economic goals with social and environmental issues (McDonough and Braungart, 2002). A company that can meet the needs of the present in terms of social and environmental impact, without compromising the needs of the future, is more likely to appeal to investors and customers alike, and thus be financially successful (Sauvante, 2001). This may be of particular relevance for firms in the tourism industry that depend crucially on unique features of the natural and social environments to maintain competitive advantage (Dwyer and Kim, 2003). For TBL reporting to be of real value to an organisation, it must be integrated into day-to-day business operations and be appropriately resourced (Gray and Bebbington, 2000).

In another contribution to this volume, Presbury and Edwards (Chapter 3) explore the implications of firms' pursuing sustainable tourism operations. The potential benefits that businesses can derive from TBL reporting can be classified under five headings: efficiencies and cost savings; improved market positioning; better stakeholder relationships; improved 'strategic' decision making; and 'wider' community benefits.

Efficiencies and cost savings

Substantial evidence is accumulating that by paying attention to social and environmental capital, companies are in fact realising better financial bottom lines (Anderson, 1999; Willard, 2002; Hawken *et al.*, 2003). TBL reporting can identify potential cost savings through:

♦ Reduced operating costs or through the detection of wasteful activities: for example, reducing materials and energy use, increasing operational and design efficiencies, recycling/reusing wastes, reduced transportation, storage, and packaging costs. These are of particular importance when TBL reporting leads to adoption of and/or is based on an environmental management system; and/or activity-based costing that provides firms with better information on the true costs of activities. Studies of materials and energy use in hotels reveal the importance of cost minimisation in maintaining viable operations (Stipanuk, 2001).

♦ Potentially lower compliance costs. Regulatory processes will run more smoothly if regulators have greater understanding of a company's performance. This applies to other business, tourism and hospitality firms which are responsible for compliance with operational development plans, planning conditions, standards and targets for sustainable tourism (Suggett and Goodsir, 2002).

♦ Attracting and retaining competent staff by demonstrating an organisation is focused on values and its long-term existence. The tourism industry is notorious for its high turnover, antisocial working hours, low pay, seasonal employment, instability and low job status (Hinkin and Tracey, 2000; UNEP, 2002: 13). A healthier working environment for employees results in reduced turnover of staff, fewer sick days, reduced penalties, insurance and workers' compensation costs, higher levels of worker satisfaction, and the ability to attract good quality staff. As a factor to help overcome this there is evidence that TBL attracts and retains high-calibre employees, improves employee morale, productivity and creativity (Sauvante, 2001).

♦ Improved access to capital from potential shareholders and financial institutions. The proliferation of 'green' and 'ethical' investment funds is making it more attractive for listed companies to meet the investment criteria of such funds (e.g. Ethical Investment Association, ttp://www.ethicalinvestment.org.uk). Tourism firms typically face strong impediments to investment due to lack of expertise in assessing high-risk tourism investments with variable cash flows, coupled with a reluctance by institutions to invest heavily or in the long term in the tourism industry (Dwyer and Forsyth, 1994). TBL reporting may help to overcome this constraint.

Improved market positioning

Adoption of TBL reporting can improve a firm's market position. TBL can have positive impacts on the branding of the organisation's products or services, thereby creating value through enhanced reputation and positive customer response (Suggett and Goodsir, 2002). TBL can help the firm to appeal to new and growing markets and encourage existing customers to return. In today's tourism industry, travellers are typically more sophisticated, have more disposable income, and are more confident about their expectations. As such, these consumers are attracted to businesses that are showing responsibility and awareness for the environment and the communities in which they operate. Further, there is a growing understanding that social responsibility implies risk minimisation, and that customers perceive the operator's duty of care to extend to the environment and the global community. Good organisational performance in relation to environmental and social issues can build the reputation of firms in the industry (Worby and DeLacy, 2003: 14).

Better stakeholder relationships

The term 'stakeholder' encompasses all individuals and bodies who have an interest in or are affected by (or potentially affected by) an activity. The term implies that the person has a 'stake' in the operation of an organisation (Freeman, 1984). Stakeholders include, inter alia, owners/shareholders/investors, employees, customers, business partners, suppliers, competitors, government regulators, pressure groups, local communities and future generations. In the tourism planning literature, the importance of meeting stakeholder needs is well recognised (Inskeep, 1991). While there is a research literature on employment issues (Olsen *et al.*, 1998) and customer (visitor) satisfaction (Toy *et al.*, 2002), there is less recognition of the importance of satisfying the wider set of stakeholders, as indicated above. Stakeholders may be categorised as primary and secondary (Freeman, 1984). The former are those who exert a direct economic influence on the company and, in turn, are directly influenced by the company's performance. Primary stakeholders would include customers, suppliers, employees, creditors, investors, and shareholders. Secondary stakeholders are those who have a less direct relationship with the economic base of the company (but may have significant expectations). Secondary stakeholders might include media, government, local communities, interest groups, non-profit organisations and the general public.

Competitive advantages can be derived from strong and meaningful relations between a company and its key stakeholders (especially those at the local community level). Effective stakeholder engagement can produce significant corporate value in the form of reputation/brand strengthening and assurance, enhanced operational certainty through achievement of social licence to operate, reduced/minimised pressure on government to implement restrictive regulatory frameworks, and enterprise agility through a strong understanding of external issues and trends (Dwyer and Kemp, 2004). TBL reporting is a vehicle for organisations to render account of their activities in relation to a wide group of stakeholders and thereby respond to society's growing expectations of transparency. The more that tourism firms and organisations adopt TBL reporting, the greater the opportunities for genuine community involvement in tourism development.

Formalising and enhancing communication with key stakeholders allow an organisation to develop a more proactive approach to addressing future needs and concerns.

Improved 'strategic' decision making

TBL reporting provides a number of advantages to company management, including:

♦ Forcing an organisation to be clear about what it is achieving: 'what gets measured gets managed'

- Improving the quality of information for decision makers, which clarifies organisational responsibilities and results in a more informed and accountable decision-making process through greater levels of transparency (Norman and MacDonald, 2003)

- Systematising and institutionalising best practice and providing the ability to benchmark both within and across sectors. TBL can foster innovation – addressing environmental and social impacts can lead to innovation that results in new markets and value creation (Suggett and Goodsir, 2002).

- Improving management of risk through stakeholder engagement, enhanced management systems, and performance monitoring (Gray and Bebbington, 2000). This may also lead to more robust resource allocation decisions and business planning, as risks are better understood and factored into decision making.

- Supporting the development of communication tools that enable information to be shared internally more effectively, thereby facilitating company learning (Gray and Bebbington, 2000)

- Helping to ensure that a values-driven culture is integrated at all levels of an organisation. The importance of organisational culture in tourism firm performance is well recognised (Dwyer et al., 1998/99, 2000; Kemp and Dwyer, 2001). Promoting integrated decision making within businesses and other organisations is a way of embedding sound corporate governance and ethics systems throughout all levels of an organisation.

There is growing evidence to suggest that over time these benefits do contribute to the increased market value of an organisation. Companies that incorporate TBL into their strategic decision making can generate substantial competitive advantages. Hence, TBL thinking is not a short-lived marketing ploy but a strategy that is designed to enhance long-term competitiveness.

Wider destination benefits

TBL reporting has potential to yield significant benefits to the wider community. Other benefits can accrue beyond the practising organisations themselves. This arises because widespread adoption of TBL reporting by companies will also enhance destination competitiveness. In the various models of destination competitiveness that have been developed, environmental and social factors are considered to play an important role as 'attractors' of tourists (Hassan, 2000; Ritchie and Crouch, 2003). The efforts of individual firms to achieve TBL reporting will have implications for the competitiveness of the destinations within which they operate. The relationship between the competitive advantage of the destination as a whole and the competitive advantage achieved by its constituent firms and organisations needs further research (Dwyer and Kim, 2003). Widespread adoption of TBL reporting would therefore also benefit policy making at the destination management level. Because the ultimate objective of achieving destination competitiveness is to improve the quality of life of residents, a TBL approach by constituent firms can help to achieve this result.

Integrating TBL into a tourism organisation

The adoption of a TBL perspective can begin with a simple shift in defining the objectives of management, as dictated by the board of directors, from maximising 'shareholder profits' to maximising 'stakeholder value', a very different goal with a broader set of beneficiaries. Not only does the company derive value but the company's wider influence also delivers community benefits. The task of integrating TBL into any organisation involves several challenges. These include: staff internalising the requisite attitudes and behaviours; identifying and selecting appropriate indicators; adopting an appropriate framework for TBL accounting and monitoring purposes; and confronting TBL implementation costs. The role of government and the role of industry codes are also recognised to be of relevance as facilitators of TBL development at the business level.

TBL reporting will only be a meaningful exercise as long as practitioners are genuinely committed to its success. TBL therefore needs to be perceived as good business practice for today as well as contributing to the more distant goal of sustainable development, and not as merely adding to the regulatory burden on business. There are several essential behaviours and attitudes that are required in those firms that seek to adopt the TBL approach (Suggett and Goodsir, 2002).

Commitment to accountability

TBL is founded on the assumption that firms are accountable not only to shareholders for generating returns but also to stakeholders for contributing, within their context and capabilities, to sustainable development. This notion of accountability is most often expressed in the 'vision' or mission statement of the firm (Kemp and Dwyer, 2003) and is inculcated in its 'organisational culture' (Kemp and Dwyer, 2001).

We can identify five accountability rationalities that may support the need for entities to report their performance (Diegling *et al.*, 1996):

♦ Legal: fundamental rules of assigning responsibility, in regulating differences and containing conflict

♦ Economic: sets out the methods for evaluating alternative uses of resources

♦ Technical: stipulates the expert or knowledge-based criteria by which means are selected in relation to ends

♦ Social: conditions which have to be met if social integration is to be maintained; and,

♦ Political: pragmatic requirements for sustaining the integration of decision-making structures and processes (adapted from: Diegling *et al.*, 1996).

These 'accountability rationalities' suggest that companies have a much greater obligation to account for their actions to a much broader audience than is presently acknowledged. Similarly, companies in their annual reports need to identify this greater obligation of accountability. Whilst the present reporting regime is directed principally at explicit users, government initiatives for example, broader based company reporting which includes environmental and social activities of business seems inevitable.

Commitment to transparency

Companies also have an obligation, within commercial limits, to be transparent about their activities and impacts beyond financial performance. Recognising the legitimacy of stakeholders' 'right to know' and disclosing multidimensional results and impacts is a powerful idea embodied in the TBL that can be included in the company 'vision' or mission statement, its communication with stakeholders, and in the actual content of its public reporting. That transparency needs to be embedded into the organisational culture, allowing the process to be viewed openly by all (Dwyer *et al.*, 1998/99; Dwyer, 2005).

Commitment to integrated planning and operations

Changes of the type required for TBL need to be well integrated into core management systems including planning, operations, employee relations, community involvement, information management, environmental management and management appraisal, and reward systems. Taking the holistic approach demanded by TBL requires significant internal cultural change in an organisation, with detailed attention paid to values, ethos, mission and long-term corporate reputation, stakeholder inclusivity, employee engagement and so on (Kemp and Dwyer, 2001). Thus, TBL is also important as a lever for cultural change within the company.

Companies are facing a number of changes in moving from old business paradigms to new business paradigms. Some main differences between the 'old' and 'new' perspectives are set out in Table 7.1.

Table 7.1: The 'old' vs 'new' reporting system

The old reporting system	The new reporting system
Shareholder focus	Stakeholder focus
Paper-based	Paper- and web-based
Standardised information	Tailored stakeholder information
Financial information	Economic, social and environmental information
Company-controlled information	Open and transparent approach including third-party information
Periodic reporting	Continuous reporting
Distribution of information	Stakeholder dialogue
Technical features and past performance	Greater emphasis on strategy, future projects, risk management and sustainability
Historical cost	Value-based assessments
Audit of accounts	Assurance of underlying system

Source: Suggett and Goodsir (2002)

As indicated above, a change in organisational culture is required if staff are to internalise the attitudes required to actualise the new perspective.

Reporting can be directed to external stakeholders and regulators, and to internal audiences, and serve in management improvement. While the reporting process will vary depending on the target audience, a main goal is to move towards a closer alignment of values between external and internal stakeholders and decision makers. This engagement is most appropriate during the stages of identifying core issues to address and at the assessment stage to ensure that the results are credible and transparent.

The concept of the TBL is intended to be integrated into the philosophies, values and business planning of the organisation. Thus, TBL accounting does not end with the first report. It is a continual process of monitoring, assessment, evaluation and amendment of organisational procedures.

Commitment to stakeholder engagement

The development of TBL strategies, activities and indicators involves collaboration with stakeholders. Businesses must understand, identify and evaluate how their activity affects stakeholders, what the main concerns/issues of stakeholders are and how they are being addressed, and need to ensure that their positive initiatives are being recognised.

Formalised, collaborative and meaningful stakeholder engagement, rather than an ad hoc approach, is an essential component to integrating TBL into business strategies and operations. This requires businesses to provide greater access for stakeholder dialogue and to build stakeholder engagement into their project time frames. At each point in the corporate decision-making process, there is an opportunity to ensure that key stakeholder concerns, perspectives, insights and priorities are addressed and integrated. Important issues include: identifying stakeholder concerns/issues about all aspects of operations; seeking input, advice and support for programmes and planning activities; identifying appropriate types of reporting; and seeking stakeholder support for stated goals (Freeman, 1984).

Effective stakeholder engagement is something that tourism firms can easily relate to. Recognition of the importance of broad community participation, of effective coordination and support between all involved parties, is crucial to the achievement of sustainable tourism (Timothy, 2002).

Challenges for tourism firms

Identifying and selecting indicators

The ability of a tourism operation to sustain itself and the environment depends on its ability to understand and manage the type of impacts that it may have. There is a substantial research literature on environmental and social indicators for tourism (Bossel, 1999; Manning, 1999; McCool et al., 2001).

Generally, the discussion has focused on indicators for sustainable development at a macro-level (destination), rather than at the micro-level of the firm. Indicators are critical to the success of environmental monitoring and reporting as they provide the basis for objective performance assessment. Indicators function as a 'measuring stick' by which companies can evaluate how they are accomplishing explicit goals (Suggett and Goodsir, 2002).

Various methodologies or templates for TBL reporting or corporate environmental and social responsibility accounting have been proposed or are still under development (Gilkison, 1999). Perhaps the best known and most widely adopted of these methodologies is the so-called Global Reporting Initiative (GRI), which provides social, environmental and economic indicators at an international level. The GRI has emerged as the internationally accepted framework for sustainability reporting. Founded by the Coalition for Environmentally Responsible Economies (CERES), the GRI is an official collaborating centre of the United Nations Environment Programme (UNEP, 2001). There is no clear-cut approach to reaching the TBL – each company situation is case-specific, and specialised solutions will have to be developed to fit their needs appropriately. Social reporting is particularly challenging. An organisation's social impacts are at least as diverse as its environmental impacts, if not more so. Additionally, social impacts are value-laden and therefore perceived differently by different stakeholder groups. (For some examples of social performance indicators see Norman and MacDonald, 2003: Appendix 1.) The GRI methodology is attractive because it: (a) allows a partial and incremental implementation; (b) involves a continuous learning process; and (c) adapts to new demands. The calibre and standing of its supporters give it credibility. It also provides a framework for reporting that promotes comparability between reporting organisations while recognising the practical considerations of collecting and presenting information across diverse reporting organisations. However, while the GRI provides an internationally accepted guide, it does not yet provide methodologies for many of its indicators, nor does it take into consideration specific conditions in different countries, particularly in relation to established indicators and methodologies. While some companies are successfully adopting the GRI and other frameworks, others take a more eclectic approach where they review indicators used by other companies and adopt the most appropriate from various sources. In general, businesses develop indicators that are most relevant to themselves. Unfortunately, to date tourism researchers have neglected the potential relevance of GRI indictors to promote a better understanding of tourism's environmental and socio-cultural impacts and as an underpinning of sustainable tourism. More research is needed in this area to apply TBL indicators to assess tourism firm performance.

Measurement

Identifying economic values for the social and environmental benefits has proven to be difficult as many of these outcomes expand over many years, flow on to other areas, and frequently do not have clear market values. As environmental and social impacts often involve benefits and costs that are not bought and sold in markets, market values will not identify people's preferences for these values.

Many of these social and environmental benefits can best be measured using qualitative techniques. However, accountability is increasingly requiring clear economic valuations of all returns (Christiansen, 2004). Attempts have been made to use money as the common denominator (e.g. by putting a monetary value on the cost of restoring environmental damage or the cost of treating an injured worker).

However, there are limits to the success of a monetary formula (e.g. what monetary value can be put on the extinction of a species, the alienation of local communities in the face of tourism development, or the exploitation of child workers in Third World factories making items for tourist shopping?). The challenge is now to understand how these factors interrelate (i.e. the 'joined-up' bottom line) rather than measuring how the economic, environmental and social dimensions fit into three separate bottom lines.

There is presently no accepted single standard for measuring the combined economic, environmental and social performance of an organisation. Some commentators argue that this is an unachievable aim (Norman and MacDonald, 2003).

Implementation costs

Companies will inevitably weigh improving environmental quality against compliance costs. The costs of preparing a TBL report will vary from organisation to organisation. But as argued above, adoption of TBL should be regarded as an investment to maintain competitive advantage over time.

Business size

Larger businesses, due to their access to resources, are well placed to make significant inroads into operating sustainably, particularly if they can utilise their own staff to become involved and committed to the principles of sustainability. Small- to medium-sized operations, which comprise the majority of firms in tourism, have fewer resources but can still achieve a great deal through the personal involvement of owners and staff together with their guests. Small to medium-sized tourism organisations also have avenues for guidance in adopting a TBL approach through local community initiatives and regional industry associations, as well as government organisations such as local councils. These can provide information, guidance training and ready-made packages for small to medium-sized operators to take advantage of. Examples and case studies can be found on the Green Globe website (http://www.greenglobe21.com/).

Role for government

Globally, governments espouse the benefits of sustainable development, including particular emphasis on a sustainable tourism industry. Some form of government support may be needed (and justified in terms of the wider destination benefit) to promote TBL measurement, reporting and auditing. TBL reporting can be promoted to the business sector as a means for improving competitiveness. Governments at all levels can act as catalysts for the development of TBL. Inter alia, governments can do the following: provide support for and facilitate TBL to allow strategic partnerships and support networks to develop and experiences to be shared; develop and promote support networks that encourage sharing of experiences among government agencies including the implementation of a TBL procurement policy for government agencies; and develop improved strategies and measurements of accountability and transparency in public-sector decision making. Governments can support research into TBL reporting and provide financial incentives (e.g. tax concessions) for firms attempting to improve their TBL performance (Allen Consulting Group, 2002). Government pressure on business to adopt TBL reporting will only be credible, however, if government bodies are subjected to the same discipline ('do as I do, not only as I say'). For any government to demonstrate a commitment to TBL, opportunities need to be created for stakeholders to genuinely engage in decision making and reporting. Views vary regarding the issue of mandatory TBL reporting. The general perception is that TBL reporting will become a commercial imperative rather than an imposed measure. Governments seriously concerned with promoting sustainable development should provide incentive-based approaches rather than imposing prescriptive requirements.

Role for industry codes

Economic, environmental and socio-cultural pressures are resulting in increasingly stringent legislation and taxation designed to encourage people to act more considerately towards the environment. Therefore, the best businesses will anticipate such action and minimise their impacts well in advance. Self-management practices will increase through the adoption of codes of practice and certification schemes. It will also minimise compliance costs. Globally, many tourism industry sectors have responded to sustainable development through the establishment of voluntary initiatives. Chief among these are codes of conduct, 'a set of expectations, behaviors or rules written by industry members (often interchangeably) with an emphasis on accreditation of operators' (Newsome *et al.*, 2002: 223). Examples in the tourism industry include: Code of Ethics and Guidelines for Sustainable Tourism (Tourism Industry Association of Canada); Environmental Codes of Conduct for Tourism (United Nations Environment Programme); Sustainable Tourism Principles (Worldwide Fund for Nature and Tourism Concern); Code for Sustainable Tourism (Pacific Asia Travel Association); Responsible Traveller Guidelines (Africa Travel Association); Declaration of Earth Friendly Travelers (Japanese Travel Association); and Agenda 21 for the Tourist and Travel Industry (promoted by the World Tourism Organization, the Earth Council and the World Travel and Tourism Council).

The codes often provide only generic principles, and businesses find it difficult to translate them to an operational level. There are a number of initiatives that can provide valuable and practical guidance to both small and large businesses, including awards, codes of conducts and certification, education and awareness programmes. Industry codes have a potentially valuable role to play in fostering a TBL approach to sustainable business operations in the tourism industry.

Conclusions

This chapter has argued that a concern by firms to cope with the challenges of the global financial crisis need not imply a neglect of sustainability. TBL reporting can be a vital part of an overall strategy aimed at encouraging the business world, government bodies and other organisations to assume responsibility for sustainable development. TBL reporting is an important means by which both the private sector and government bodies in tourism at all levels can demonstrate they are assuming their part of the responsibility for sustainable development. TBL is not about compartmentalising activities/projects in the 'three bottom lines', but rather is about integrating core principles that reflect a commitment to a sustainable organisation and society. TBL is continual learning processes with no one best approach. The exciting challenge for organisations is to now discover new pioneering ways to join the economic, environmental and social bottom lines together. Some tourism operators in fact, practise TBL even if they don't call it that. See the case study on BikeHike Adventures.

TBL reporting will be worthwhile as long as managers see it as good business practice as well as contributing to sustainable development. TBL reporting will fail as an instrument for integrated decision making if it is perceived mainly as an obligation to satisfy outsiders with no stake in the business. Despite the enthusiasm and energy with which TBL is being adopted internationally, it is still too early to tell whether this will lead to major, sustainable changes in the operation of the business community and the public sector. However, the momentum for change is growing and 'sustainability' and 'triple bottom line' terminology will soon be standard parlance in boardroom discussions around the world. Many national and multinational corporations have already demonstrated a clear commitment to TBL reporting. Tourism firms may be expected, increasingly, to adopt TBL philosophy and practice.

The significance of planning for sustainable tourism operations through new TBL-based management practices cannot be overemphasised. The monitoring of management practices against performance indicators and baseline measures is becoming an increasingly influential component of tourism operations. Tourism operators will need to identify their own indicators and set them within the context of their broader business environments, working in partnerships with their communities and matching them with their business objectives. They will also need to confront the challenges of adopting the new paradigm of reporting that have been outlined above. The aim of this scoping study has been to highlight issues that will need to be addressed by tourism firms as they adopt the new paradigm of TBL reporting.

Case Study: BikeHike Adventures Commitment to Sustainable Tourism Practices

Sustainable tourism is the banner under which BikeHike Adventures operates and is committed to. It's the kind of tourism that benefits local communities and travellers without compromising the enjoyment of future generations. Each year we look for different projects worldwide to support and help to raise social and cultural awareness. In 2008 we supported a small community in Vietnam when Typhoon Hagupit hit and contributed to the worst flooding and landslide activity in two decades in the northern border districts of Vietnam. Bat Xat, a Vietnamese region that BikeHike supports through its 'Paddle and Play Adventure', was severely impacted, particularly in the Coc My and Si Ma Cai villages where hardworking, but poor, hill-tribe people live in traditional houses of earthen walls and thatched roofs. The storm destroyed homes, their seasonal crop, and the popular and fascinating open-air market. A few BikeHike guides immediately brought two tons of rice, eight bags of second-hand clothes, and 100 children's sweaters to the community, but people are still desperate for more food and clothes.

Since BikeHike Adventures Inc. was founded in 1994, it has worked to support sustainable tourism practices. Here are some of the specifics:

- BikeHike Adventures has a maximum of 12 travellers per trip. On average it is more likely to be 6 to 8 people.

- e respect local cultures by operating sensitive adventures that view local communities as our partners.

- We strive to reduce our environmental footprint by working with socially responsible suppliers who care about the impact of their operations.

- We contribute to the conservation of the natural, welfare and cultural heritage of the areas we visit. For example, we financially supported typhoon victims in Vietnam, the Manjari Sankurathri Memorial Foundation in India and the Bicycles Crossing Borders programme in Cuba, as well as a project to educate street kids in Nicaragua. We donated school supplies to a remote village in Patachanca, Peru.

- In our Granville Island, Vancouver, British Columbia headquarters, we employ best environmental practices in our daily work by supporting the ongoing efforts of the recycling industry, using recycled paper products, and we all bike or walk to work every morning.

- We actively communicate our values to our travellers and the local operators, educating them in sustainable tourism practices.

- BikeHike is actually fairly unique in the tourism world as we are a multi-sport tour operator. This means that as much as possible our trips are 'self-propelled adventures', so there is minimal time spent in carbon dioxide-emitting vehicles (cars, buses, planes). The ways in which our travellers explore and experience a destination is very important to us. By being self-propelled we reduce our emissions of gases that contribute to climate change and to us that is a good thing! Anything we can do to reduce our footprint on the earth is good business and makes good sense!

- BikeHike is a proud member of Sustainable Travel International and the International Ecotourism Society.

Source: BikeHike Adventures, www.bikehike.com

References

Allen Consulting Group (2002) *The 'Triple Bottom Line' in the Australian Public Sector: A Collaborative Exploration*, Public Sector Collaborative Research Project, Canberra.

Anderson, R. (1999) *Mid-course Correction: Toward a Sustainable Enterprise – The Interface Model*, White River Junction, VT: Chelsea Green Publishing.

Blowfield, M. (2005) 'Corporate social responsibility: reinventing the meaning of development?', *International Affairs*, **81** (3), 515-524.

Bossel, H. (1999) *Indicators for Sustainable Development: Theory, Methods, Applications*, Winnipeg, Manitoba: International Institute for Sustainable Development.

Brundtland, M. (1987) *Our Common Future, Report of the World Commission on Environment and Development*, published as Annex to General Assembly document A/42/427, Development and International Co-operation: Environment.

Christiansen, I. (2004) *Strategic Approaches for Evaluation in Agricultural and Natural Resources Management Research Programs: A Literature Review*, Australian Cotton Cooperative Research Centre: Queensland Government.

Diegling, P. Anderson, J. and Guthrie, J. (1996) 'Accounting for public accounts committees', *Accounting, Auditing and Accountability Journal*, **2** (9), 30-49.

Dwyer, L. (2005) 'Relevance of Triple Bottom Line reporting to achievement of sustainable tourism: a scoping study', *Tourism Review International*, **9** (1), 79-94.

Dwyer, L. and Kemp, S. (2004) 'Closure of an ecolodge: a failure of strategic management?', *Journal of Pacific Studies*, **26** (1 & 2), 51–75.

Dwyer, L. and Kim, C.W. (2003) 'Destination competitiveness: a model and indicators', *Current Issues in Tourism*, **6** (5), 369–413.

Dwyer, L. and Forsyth, P. (1994) 'Motivation and impacts of foreign tourism investment', *Annals of Tourism Research*, **21** (3), 512-537.

Dwyer, L., Teal, G. and Kemp, S. (1998/99) 'Organisational culture and strategic management in a resort hotel', *Asia Pacific Journal of Tourism Research*, **3** (1), 27–36.

Dwyer, L., Teal, G., Kemp, S. and Wah, C.Y. (2000) 'Organisational culture and human resource management in an Indonesian resort hotel', *Tourism, Culture and Communication*, **2** (1), 1–11.

Dyllick, T. and Hockerts, K. (2002) 'Beyond the business case for corporate sustainability', *Business Strategy and the Environment*, **11** (2), 130-141. http://www3.interscience.wiley.com/cgi-bin/fulltext/91014927/PDFSTART, accessed 23 March 2006.

Elkington, J. (1998) *Cannibals with Forks: The Triple Bottom Line of 21st Century Business*, Stony Creek, CT: New Society Publishers.

Freeman, R.E. (1984) *Strategic Management: A Stakeholder Approach*, Boston, MA: Pitman.

Gilkison, B. (1999) *Accounting for a Clean Green Environment: Obligations and Opportunities for New Zealand Businesses and Their Accountants*, Nelson, New Zealand: Anchor Press.

GRI (Global Reporting Initiative) (2002), http://www.globalreporting.org/guidlines/2002/c52 accessed 20 January 2 2010

Gray, R. and Bebbington, J. (2000) 'Environmental accounting, managerialism and sustainability', *Advances in Environmental Accounting and Management*, **1**, 1–44.

Hassan, S. (2000) 'Determinants of market competitiveness in an environmentally sustainable tourism industry', *Journal of Travel Research*, **38** (3), 239–245.

Hawken, P., Lovins, A. and Lovins, H. (2003) *Natural Capitalism: Creating the Next Industrial Revolution*, Snowmass, CO: Rocky Mountain Institute.

Hinkin, T.R. and Tracey, J.B. (2000) 'The cost of turnover', *Cornell Hotel and Restaurant Administration Quarterly*, **41** (3), 14–21.

Inskeep, E. (1991) *Tourism Planning: An Integrated and Sustainable Development Approach*, New York: International Thomson Publishing.

Kemp, S. and Dwyer, L. (2001) 'An examination of organisational culture: the Regent Hotel, Sydney', *International Journal of Hospitality Management*, **20**, 77–93.

Kemp, S. and Dwyer, L. (2003) 'Mission statements of 50 international airlines: a content analysis', *Tourism Management*, **24** (6), 635–653.

Manning, T. (1999) 'Indicators of tourism sustainability', *Tourism Management*, **20** (2), 179–181.

McCool, S., Moisey, N. and Nickerson, N. (2001) 'What should tourism sustain? The disconnect with industry perceptions of useful indicators', *Journal of Travel Research*, **40** (2), 124–131.

McDonough, W. and Braungart, M. (2002) 'Design for the triple top line: new tools for sustainable commerce', *Corporate Environmental Strategy*, **9** (3), 251–258.

Newsome, D., Moore, S.A. and Dowling, R.K. (2002) *Natural Area Tourism: Ecology, Impacts and Management*, Clevedon: Channel View Publications.

Norman, W., and MacDonald, C. (2003) 'Getting to the bottom of the "Triple Bottom Line"', *Business Ethics Quarterly*, March, 1–19.

Olsen, M., Tse, E. and West, J. (1998) *Strategic Management in the Hospitality Industry*, 2nd edn, New York: John Wiley.

Ritchie, J.B.R. and Crouch, G. (2003) *The Competitive Destination: A Sustainability Perspective*, Wallingford: CAB International.

Sauvante, M. (2001) 'The "Triple Bottom Line": a boardroom guide', *Directors Monthly*, **25** (11), 1–6.

Stipanuk, D.M. (2001) 'Energy management in 2001 and beyond', *Cornell Hotel and Restaurant Administration Quarterly*, **42** (3), 57–71.

Suggett, D. and Goodsir, B. (2002) *Triple Bottom Line Measurement and Reporting in Australia: Making It Tangible*, Canberra: Allen Consulting Group.

Timothy, D. J. (2002) 'Tourism and community development issues' in R. Sharpley and D. Telfer (eds), *Tourism and Development: Concepts and Issues*, Clevedon: Channel View Publications, pp. 149-164.

Toy, D., Kerstetter, D. and Rager, R. (2002) 'Evaluating customer satisfaction: a contingency model approach', *Tourism Analysis*, **6** (3), 99–108.

UNEP (United Nations Environment Programme) (2001) 'Ecotourism and sustainability', *Industry and Environment*, 24, (3–4).

UNEP (United Nations Environment Programme) (2002) Biological Diversity and Tourism: International Guidelines for Sustainable Tourism, Secretariat of the Convention on Biological Diversity, UNEP. http://www.biodiv.org/programmes/socio-eco/tourism/guidelines accessed January 19 2010

Utting, P. (2005) 'Corporate responsibility and the movement in business', *Development in Practice*, **15** (3 & 4), 375-388.

Willard, B. (2002) *The Sustainability Advantage*, Gabriola Island, British Columbia: New Society Publishers.

Worboy, G. and DeLacy, T. (2003) 'Tourism and the environment: it's time!', paper presented to the 2003 Ecotourism Australia 11th National Conference, National Wine Centre, Adelaide, Australia. http://www.crctourism.com.au/CRCBookshop/Documents/WorboysPaper-Tourism&Environment.pdf.

8 Supplier-driven Innovations for Sustainable Tourism

Anne-Mette Hjalager

Rationale

The purpose of this chapter is to introduce a conceptual approach to driving forces for innovation in sustainable tourism. The model underpins the fact that innovation in tourism is not solely the effect of a strategic and wilful internal action in tourism firms and organisations, but also the consequences of external driving forces. Further, the chapter offers a more detailed review of the importance of suppliers as (one of several) push factors for sustainable tourism. Examples are provided, and possibilities and limitations in terms of a rapid development of more sustainable practices in tourism are discussed. A four-field model aims at stimulating the search for new forms of collaboration between tourism firms and their suppliers, and it adds dimensions to the traditional views in supply chain management.

Learning objectives

On completion of this chapter students should be able to:

- Define and understand the driving forces for sustainable tourism innovation
- Identify the capacity of tourism suppliers to undertake sustainable innovations that affect tourism
- Explain the sustainability issues from a supply chain perspective
- Evaluate types of innovations for sustainable tourism
- Track tourism innovations back to suppliers
- Understand how suppliers can be promoters or inhibitors of sustainability in tourism;
- Discuss appropriate sustainability incentives and measures.

What promotes innovation?

The context of innovation in tourism

There are many definitions of the term 'innovation'. At the broad level, innovation implies the materialising of something new and the successful exploitation of ideas. Joseph Schumpeter (1934) distinguished between the introduction of new goods, new methods of production, the opening of new markets, the conquest of new sources of supply, and the setting up of a new organisation.

Innovation takes place in all sectors of the economy, including the public and voluntary sectors, but with variations in intensity. Investigations of innovations in tourism firms often come up with very bleak results. The observation is that, understood as individual entities, tourism firms are not particularly innovative (Sundbo, 1997; Christensen, 2008; Hjalager, 2010). Even the largest corporations seldom employ people in research and development departments (R&D). At best, innovations consist of small changes, mostly aimed at obtaining higher productivity and cost savings. Supplementary studies of management attitudes and practices reveal a distinct conservatism and high risk aversion that is likely to counteract the inclination to innovate or hinder the implementation of new products and services (Orfila-Sintes *et al.*, 2005; Jacob and Groizard, 2007; Pikkemat, 2008). In small and medium-size firms, changes often do not take place until the facilities are closed and restarted by new proprietors with novel concepts or ideas.

Nevertheless, tourism as it is experienced by the customer is undergoing quite dramatic changes. Specifically in the field of sustainable tourism, green labelling as auditing started more than a decade ago and represented major steps forward both for protection of the environment and for the image of tourism products (Buckley, 2002; Cater *et al.*, 2004, Presbury and Edwards, this volume). Likewise, the conceptualisation and re-launching of destinations as eco-friendly embody innovations in the larger geographical scale. Such initiatives require inclusive and collaborative attitudes in their local settings to harvest the benefits of the sustainability wave. For example, Costa Rica focuses on sustainability issues in tropical rainforests, and the Alpine region attempts to address the challenges of the immense environmental pressure from winter sport enthusiasts without compromising the economic potentials (Liu, 2003; Holden, 2008).

Unlike other sectors – for example, the automobile or pharmaceutical industries – innovations in tourism are not noticeably embedded inside existing corporative structures. Rather, they are to a greater extent associated with external collaboration and entrepreneurship. Accordingly, the search for, the discovery and creation, the experimentation and development of products and services take place in association with recently started firms or through networks for which the tourism aspect represents a new business strategy (Hall and Williams, 2008). Knowledge needed for the innovative processes is shared with many actors and flows across sectors.

In his book *Innovation and Entrepreneurship*, Drucker (1985) elaborates on the various sources of innovation. Drucker finds that during an innovation process, actors search consistently and purposefully and are organised for changes in the surrounding environment. Innovations exploit changes. His approach and examples demonstrate the existence of a range of external factors that may promote an innovative activity, and which open new profitable niches. They include the unexpected, incongruence, process need, industry and market structure, demographics, changes in perception and new knowledge.

♦ **The unexpected**: for example, a success or a failure that can be enhanced. The first Icehotel in Sweden was based on the unexpectedly positive feedback of guests who happened to spend a night in an igloo which was – reluctantly – provided for them.

♦ **Incongruence**: misunderstandings about the customers' needs and preferences. For example, tour operators believed that travellers invariably want extensive service packages, luxury and relaxation. That made room for contrasts to luxury 'back to basics' and 'rough adventure trips'.

♦ **Process need**: Sometimes it becomes a necessity to break routines and invent new modes of operation. For example, congestion on roads has led to electronic traffic control and management systems, and more recently GPS systems are leading to the smoothing of traffic flows and (potentially) the saving of energy.

♦ **Industry and market structure**: Refocused political agendas lead to changes in industry and market structures. Future climate agendas will influence the operations of fuel-intensive airlines and cruise ships and challenge the business models in these sectors.

♦ **Demographics**: It is recognised that demographic changes affect the nature of tourism. For example, an increase in the average age of tourists shifts the demand patterns. But demographics that are important for sustainability issues also include changes in education, employment status, income distribution, etc.

♦ **Changes in perceptions**: Changing consumer perceptions require industries to adapt. Tourists are influenced by public opinion in terms of what tourism destinations are worthwhile to visit. For example, the perception of destinations such as Bangladesh and the Arctic/Antarctic are shifting from 'no-go' places towards an image as destinations to visit as a last chance before they sink into the sea.

♦ **New knowledge**: Technical and scientific knowledge is often regarded as a prime source of innovation, and indeed they are essential in many respects. Achievements from hardcore scientific research will, however, often only indirectly affect tourism, as they will be embedded in supplies and machinery.

A concise understanding of what drives the development of tourism will have to take into account not one of these factors, but all of them. Drucker's point is that existing and well-established firms will only reluctantly observe new developments and that opens up opportunities for new entrepreneurs in the field. As observed by Ateljevic and Doorne (2000), entrepreneurs play a key role in the renewal of the sustainable tourism product as they bring in inspiration and knowledge from other categories of economic activity.

Driving forces – a systematic overview

Classic academic authors such as Rogers (1995) and Rosenberg (1976) emphasise R&D as drivers for innovation. They include the firm's own R&D as well as R&D mediated through universities and public research units. Increasingly, research in innovation has taken into account other driving forces. Ideas and inspiration for innovation are fostered in diverse ways, and studies increasingly recognise that many firms are innovative even though they do not invest in formal R&D (von Hippel 1988). It is helpful to distinguish between the following driving forces:

♦ **Technology**: innovations in tourism which are the result of technical progress for example new types of sustainable guiding practice due to development such as GPS, smart-phones, etc. (Maxwell, 2009).

♦ **Research**: innovations that would not have been possible without integration with academic research efforts. An example is Ecocean, which combines whale-shark habitat and migration research with tourism experiences (Hughes, 2008).

♦ **Price:** Tourism businesses are often cost-constrained, and innovations are occurring to maintain acceptable yields under aggressive competition. It is an ongoing and non-settled discussion whether customers are willing to pay a price premium for sustainable products (Masau and Prideaux, 2003).

♦ **Employees**: Innovation frequently depends on the knowledge and creativity of the staff, particularly under circumstances where they are encouraged through appropriate management systems and incentives (Cooper, 2006).

♦ **Users:** Some niche tourists are 'lead users' in the sense that they are months or years ahead of what will eventually become products in high demand. Learning from these users is becoming a method that is applicable in sustainable tourism as shown by Damsholt and Ren (2009), who studied the use of focus groups, observations, anthropological experimentation, etc.

♦ **Legislation**: Regulation is often considered negative for business development. However, regulation and taxing can urge the industry to look for new ways of organisation and operation, for example in terms of radical energy savings. Peeters *et al.* (2006) discuss the case of an environmentally critical sector, namely aviation.

♦ **Suppliers:** Tourism firms are directly or indirectly dependent on a broad range of services and sectors: information technology, food services, mechanics, building materials etc. Some suppliers are advanced innovators. When tourism firms are purchasing a product or a service, the innovation is embedded therein. In this understanding, the acquisition of a product/service represents a shortcut to innovations for the tourism firm.

All of these seven driving forces deserve separate analytical attention. Quite overwhelmingly, the tourism debate focuses on the market-related driving forces for innovations – what do the customers want and what are their attitudes? In this chapter only the last-mentioned – supplier-driven innovation – will be unfolded and discussed. There is a need to bring suppliers out of anonymity in order to use their full capacity in the drive for a more sustainable tourism. A higher level of transparency throughout the value chain is essential.

Suppliers' roles in sustainable tourism – a review

The academic literature views the tourism experience as a collection of many components delivered by a variety of providers, and consumed in a continuous process (Tremblay, 1998). There is less research attention paid to those suppliers who have an earlier position in the value chain, i.e. those who are delivering goods or services to core tourism firms (transportation, accommodation, catering and attractions). Following a review of value chains in tourism, Zhang *et al.* (2009) identify some examples of studies of value chains in tourism and emphasise that the strategic role of suppliers and the collaboration between tourism firms and suppliers is a neglected research theme. Likewise, the discipline of supply chain management (SCM), which is well known in other sectors of the economy, has received limited attention in the case of tourism. The financial and operational benefits of a distinctive supply chain management endeavour seem to remain to be addressed in most categories of tourism firms.

The potential of collaboration with suppliers for innovative product and process developments has also received considerable attention in the general business literature and research. In manufacturing, for example, firms are often dependent on suppliers who feel a responsibility not only to deliver required qualities, but also to be visionary on behalf of their customers and their customers' customers. Such suppliers may be the origin of an innovative 'push' and contribute with knowledge that leads to a comprehensive competitive capability for both suppliers and buyers (Möller and Törrönen, 2003; McEvily and Marcus, 2005).

Orfila-Sintes *et al.* (2005) suggest that tourism firms lack awareness of the possibilities of learning from suppliers. They observe that when hotels purchase technical equipment, only 6% of them develop equipment jointly with their supplier, while nearly 80% just buy and install equipment. Radical innovations are mostly seen in connection with ICT investments. Environmental quality management is found to be affected very modestly in an innovative direction by suppliers (Orfila-Sintes *et al.*, 2005).

Some research addresses specifically the sustainability issues of supply chains. Quite uniformly, however, they accentuate the 'trend to use purchasing policies and practices to facilitate sustainable development at the tourist destination' (Font *et al.*, 2008: 260; see also Schwartz *et al.*, 2008). Sigala (2008) investigates the influence of tour operators on suppliers, the rationale being that tour operators' contribution to sustainable tourism will be more effective, as they are able to set (new and enhanced) standards for the suppliers. Tour operators are concerned with the sustainability performance of hotels, transportation companies, local guides and attractions, while stepping back in the value chain to suppliers is less common.

Generally, it is interesting to observe that suppliers are mainly seen as passive providers who must comply with standards set by the buyers in the tourism industry. That is hardly the full picture, as suggested by Zhang *et al.* (2009) who point to underlying interrelationships which are far more complex. In order to understand suppliers as driving forces for innovation it is essential to address the nature of the interrelationships in greater detail.

A model of suppliers' roles and capacities in sustainable tourism

The model in Figure 8.1 is applied in order to spell out the complexities of the interrelationships between tourism firms and their suppliers. The horizontal axis describes a continuum of collaborative distance between suppliers and tourism actors – from a greater distance (culturally, geographically and in terms of communication) on the left side to a close relationship on the right side. The vertical axis demonstrates the nature of suppliers' business strategy – from the lower situation where suppliers are only passively responding to the demands from tourism firms to the situation at the top of the figure where they aim at affecting the behaviour of tourism actors, and interact in the total value chain.

The four fields in Figure 8.1 represent different supplier-driven innovation situations: the reactive suppliers, the proactive suppliers, the co-branding suppliers and the co-developing suppliers.

Figure 8.1: Model of suppliers' roles in sustainable tourism development

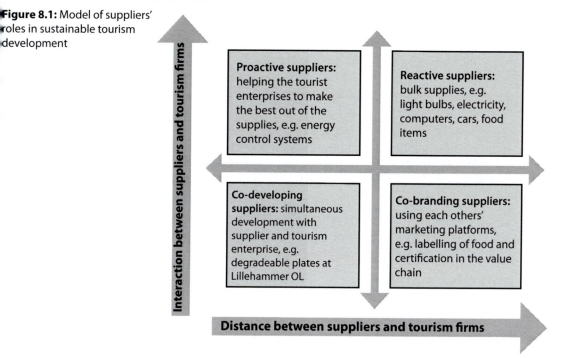

The following section examines these four fields with examples from sustainable tourism.

The reactive suppliers

By definition, reactive suppliers distribute products and services to the tourism sector with a minimum of formal or informal collaboration and without significant attempts to adapt to the particular needs of purchasing firms in (sustainable) tourism. To judge from the literature on purchasing practices in tourism, the majority of supplies seem to be repetitive standard purchases, where the price is a decisive determining factor (Crotts *et al.*, 1998; Kirstges, 2002).

Much supply to tourism consists of indistinguishable bulk products that are shipped off to a broad variety of consumers, for example electricity and food supplies. Several categories of products are highly standardised, for example light bulbs, paper, gardening equipment, cars, etc. For producers of such supplies, tourism is one of many customer groups, and there is limited capacity or motivation to differentiate products or marketing methods in order to reach tourism in special ways or to adapt to individual needs of tourism firms. As noted in Bloch (2008), purchasing traditions, which have been built over long periods of time, may be complicated to revolutionise.

Manufacturers of machinery, information and communication technology (ICT) and food are, on average, found to be in closer contact with the needs of their customers than, for example, transport companies, sellers of materials and wholesale companies (Schiele, 2006). Tourism firms do not often hold strong links to their primary producers in agriculture and manufacturing, but find it more feasible to purchase through intermediaries, such as wholesalers and retailers. This stifles communication is as it has to go through filtering layers. If individual tourism firms have comments and suggestions that could lead to improvements and adaptations by the manufacturer, such communication is unlikely to reach the producer at all.

As previously mentioned, the sustainable tourism literature has focused on setting environmental standards as part of a sustainable business strategy. The standards are translated into requirements throughout the supply chain. Processes towards consistent strategies and sustainability programmes include the gathering of information about and monitoring of the suppliers' environmental compliance status. Further, tourism firms may influence their suppliers through systematic supplier meetings and workshops, and offer suppliers' staff training in the tourism firms' standards. These strategies can assist the supplier to better respond to the tourism firms' environmental requests (Font et al., 2008: Sigala, 2008). Tourism firms with significant purchasing power have better opportunities to influence suppliers in a backward supplier chain.

The proactive suppliers

Proactive suppliers have an opposite profile to reactive suppliers, mainly because they deliver other categories of products and services. When a tourism firm, such as a large hotel or attraction, purchases a new heating or air-conditioning system, it is likely to get into dialogue with the provider of the equipment in order to ensure an adaptation to the firm's particular needs. The supplier may then be in a position to affect the choice of solutions, for example by promoting systems with higher energy-saving potential. Construction work is also in this category, where design measures include a broad variety of issues that have to be adapted to the tourism firm. Suppliers should be in a position to provide relevant advice.

An expanding number of suppliers are offering packaged solutions of equipment that simultaneously give promises of CO_2 reductions and cost savings. As suggested by Swarbrooke (1999), suppliers with the ability to argue for combined cost and resource efficiency initiate efficient supplier-driven influence on tourism firms.

Suppliers' creativity has increased over recent years, and there are quite a number of sustainability compliant offers available, ranging from stationery items to recycled materials and thinner towels that will help save water and washing detergents. Not surprisingly, we also see a variety of waste handling systems and bio-fuel provisions for heating purposes (see, for example, Green Lodging News).

Trade fairs and exhibitions are intermediary events and locations where suppliers can indirectly affect innovations in tourism. Judging from exhibitor lists, the suppliers with distinct sustainability profiles continue to show strongly at traditional hospitality fairs. However, as an example of new measures, the European

Union has supported the Green Travel Market website that adopts a value chain approach where facilities are giving priority to suppliers who can be proven to offer sustainable products to the tourism industry.

Proactive suppliers are most likely to be successful if there is a direct interface and, possibly, also a personal contact. That is most evidently the case in non-standard, incidental and non-routine purchases. If a tourism firm has a distinct environmental agenda and if it is known to be actively in search of innovative supplies, there is scope for suppliers to come up with solutions. Interaction of a proactive nature has been found to lead to improved financial performance in the restaurant sector (Kim, 2006), and this is an argument for tourism firms to become more involved with their suppliers.

In recent years, the gastronomy field has become an important driver in sustainable tourism (Scarpato, 2002). Suppliers are essential in achieving local employment, low waste, few food miles, etc., while the integrated image of a sustainable tourism destination requires proactivity among small-scale producers. Font *et al.* (2008) stress that while small local food producers have the potential to operate as both reactive and proactive suppliers, working with them requires constant supervision and commitment from purchasing tourism firms. Crucial in this context, suppliers must address key operational issues such as lead times, delivery reliability and costs, which are often given a higher priority than sustainable ingredients or production methods in the restaurant sector (Murphy and Smith, 2009).

Co-branding suppliers

The third field in the model suggests a closer collaboration between suppliers and tourism firms, but based on well-recognised and accepted products and services. Co-branding is when two companies form an alliance to work together, thereby creating a marketing synergy. In this situation, a tourism firm will enhance its image by using respected and, preferably, already well-branded products, while the suppliers can achieve an extra marketing platform for its products. Most simply, hotels or restaurants may add environmentally labelled food items on the menu, and tourists can also find the same products in the hotel shop to bring back as souvenirs. The co-branding can also take place on the websites of firms, sometimes even including e-shopping opportunities (Lee *et al.*, 2006).

Co-branding initiatives may be wider in scope and 'sponge' image elements from more general reputations of a nation or a region. Scandinavian hotels and conference centres, for example, are often consciously furnished with trendy designer items. In this sense they are 'showrooms' vis-à-vis a large audience of visitors. Sometimes there are explicit alliances between hotels the producers of the furniture to promote an image of Scandinavian design.

The brand equity literature elaborates on the many dimensions of effective co-branding. Aaker (1996) demonstrates that the companies in collaboration must have deep understanding of their customers' motivations in order to create and enhance loyalty for more products in a co-branding group. Furthermore, the quality levels must be comparable, and the product character stable and untouchable, as compromising will harm the collaborating partners. In the cases of successful co-branding, a mutual respect and trust have been built over time. Suppliers are likely to be more willing to launch into risky partnerships if they have the prospect of lasting contracts that guarantee a return on their innovation and other investment (Crotts *et al.*, 1998).

In tourism much co-branding is embedded in destination management initiatives, where the main activity is joint marketing. Co-branding is also part of bonus systems, for example airlines' loyalty programmes, where miles can be spent on hotels, rental cars and other services. In these cases the sustainability features tend to be weak, if existent at all. This demonstrates the struggle for suppliers of sustainable products and services to obtain a place on the most influential tourism providers' marketing platforms.

Co-branding in the sustainable tourism sector is still quite limited, but tends to be emerging as both tourism firms and their suppliers see the wider perspectives of achieving an image as climate conscious and ethical players on the market. Examples are seen in terms of 'fair' tourism in developing countries and economically challenged regions, which may mean, for example, that food comes from the local area rather than being flown in, and that furniture is local and authentic (Carlsen and Edwards, 2008; Jensen, 2009). Fair trade and fair tourism are increasingly intermingling, and branding alliances can be one of the ways to break the strong co-marketing dominance of the international airlines, hotels and similar tourism corporations.

Co-developing suppliers

Co-developing represents the most integrated manner for supplier-driven innovation in the tourism sector. According to our definition, a supplier will collaborate with one or more tourism firms to develop new products specifically for those tourism firms. The argumentation behind co-creation is that value is generated by a firm and its customer, rather than being created entirely by a closed entity. The open process leads to cross-fertilisation of knowledge. It opens extra dimensions of reflexivity. During co-creation the intention for the supplier is to gain new ideas and insights, which may eventually lead to new products for a wider market (Möller and Törrönen, 2003). Accordingly, tourism firms and suppliers are partners in an innovation process, and leading tourism firms are responsive test opportunities for new supplies with higher quality and better specifications in terms of environmental sustainability.

Crotts *et al.* (1998) touch upon co-creation at a general level. They emphasise that cooperative relationships are typically enduring alliances, where a trust has been built, and where both sides in the relationship have a readiness to adapt to ensure a satisfactory aggregate performance. The objective is to ensure a marketable product in the hands of the supplier. However, this objective should not overshadow the need to create solutions that fit the immediate needs and objectives of the tourism firm, both as a 'first-mover' in a new field and also in a longer perspective. Co-developing partnerships are risky, and a continual mitigation of the risk, the related costs and benefits must be part of the process. Hall (2009) refers to the obvious asymmetries as a hampering factor. Suppliers and tourism firms have to be at something like the same level in terms of values and organisational culture and possibly also in more or less the same financial league.

A practical example of the difficulties is provided Murphy and Smith (2009). In a study of the relationship between upscale restaurants and suppliers, they found that some suppliers lacked the ability to be alert and proactive, while others during a period of collaboration began to see themselves in new and more active roles of alliances with groups in the high-end market. Thus, suppliers developed their businesses simultaneously with the restaurants towards a higher degree of authenticity.

Sustainable tourism strategies in the developing world often include the establishment of durable partnerships with local producers as part of building a development capacity in the area and to ensure induced employment impacts. The experience is that non-governmental organisations (NGOs) take a leadership role to release any innovative abilities of local actors (Liburd, 2004), and to direct their entrepreneurial aptitude into directions complying with general sustainability measures (Swarbrooke, 1999; Jensen, 2009).

Co-creation in tourism is often connected with events, festivals, sports games, etc. Here, boundaries between the various actors from production to consumption in the value chain tend to be rather fluid, a feature that facilitates innovation. In these situations, leadership roles are also momentarily made flexible, which is an invitation to creativity and non-standard employee behaviour. Last but not least, events provide excellent opportunities to create media attention and exposure which can benefit producers of novel products and services. This was the case when the Lillehammer Winter Games were launched as the first Green Games in 1994. One innovative practice was that the supplies of plates and utensils were made of potato-based starch, allowing them to be recycled and used as animal feed and compost.

The 2009 Copenhagen Climate Change Conference (COP15) was regarded as an excellent opportunity by suppliers to become a distinct part of a tourist experience, which also attracted considerable media interest. The bicycle-producing firm Christiania Bicycles was key promoter of an exhibition of the history and future of urban transportation. A competitive race between zero-pollution electrical motorcycles was organised for the experience of a soundless event and to demonstrate new technology. Building materials, wind turbines and other facilities were exhibited under new circumstances and in new designs. Restaurants started a network 'Eat climate-friendly food', where they agreed to introduce food items which had travelled a short distance and which had been processed using sustainable practices.

The annual Roskilde Festival in Denmark makes a special effort to invite young entrepreneurs into the festival programme, who for example offer new forms of environmental control, waste management, etc. Meeting a large festival audience can provide entrepreneurs with relevant feedback. The festival achieves early access to new technologies/products/services, and the audience witnesses new services that could enhance the festival experience and/or quality (Hjalager, 2009).

Future challenges and issues

This chapter has focused on the functions of suppliers in sustainable tourism. It investigated the early steps in the sometimes long and often complex tourism supply chain. It must be concluded that the many suppliers to tourism firms of products, concepts and services represent considerable innovative capacity. Inclusion of the suppliers into the full picture of what makes tourism sustainable is still weak, and their position as proactive agents on the wider sustainable tourism agenda is lagging behind.

In order to achieve comprehensive joint innovations, it is necessary to develop a new and more balanced mode of sustainable supply chain management for tourism. Sigala (2008) argues that beneficial management processes include:

♦ Better information sharing, including early warnings of problems that need to be solved, specifications of requirements etc. Information sharing also includes performance parameters for new supplies. External certification bodies have an important complementary role in ensuring reliability in information flows.

♦ Decision synchronisation which comes out of closer collaboration where both the suppliers and the purchaser are able to schedule and plan their strategies. It is important for actors to meet at various events and in an ambiance of honesty and mutuality.

♦ Incentive alignment where the risk and the benefits of innovation processes are properly balanced. New business models have to be created.

Additionally, leadership is required. It could be either the tourism enterprise or the supplier, depending on the nature of collaboration or development aspirations.

There is a need for more efficient intermediaries and 'translators'. Research points towards a requirement for institutional measures to improve the links between tourism firms that foster partnerships throughout the value chain at a destination or in a wider context. Destination management organisations (DMOs) sometimes line up to undertake this task (Pechlaner *et al.*, 2009). However, DMOs have to serve all tourism firms and organisations in an area. Consequently sustainability objectives are often given a lower priority. Other types of organisations with a distinctive green profile have a propensity to fill the institutional gap. There are many already, such as National Geographic, Ecotour, UNWTO and Sustainable Travel International. Typically, however, these organisations lay emphasis on communication with consumers, and they are not geared to encourage the perspectives of supplier-driven innovation.

There is also a challenge for those tourism firms who are already in the forefront of sustainable management. They ought to enhance their functions as role models for others in terms of collaborating in new ways and more extensively with suppliers. Font *et al.* (2008) and Sigala (2008) accentuate the responsibility of tour operators as powerful initiators, but when examining their codes of conduct it becomes clear that they typically do not exercise their purchasing throughout the supply chain, and their certification procedures tend to be rather superficial.

Many festivals and events are publicly supported. Public funds can be regarded as more than just a way to help to create tourism activity and help organisers; they can be mechanisms to stimulate innovations in the value chain and in experience economy clusters (Flemig, 2007).

Supplier relations and sustainable supply chain management are not quick-fix solutions to innovation in sustainable tourism (Font et al., 2008). There is still a lack of genuine, research-based observation and interpretation of 'supplier power' compared to other driving forces in innovation. Motivational aspects and institutional structures require closer inspection.

There is a lack of attention on both sides – the supplier and the tourism firm – which is a main barrier for integrated sustainability measures and innovations. However, there are also structural barriers, as many suppliers may regard tourism firms as less attractive customers and partners as they are, on average, small and lack a qualified supply chain management capacity. Tourism firms are frequently only in their initial phases of environmental management, and comprehensive strategic approaches appear to be still glaringly infrequent (Roberts and Tribe, 2008).

Some alliances between suppliers and tourism firms may be innovative in controversial ways. 'Greenwashing' – when firms disingenuously spin their products and policies as environmentally friendly – is sometimes carried out instead of action with deeper impacts (Buckley, 2002), and suppliers might help tourism enterprises to give the impression of being green and environmentally conscious. The ethical dimension of sustainable tourism remains to be addressed, even when professional segments of suppliers are invited into innovation strategies.

Moving towards sustainability is a complex political and practical mission, which is at risk of being compromised at any time and during many stages (Hjalager, 1997, 2002). On behalf of the UN Environment Programme (UNEP), Simpson et al. (2008) work systematically through a large of number of mitigation tools for industries and destinations. They claim that reducing, eliminating and substituting emissions that threaten the climate and the environment are a key responsibility to address. In this perspective, suppliers to the tourism sector are indispensable allies for tourism leaders who want to commit themselves to work towards sustainable tourism.

Review questions

1   Think of a tourism firm that you are well acquainted with. Identify the firm's suppliers. Group the suppliers into two categories: (a) innovative suppliers; and (b) non-innovative suppliers. Explain the criteria you used to differentiate these suppliers. Specify the suppliers' potential in terms of affecting the sustainable operations of the tourism firm.

2   Discuss how the following categories of suppliers can co-brand themselves as sustainable suppliers with tourism firms: (a) suppliers of saunas, jacuzzis and other spa/wellness equipment; (b) suppliers of electricity; and (c) suppliers of souvenirs.

3   Review the driving forces of innovation discussed in this chapter. Can you think of other driving forces of sustainable tourism than those mentioned here? Find literature and web-sources to support your points of view.

References

Aaker, D.A. (1996) Building Strong Brands, New York: Free Press.

Ateljevic, I. and Doorne, S. (2000) '"Staying within the fence": lifestyle entrepreneurship in tourism', *Journal of Sustainable Tourism*, **8** (5), 378-392.

Bloch, C. (2008) *Innovation Indicators and Performance – An Analysis for Danish Firms*, Danish Centre for Studies in Research and Research Policy, University of Aarhus, available at http://www.cfa.au.dk/fileadmin/site_files/filer_forskningsanalyse/dokumenter/Diverse/Innovation_indicators_Ignored.pdf, accessed 1 February 2010.

Buckley, R. (2002) 'Tourism ecolabels', *Annals of Tourism Research*, **29** (1), 183-208.

Carlsen, J. and Edwards, D. (2008) 'Tasting Arizona, USA', in J. Carlsen, J. Liburd, D. Edwards, and P. Forde (eds), *Innovation for Sustainable Tourism*, International Case Studies BEST Education Network, University of Southern Denmark, pp. 48-56.

Cater, R.W., Whiley, D. and Knight, C. (2004) 'Improving environmental performance in the tourism accommodation sector', *Journal of Ecotourism*, **3** (1), 46-68.

Christensen, J.L. (2008) 'Innovation and management in North Jutland tourism firms', paper for the RSA-workshop, 28 November, Aalborg University Department of Business Studies.

Cooper, C. (2006) 'Knowledge management and tourism', *Annals of Tourism Research*, **33** (1), 47-64.

Crotts, J., Aziz, A. and Rashid, A. (1998) 'Antecedents of supplier's commitment to wholesale buyers in the international travel trade', *Tourism Management*, **19** (2), 127-134.

Damsholt, T. and Ren, C. (2009) 'Fieldwork and games. A discussion of user-centered methods in green tourism development', paper for the 18th Nordic Tourism Symposium, Esbjerg.

Drucker, P. (1985) *Innovation and Entrepreneurship: Practice and Principles*, London: Heinemann.

Flemig, T. (2007) *A Creative Economy. Green Paper for the Nordic Region*, Oslo: NICe.

Font, X., Tapper, R., Schwartz, K. and Kornilaki, M. (2008) 'Sustainable supply management in tourism', *Business Strategy and the Environment*, **17**, 260-271.

Green Lodging News, http://www.greenlodgingnews.com/Content.aspx?ID=1690.

Hall, C.M. (2009) 'Tourism firm innovation and sustainability', in S. Gösling, C.M. Hall and D. Weaver (eds), *Sustainable Tourism Futures: perspectives on systems, restructuring and innovations*, New York: Routledge, 282–298.

Hall, C. M. and Williams, A.M. (2008) *Tourism and Innovation*, London: Routledge.

Hjalager, A.-M. (1997) 'Innovation patterns in sustainable tourism – an analytical typology', *Tourism Management*, **18** (1), 35-41.

Hjalager, A.-M. (2002) 'Repairing innovation defectiveness in tourism', *Tourism Management*, **23** (5), 465-474.

Hjalager, A.-M. (2009) 'The Roskilde Festival as a tourism innovation system', *Scandinavian Journal of Tourism and Hospitality Management*, **9** (3/4), 266-287.

Hjalager, A.-M. (2010) 'A review of the innovation research in tourism', *Tourism Management*, **31** (1), 1-12.

Holden, A. (2008) *Environment and Tourism*, London: Routledge.

Hughes, M. (2008) 'Ecocean, Western Australia', in J. Carlsen, J. Liburd, D. Edwards and P. Forde (eds), *Innovation for Sustainable Tourism*, International Case Studies BEST Education Network.

http://www.besteducationnetwork.org/books/2007.php accessed 1 February 2010.

Jacob, M. and Groizard, J.L. (2007) 'Technology transfer and multinationals: the case of Balearic hotel chains' investments in two developing economies', *Tourism Management*, **28** (4), 976-992.

Jensen, K. (2009) 'The activation of local service suppliers by incoming tour operators in a "developing" destination', *Current Issues in Tourism*, **12** (2), 133-163.

Kim, B.-Y. (2006) 'The impact of supplier development on financial performance in the restaurant industry', *International Journal of Hospitality and Tourism Administration*, **7** (4), 81-103.

Kirstges, T. (2002) 'Basic questions in sustainable tourism: does ecological and socially acceptable tourism have a chance?', *Current Issues in Tourism*, **5** (3), 173-192.

Lee, S., Kim, W.G. and Kim, H.J. (2006) 'The impact of co-branding on post-purchase behaviours in family restaurants', *International Journal of Hospitality Management*, **25** (2), 245-261.

Liburd, J.J. (2004) 'NGOs in tourism and preservation: democratic accountability and sustainability in question', *Tourism Recreation Research*, **29** (2), 105-110.

Liu, X. (2003) 'Sustainable tourism development: a critique', *Journal of Sustainable Tourism*, **11** (6), 459-475.

Masau, P. and Prideaux, B. (2003) 'Sustainable tourism: a role for Kenya's hotel industry', *Current Issues in Tourism*, **6** (3), 197-208.

Maxwell, I. (2009) *Managing Sustainable Innovation*, New York: Springer.

McEvily, B. and Marcus, A. (2005) 'Embedded ties and the acquisition of competitive capabilities', *Strategic Management Journal*, **26** (11), 1033-1055.

Möller, K.E. and Törrönen, P. (2003) 'Business suppliers' value creation potential: a capacity-based analysis', *Industrial Marketing Management*, **32** (2), 109-118.

Murphy, J. and Smith, S. (2009) 'Chefs and suppliers: an exploratory look at supply chain issues in an upscale restaurant alliance', *International Journal of Hospitality Management*, **28** (2), 212-220.

Orfila-Sintes, F., Crespi-Cladera and Martinez-Ros, E. (2005) 'Innovation activity in the hotel industry: evidence from Balearic hotels', *Tourism Management*, 26 (6), 851-865.

Pechlaner, H., Raich, F. and Fisher, E. (2009) 'The role of tourism organizations in location management: the case of beer tourism in Bavaria', *Tourism Review*, **64** (2), 28-40.

Peeters, P., Gössling, S. and Becken, S. (2006) 'Innovation towards tourism sustainability: climate change and aviation', *International Journal of Innovation and Sustainable Development*, **1** (3), 184-200.

Pikkemaat, B. (2008) 'Innovation in small and medium-sized tourism enterprises in Tyrol, Austria', *Entrepreneurship and Innovation*, **9** (3), 187-197.

Pikkemaat, B. and Peters, M. (2005) 'Towards the measurement of innovation – a pilot study in the small and medium sized hotel industry', *Journal of Quality Assurance in Hospitality and Tourism*, **6** (3/4), 89-112.

Presbury, R. and Edwards, D. (2010) Managing Sustainable Festivals, Meetings and Events in Liburd, J. and Edwards, D. (eds) *Understanding Sustainable Tourism Development*, Oxford: Goodfellow Publishers.

Roberts, S. and Tribe, J. (2008) 'Sustainability indicators for small tourism enterprises – an exploratory perspective', *Journal of Sustainable Tourism*, 16 (5), 575-594.

Rogers, E.M. (1995) *Diffusion of Innovations*, 4th edn, New York: Free Press.

Rosenberg, N. (1976) *Perspectives on Technology*, Cambridge: Cambridge University Press.

Scarpato, R. (2002) 'Sustainable gastronomy as a tourist product', in A.-M. Hjalager and G. Richards (eds), *Tourism and Gastronomy*, London: Routledge, pp. 132-152.

Schiele, H. (2006) 'How to distinguish innovative suppliers?', *Industrial Marketing Management*, **35** (8), 925-935.

Schumpeter, J.A. (1934) *The Theory of Economic Development: An Inquiry into Profits, Capital, Credit, Interest and the Business Cycle*, Cambridge, MA: Harvard University Press.

Schwartz, K, Tapper, R. and Font, X. (2008) 'A sustainable supply chain management framework for tour operators', *Journal of Sustainable Tourism*, **16** (3), 298-314.

Sigala, M. (2008) 'A supply chain management approach for investigating the role of tour operators on sustainable tourism: the case of TUI', *Journal of Cleaner Production*, **16**, 1589-1599.

Simpson, M.C., Gössling, S., Scott, D., Hall, C.M. and Gladin, E. (2008) *Climate Change Adaptation and Mitigation in the Tourism Sector: Frameworks, Tools and Practices*, Oxford: UNEP, University of Oxford.

Sundbo, J. (1997) 'Management of innovations in services', *Service Industries Journal*, **17** (3), 432-455.

Swarbrooke, J. (1999) *Sustainable Tourism Management*, Wallingford: CABI.

Tremblay, P. (1998) 'The economic organization of tourism', *Annals of Tourism Research*, **25** (4), 837-859.

von Hippel, E. (1988) *The Sources of Innovation*, New York: Oxford University Press.

Zhang, X., Song, H. and Huang, G.Q. (2009) 'Tourism supply chain management: a new research agenda', *Tourism Management*, **30**, 345-358.

9 Managing Sustainable Festivals, Meetings and Events

Rajka Presbury and Deborah Edwards

Rationale

Festivals, meetings and events (FMEs) are an important component of the tourism industry. FMEs provide opportunities for social and cultural exchange, exchange of new and innovative ideas, business contacts, and learning. They play a key role in many destinations in attracting tourists, providing recreational activities for the community and developing and strengthening a destination's image. Each FME provides a specific kind of appeal and experience, which in most cases cannot be repeated. As the appreciation of the benefits of holding festivals, meetings and events grows, governments and operators are continuing to invest in developing the necessary facilities and infrastructure to accommodate this tourism activity.

While FMEs are often a representation of a community's culture and way of life, the host community bears the burden of the FMEs. They are required to accept its activities, open their doors to welcome the gaze of the visitor, and pay for the costs of the additional infrastructure and pressure on essential resources that may be required to host them. Thus FMEs affect the quality of life of local residents. Therefore, if not planned well, this kind of development puts at risk the quality of the economic, social and natural environments in which such activity takes place. For long-term sustainability it is essential for all stakeholders to take responsibility and clearly evidence accountability when organising and managing FMEs.

This chapter defines a sustainable FME as one that adopts a best practice approach to the management and operation of an FME that is underpinned by the principles of sustainable development, sustainable tourism ethics and the guiding values of sustainable tourism education. These principles form the basis for establishing sustainability criteria in FMEs.

Learning objectives

On completion of this chapter the student should be able to:

+ Discuss the role and nature of FMEs in society
+ Identify and assess the impacts of FMEs to promote and enhance the quality of life and social wellbeing for local and regional development
+ Explain the principles that underpin sustainable FMEs
+ Plan for sustainable FMEs
+ Design and implement a flexible FMEs process, which offers products and services that incorporate principles and practices of sustainability; and
+ Evaluate the implementation of an FME to ensure sustainable outcomes are achieved.

The role and nature of FMEs in society

FMEs represent different themes of the same phenomenon. Each theme is described below.

◆ **Festivals** are an important expression of human activity that contribute to a community's cultural and social life (Allen *et al.*, 2008). Festivals are commonly referred to as public, themed celebrations designed to occur for a limited duration that celebrate valued aspects of a community's way of life and can educate those engaged about the host culture and community (Getz, 1997; Small and Edwards, 2006). Festivals are generally cultural celebrations that may be displayed in carnivals, religious events, parades or heritage commemorations. Festivals are important components of community pride, cohesion, fun and relaxation. Opportunities exist for festivals to advance educational values, demonstrate arts and crafts, enhance community engagement and showcase endeavours in music, art, drama, sports and culture.

◆ **A meeting** is defined as 'an off-site gathering, including conventions, congress, conferences, seminars, workshops and symposiums, which bring together people for a common purpose – the sharing of information' (Allen *et al.*, 2008, 16). Meetings are part of the wider MICE industry (meetings, incentives, conventions and exhibitions). The MICE industry encompasses related but diverse elements including conferences, congresses and trade shows which attract local, national and international visitors and enable business and individuals to receive benefits in the field of sales, marketing, education, communication, motivation and evaluation.

◆ **An event** is defined as a 'celebration or display of some theme to which the public is invited for a limited time only, annually or less frequently' (Getz, 1997: 28). Community events are 'themed public occasions designed to celebrate valued aspects of a community's way of life' (Douglas and Douglas, 2001: 358). There are many types of events including cultural celebrations, arts and entertainment, business and trade, sport competitions, educational and scientific seminars, and political events. For the event organiser (and sponsors), an event is an opportunity to communicate with the public outside their normal activities. For the public, it is an opportunity for social and cultural interaction during their leisure time.

All FMEs represent gatherings of people for some common purpose. Such activities require a concentrated and coordinated effort in their formulation, implementation, monitoring and evaluation. FMEs can be generated by government, private or business groups at many different levels, including:

◆ Local – a local Rotary meeting, or a community market
◆ Regional – food and wine festivals showcasing the produce of the region
◆ State – sporting event or carnival
◆ National – Clean Up Australia Day, Republic Day of India, Chinese New Year;
◆ Global – the Olympics; Rugby World Cup; Earth Day.

Each FME has a responsibility to the community and other stakeholders to effectively manage these activities in a sustainable way. A central focus of a sustainable FME is to build relationships and alliances underpinned by a sustainability philosophy as reflected in Figure 9.1.

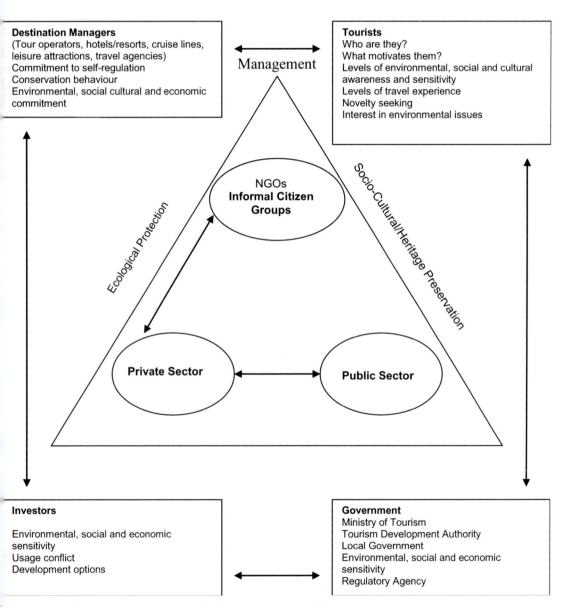

Destination Managers
(Tour operators, hotels/resorts, cruise lines, leisure attractions, travel agencies)
Commitment to self-regulation
Conservation behaviour
Environmental, social cultural and economic commitment

Management

Tourists
Who are they?
What motivates them?
Levels of environmental, social and cultural awareness and sensitivity
Levels of travel experience
Novelty seeking
Interest in environmental issues

Ecological Protection

Socio-Cultural/Heritage Preservation

NGOs
Informal Citizen Groups

Private Sector

Public Sector

Investors

Environmental, social and economic sensitivity
Usage conflict
Development options

Government
Ministry of Tourism
Tourism Development Authority
Local Government
Environmental, social and economic sensitivity
Regulatory Agency

Figure 9.1: Relationships between stakeholders, Source: Adapted from Hassan (2000)

This means actively decreasing the existing use of scarce resources, reducing current outputs of waste and pollution, promoting awareness of the environmental qualities of destinations and influencing ways in which customers understand, respond and are sensitive to the local destination (Presbury and Edwards, this volume).

Impacts of FMEs

Organisations and individuals attempting to facilitate sustainability in tourism activities are frequently faced with conflicting expectations of tourists and the local population; and FME activities are no exception. FMEs result in outcomes that can affect communities both positively and negatively and these outcomes are dependent on the particular context in which the FME takes place.

The task of the organising committee is to identify and assess the potential impacts to ensure sustainable outcomes, that is, adopting strategies and activities that will meet the needs of all stakeholders. Examples of socio-cultural, environmental and economic impacts that may arise from the staging of an FME are presented in Table 9.1.

Table 9.1: Potential socio-cultural, environmental and economic impacts

FME impact	Positive impacts	Negative impacts
Social and cultural	Shared experiences Revitalisation of culture and traditions Increased community participation and pride Introduction of new and innovative ideas Respect for other cultures	Community alienation Manipulation of community values and traditions Poor social behaviour Substance abuse Social dislocation Loss of amenities Increased crime
Environmental	Showcasing the environment Renewal of urban and natural environments Providing models of best practice Increased environmental awareness Extend local infrastructure Improved transport and communication	Environmental damage Pollution Destruction of heritage Noise disturbance Traffic congestion Overuse of sensitive sites and natural resources
Economic	Destination promotion and increased tourist visits Extended length of stay Higher yield Increased revenue Job creation Source local products	Loss of authenticity Damage to reputation Exploitation Inflated prices Opportunity cost Community resistance Community burdened with the cost of the event

Source: Author, adapted from Allen *et al.* (2008)

A sustainable FME is one that is underpinned by a sustainable philosophy and meets the following criteria:

♦ Minimises resource use and the generation of wastes by using environmentally sound technologies (ESTs)

♦ Ensures compliance with operational development plans, planning conditions, standards and targets for sustainable tourism by providing incentives, monitoring compliance, and enforcement activities where necessary

♦ Involves all primary stakeholders, including the community, the tourism industry and government, in the development and implementation of tourism plans so as to increase the long-term success of projects

♦ Raises awareness of the principles of 'best practice' in sustainable tourism by promoting the exchange of information between stakeholders; establishes networks for dialogue on implementation of these principles; promotes broad understanding and awareness to help strengthen attitudes, values and actions that are compatible with sustainable tourism operations (UNEP 2002a)

♦ Ensures consistent monitoring and review of activities to detect problems at an early stage and to enable action to prevent more serious damage.

Principles that underpin sustainable FMEs

A number of principles underpin FMEs. These include: responsibility, commitment and leadership, cooperation, knowledge creation, social creativity and freedom and adopting ethical standards (Dwyer and Edwards, 2004). Each is discussed below as they relate to FMEs.

Responsibility to protect natural and built cultural/heritage environments

The FME has a responsibility to share with residents, governments and all people, the obligation to protect and maintain the natural, built and heritage resources of communities, to sustain economies and to be passed on to future generations. This recognises the importance of the continuity of natural resources and the continuity of culture and the balances within culture (Sharpley and Tefler, 2002).

Commitment and leadership

Many FMEs fail or are no longer staged because there has been a lack of commitment and leadership. Sustainable FMEs require strong, committed and effective leadership. A proactive role, rather than a passive one, is required to ensure that heritage, community and environmental values are fully sustained. A sustainable FME will require a long-term commitment by stakeholders to sustainable development principles at all stages of an event.

Sustainable leadership matters, spreads and lasts. It is a shared responsibility, that does not unduly deplete human or financial resources, and that cares for and avoids exerting negative impacts on the community environment (Hargreaves and Fink, 2003). We suggest 12 attributes that define the sustainable FME leader:

♦ Practical

♦ Service-orientated

♦ Relevant

♦ Time-conscious

♦ Reflexive

♦ Team-orientated

♦ Proactive

♦ Ethical

◆ Leads by example
◆ Socially responsible
◆ Committed
◆ Promotes diversity and builds capacity.

Cooperation and working together

Cooperating with diverse stakeholders is important for achieving the sustainable goals of an FME. A stakeholder can be defined as 'those individuals or groups who have the ability to affect or be affected by the existence of an event' (Reid and Arcodia, 2002: 492). Working with stakeholders requires identification and inclusion of diverse groups and agencies that can contribute to a sustainable FME. Stakeholders will be discussed in more detail later in this chapter.

Knowledge

A sustainable FME should create enduring legacies for the communities in which they are staged. 'Learning forward' the knowledge arising from FMEs is important for assisting event organisers to improve the sustainability of future FMEs. Learning forward requires critical thinking, reflection, innovation, creativity and networking.

Social creativity and freedom

There is a need to strike a balance between economic, environmental and social considerations. The attributes of a healthy community extend beyond standard economic measurements to include whether or not it meets the basic needs of its citizens (food, water, housing, safety, employment); the quality of the environment (natural and built); the vitality of its social fabric (including diversity, tolerance and commitment); its efficient use of material resources; and its cultural accomplishments. This recognises that staging a sustainable FME can enhance the 'quality of life' of communities, a broader notion than economic prosperity.

Adopting ethical standards

'Ethics must have a role in protecting the vital needs of minorities and those without political clout and economic power' (Smith and Duffy, 2003: 89). Organisers of sustainable FMEs have a responsibility to maintain honesty, transparency, authenticity, a genuine ethical concern and a sense of moral duty in their daily business activities that is conscious of their own duty and others' rights. In this regard the WTO Global Code of Ethics can assist.

Why incorporating sustainability is important

Four factors have influenced the importance of incorporating sustainability in FMEs: global growth, global media coverage, increased scrutiny of FMEs and a more socially and environmentally aware traveller.

The tremendous global growth in the staging of FMEs has to a large extent been due to the increase in leisure time and discretionary spending. Events have been held to fund small and large community projects, and the corporate world has taken advantage of meetings to promote business opportunities.

Widespread media coverage attracts substantial commercial interests and related sponsorship. Sponsors are cautious of being implicated in FMEs that may receive negative publicity as a result of poor planning or management. Future growth will need to be guided by a global focus that responds to trends related to sustainability values and motivations of the community, visitors and sponsors.

As the amount of money that is poured into FMEs grows, there are increased calls for accountability. Private and public companies question costs and benefits, and experts and interest groups conducting analysis scrutinise impacts.

The global environmental and conservation movement has increased awareness of the travelling public. The 'new traveller' is more discerning and responsible for their travel decisions and behaviour making travel decisions based on the expectation of experiencing quality tourism that maintains environmental, social and cultural integrity (Hassan, 2000).

Leveraging FMEs for short and long-term opportunities

FME organisers must learn to manage the increasing interest in sustainability as part of their sustainable FME strategy. A sustainable FME strategy requires a critical evaluation on the part of the organisers of the economic, environmental, social and governance aspects such that benefits of the FME can be realised for communities beyond the staging of the event. The application of sustainable tourism practices can result in significant economic, environmental and cultural benefits for stakeholders of FMEs including the following.

Economic

Leveraging economic opportunities can be measured by looking at the benefits accruing from the FME against the cost of actually staging these activities. Such assessments would look at the output, the income, any value-added products and services, and employment generated by the FME. Although these costs and benefits need to have measurable values, efforts should be made to include intangible benefits, such as favourable publicity, enhanced community engagement or community pride. Assessment of the economic impacts of events should take into account factor constraints that result in changes in input and output prices and industry interactive effects that reduce the value of any multiplier effects (Dwyer *et al.*, 2000).

Proactive environmental behaviour has its own benefits through positive local publicity that in turn may heighten the image of the event or meeting, giving it a competitive market position.

Environmental

The adoption of environmental practices appeals to a new and growing visitor market: visitors who are becoming more environmentally aware and can be influenced to attend events and meetings through positive environmental messages.

Assessing the impact an FME may have on the natural resources and environmental quality of a destination requires the development of indicators that describe and quantify the extent of human impact on the environment that may be generated as a result of the FME.

This kind of commitment to the environment indicates that organisers value the local community and will in many instances create staff loyalty and the generation of enthusiasm to act as a team in the achievements of programmes to serve the community.

Social

It is necessary to assess how the actions connected to the FME might affect the quality of life and wellbeing of individuals or groups within the community. The establishment of sustainable management practices can and does result in long-lasting improvement of relations within and between communities and local authorities. Also, participants will experience the 'feel good' factor knowing that they have had a low impact event and used the services of environmentally and socially responsible operators (UNEP, 2002a).

Governance

Government authorities and the public at large are much more likely to support organisations that can show they care for their environment and community and are sensitive to the impacts they have. The fact that an operator has policies and systems in place demonstrates 'due diligence' in their operation and may also make it easier for that operator to obtain operational permits or licences for future projects.

Sustainability requires a holistic approach based on highly detailed information, that keeps in mind all the rights and responsibilities of all stakeholders now and into the future.

Criteria for sustainable FMEs

FMEs can be held at five major levels: local, regional, state, national and global. At each level there are eight broad criteria that guide the staging of a sustainable FME including leveraging the event; gaining management, sponsor and stakeholder support for a sustainable FME; setting environmental, socio-cultural and economic priorities representative of the community; site or venue selection; FME inputs, timing; educating exhibitors, vendors, community and visitors; monitoring and evaluating the FME and communicating its successes. Each of these criteria will be discussed in turn.

Leveraging the event – why is the FME being held?

Identifying the reason for hosting a festival can assist organisers to focus their decision making and priority setting. FMEs can be used as catalysts for:

♦ Revitalisation of a destination

♦ Positioning and branding destinations

♦ Increasing community activities and entertainment

♦ Promoting economic growth

♦ Enhancing visitor experiences; and/or

♦ Celebrating cultural and spiritual occasions.

The reason for staging an FME will have implications for sustainable choices in services providers and operational decisions.

Gaining management, sponsor and stakeholder support for a sustainable FME

Management and stakeholder support can be gained by emphasising that a range of environmental, socio-cultural and economic benefits (such as potential cost savings and enhanced public image) can result from incorporating sustainable principles into the FME planning process.

Setting environmental, socio-cultural and economic priorities representative of the community

It is important to first identify the environmental, socio-cultural and economic issues that are especially significant to the committee, organisation and host community. By defining these priorities, specific resources can be allocated and action taken that will help meet these objectives. Specific priorities of an FME will differ between communities and it is important that all stakeholders have input into this process.

It is necessary to translate identified priorities into actions. At this stage it is helpful to draw up a priorities checklist. A checklist will vary according to the type and size of FME being held and the reason for holding that FEM. The checklist should include priorities and actions related to:

Site or venue selection

Look for a site or venue that best addresses your environmental, socio-cultural and economic priorities and reasons for staging the FME. For example, the site chosen for the Sydney 2000 Olympics was based on the opportunity for the rejuvenation and regeneration of a previously denigrated area. The site now serves as a destination for community activities and recreation. On a smaller scale the hosting of an FEM can promote historic buildings, precincts or natural areas that would otherwise go undervalued.

FME inputs

'Using local goods and services, materials, local expertise and local design can help to reduce 'leakages' of tourism expenditure and maximise economic impacts of tourism to the destination' (Dwyer and Edwards, 2004: 41). The selection of local service providers and contractors for items such as equipment and food who incorporate sustainability principles into their business can encourage broader sustainability practices in communities.

Timing

Timing can be critical to success. Staging an FME to extend the holiday season, to boost an off-season, to avoid clashing with another FME, or to allow enough time for proper event organisation are some of the factors that will affect its sustainability and contribute to the wellbeing of host communities. Correct timing can enable event organisers to undertake appropriate environmental, socio-cultural and economic assessment procedures (Yeoman *et al.*, 2004). It will also avoid the temptation to fast track processes, which can lead to negative outcomes on host communities.

Educating exhibitors, vendors, community and visitors

By ensuring that stakeholders are aware of an FME's sustainable features, organisers can gain their commitment for sustainable procedures prior, during and after the event.

Monitoring and evaluating the FME and communicating its successes

Monitoring activities during the FME can facilitate early detection of problems. Early detection of problems can assist organisers to identify the causes and take action to prevent further problems from occurring. The hosting of a sustainable FME is a major accomplishment. Therefore consideration should also be given to celebrating the FME's success before, during and after the FME. Management, shareholders, sponsors, contractors and the public can be informed via public announcements, press releases, internal newsletters, bulletin boards and annual reports.

Thinking through these criteria can ensure that the responsibility and accountability put in place at the start of FME planning will assist in identifying and correcting risks and problems before they escalate.

Industry Insight: the Roskilde Festival

The organisers of the Roskilde Festival in Denmark are drawing on the community to improve the sustainability of the festival:

The festival organizers are directly inviting young entrepreneurs to develop innovative ways to deliver services and products to festival attendees. The Festival has a focus on the surrounding environment as well as a wide selection of stalls that have to meet sustainable criteria such as organic food and beverage outlets and fair-trade and recycled clothing. All these activities have been found to add to a positive experience for the audience.

(Hjalager, 2009: 270)

Planning for sustainable FMEs

An FME is planned and implemented by a variety of interested individuals and entities (Andersson and Getz, 2008). To realise a sustainable FME it is necessary to balance the competing needs, expectations and interests of these diverse stakeholders. This section discusses those elements that will assist in realising this objective and includes taking a community approach, stakeholder leadership and empowerment, connecting communities with FME visitors, creating educational opportunities and engagement for visitors at every step, and a flexible approach to FME implementation.

Taking a community approach

A community approach to FME management can provide a framework for building strong partnerships. However, it will not in itself ensure an equitable or 'fair' distribution of the costs and benefits of the FME or the engagement of visitors. Nonetheless a community approach can lead to greater community involvement and increased business linkages between FME activity and other, formal and informal, activity in the community. The range of benefits in this approach may include:

♦ An FME that is acceptable to local residents

♦ The perception of local involvement as one way of integrating FMEs with community activities and creating products that are more creative, engaging and authentic

♦ Facilitation of an ongoing forum for the sharing of ideas, communicating positive practices and reinforcing behaviour of operators and businesses involved in the FME

♦ Facilitation of the preparation of codes of conduct for specific groupings of businesses/operators, governments, community members and visitors.

Stakeholder leadership and empowerment

The communities that host FMEs differ in their composition due to size, geographic location, population, resources, skills, government structure and resource capabilities. Therefore every community will have its own particular set of stakeholders. Stakeholders are described by Goldblatt and Nelson (2001) as organisations, municipal councils, political officials, guests, vendors, media and others who are invested in the event. FME organisers have to be adept at stakeholder relationship management, especially in relation to those groups that can provide resources (Andersson and Getz, 2008).

Stakeholders can be categorised into three broad groups: primary, secondary and external (Karl, 2000). Primary stakeholders are those people and groups who are ultimately affected by the FME. Secondary stakeholders are intermediaries in the process of working with the FME. External stakeholders are those not formally involved in a project, but who may impact or be impacted by it.

Ten generic stakeholder entities have been identified by Allen *et al.* (2008) and at any one time they can fall into one of the three stakeholder groups outlined above. The ten different types of stakeholders and the relationship between each of them and a sustainable FME are:

♦ **Host organisation** – corporations, industry associations, local government

♦ **Workers** – who provide paid labour and voluntary support to operationalise the FME

♦ **Local businesses** – who derive an income directly or indirectly from the staging of an FME

♦ **Media** – who promote and advertise the FME

♦ **Emergency services** – who provide a safe environment and services for participants and visitors

♦ **Participants and visitors** – who make the FME viable

♦ **Local government** – who promote economic development, and a regulatory and guideline framework in which the FME operates

♦ **Sponsors** – who provide much-needed financial or in-kind support

♦ **Tourism organisations** – who can promote the FME to appropriate markets;

♦ **Host community** – who share their area.

Each of these stakeholder entities has different members with different agendas, aspirations and interests. A sustainable FME is contingent on each stakeholder being considered for their own sake and not merely because of their ability to further the interests of some other group.

Methods for identifying stakeholders and their interactions

Different stakeholders can perceive the same FME in quite different ways depending on their vested interests, their particular priorities at the time, their previous experiences with FMEs and organising committees. An early brainstorming session by the organising committee devoted to stakeholder identification is an effective means of capturing a list of all likely stakeholders. It is useful to keep a record of identified stakeholders and their contact details. To manage stakeholders effectively it is important to understand:

◆ Their goals

◆ Expected outcomes

◆ Past reactions

◆ The likely impact the FME will have on them (positive or negative); and

◆ The extent of buy-in and level of support.

It is suggested that discussions are held with identified stakeholders to establish the nature of their interest, ways they can contribute and any concerns they may have about staging the FME. Combining this with an understanding of how supportive each stakeholder is likely to be will then enable the organising committee to differentiate their approach to engaging with them. A simple matrix can help in this process and is presented in Figure 9.1.

		Low	High
Importance How influential How affected	High	Manage – increase their level of support	Involve – closely involve with the work of the team
	Low	Monitor – but should not distract the organising committee	Acknowledge – then manage accordingly
		Low	High
			Support

Figure 9.1: Stakeholder identification matrix
Source: http://interactive.cabinetoffice.gov.uk/strategy/survivalguide/skills/ms_effectively.htm, 2010

It is recommended that the matrix is plotted twice – once to consider the degree of influence of each stakeholder, and once to consider the degree to which each stakeholder is affected by the FME. The first matrix will inform the level of involvement, and the second will help focus the team on working with key customers of the strategy.

Managing the stakeholder relationship

Having identified the FME's stakeholders and their relevant level of participation, it is necessary to manage that relationship to ensure the smooth running of the

FME. There are a number of key elements that organisers need to be mindful of in facilitating a positive stakeholder relationship including:

♦ A shared vision and philosophy of the FME

♦ Early agreement of the need to work together to deliver results

♦ Meetings to establish project parameters, success criteria and potential constraints or barriers

♦ Review and agreement of key issues

♦ Constant updates on progress; and

♦ Early flagging of problems.

Four steps can be followed to facilitate the sustainable management of the stakeholder relationship that incorporates the above key elements. These steps are presented in Table 9.2.

Table 9.2: Steps involved in managing the stakeholder process

Steps	Key stakeholder management tasks
Research and analysis	Identify key concerns/issues and collect knowledge Discussion of broad issues, success criteria and potential constraints or barriers Identify emerging relationship options Communicate chosen option Identify economic, socio-cultural, environmental and governance goals
Set up the relationship	Agree on shared vision and philosophy Determine process for consultation Agree on strategies to leverage economic, socio-cultural, environmental and governance goals
Monitoring the relationship	Update on progress Flag early problems
Evaluating the relationship	Extent and quality of participation Costs and benefits of participation to the different stakeholders; and Impact of participation on FME outcomes, performance, and sustainability

Source: Adapted from http://interactive.cabinetoffice.gov.uk/strategy/survivalguide/skills/ms_effectively.htm, 2010

It is important to manage the stakeholder relationship for ethical reasons. Seven principles of stakeholder management (Clarkson Centre for Business Ethics, 2000) have been adapted for application to FMEs including managers:

♦ Acknowledging and actively monitoring the concerns of all legitimate stakeholders and taking their interest appropriately into account in decision making and operations of FMEs

♦ Listening to and openly communicating with stakeholders about their respective concerns and contributions, and about the risks that they assume because of their involvement with the FME

♦ Adopting processes and modes of behaviour that are sensitive to the concerns and capabilities of each stakeholder constituency

♦ Recognising the interdependence of efforts and rewards among stakeholders and attempting to achieve a fair distribution of the benefits and burdens of FME activity among them, taking into account their respective risks and vulnerabilities

♦ Working cooperatively with other entities, both public and private, to ensure that risks and harms arising from FME activities are minimised or appropriately compensated

♦ Avoiding altogether activities that might jeopardise inalienable human rights (e.g. the right of life) or give rise to risks which would be patently unacceptable to relevant stakeholders

♦ Acknowledging the potential conflicts between (a) their own role as FME stakeholders and (b) their legal and moral responsibilities for the interests of stakeholders, and addressing conflicts through open communication, appropriate reporting and incentive systems and, where necessary, third-party review.

Communicating with stakeholders

Continuous communication is important for a mutually rewarding relationship with stakeholders, for ensuring that sustainable approaches are being followed in the staging of the event and for managing problems and issues when they arise. The communication process can be undertaken in a number of ways including:

♦ One to one meetings

♦ Inviting stakeholders to sit on steering, advisory or working groups

♦ Presentations – by stakeholders to the organising committee or by the organising committee to stakeholders (such as sponsors)

♦ Recruiting team members from stakeholder organisations

♦ Joint working with stakeholder organisations

♦ Written communications such as newsletters, updates or drafts of papers

♦ Email updates

♦ Websites posting progressive information; and

♦ Information booths set up in the community.

It is appropriate for different stakeholders to undertake a combination of different approaches.

Connecting communities with FME visitors

Communities are characterised by their identity, sense of place and political ties. FMEs represent opportunities for visitors to connect to a destination's 'place' and strengthen relationships between visitors and the community: they can provide a natural medium for interpretation of place through the naming of the event; visual identification with the landscape; or where the mood of the place is integrated into the content of the programme. Community identity, sense of place and political ties are elements that represent opportunities for the FME to connect visitors with communities.

Community identity

Communities are linked to their geographic location through, food, music, religion, art and festivals. Local distinctiveness can be communicated through festivals. An

FME can be a tangible demonstration of a community and its culture. A sustainable FME will incorporate the use of products and services that promote the community's identity such as locally grown produce, locally made arts and crafts, and local musicians (Yeoman *et al.*, 2004).

Sense of place

'Place is the mental construct of the temporal–spatial experience that occurs as an individual ascribes meaning to settings, through environmental perception and cognition' (Motloch, 1991: 279). The spatial experience of a destination is the experience of such things as architecture and the way in which visitors move through exterior and interior spaces. Public environments like town squares, harbour and river foreshores, parklands, zoos and coastal zones are areas in which a well-organised FME can provide opportunities for pauses through timing and programming.

Visitor impressions and experiences vary with time. An FME can take advantage of a destination's unique temporal characteristics by factoring them into the location and timing of activities to maximise positive visitor experiences.

As a general rule, the older a place the greater the amenities and accumulated meaning that it has to offer. However, what people hold sacred are their own memories and it is these memories that attach sacredness to places. FMEs can develop creative activities and products that maintain a destination's integrity and authenticity which encourage the development of meaningful visitor memories.

FMEs without interesting and descriptive names would have trouble in attracting visitor interest. Imagery communicates the identity of a community and assists in creating an appealing authenticity (Yeoman *et al.*, 2004). The festival name can shape the image of the host community.

Industry Insight: The Australian Festival of the Book

The Australian Festival of the Book was a small community festival held in the Southern Highlands of New South Wales, Australia. It was run by a small committee who worked on a voluntary basis. Visitors to the inaugural festival in 2002 were disappointed with the range of festival activities on offer. This disappointment came about in part because they expected the term 'Australian' to signify a very large event. Hence, their disappointment when these expectations weren't met.

Political forces within communities

Ideally government should play an active role in supporting or producing FMEs. Various government agencies may be required to:

♦ Create the appropriate institutional, legal, economic, social and environmental framework by developing and applying a mix of instruments, such as FME economic instruments, social and environmental impact assessment for FMEs

♦ Facilitate the coordination and cooperation of different agencies, authorities and organisations concerned

♦ Support implementation of sustainable FMEs through effective regulatory and legislative frameworks that establish standards for FME management and staging

♦ Enforce regulations to promote ethical business behaviour with penalties for non-compliance

♦ Assist in the design and implementation of public consultation techniques and processes

♦ Establish common approaches to environmental policies and FME planning

♦ Raise awareness of sustainable FMEs by promoting exchange of information between governments and all stakeholders, on best practice for sustainable FME; and

♦ Promote broad understanding and awareness to strengthen attitudes, values and actions that are compatible with sustainable FME management.
(adapted from Dwyer and Edwards, 2004)

Creating educational opportunities and engagement for visitors at every stage of the trip

An FME can be used as a means of engaging the visitor more sustainably with the destination at every stage of the visitor's trip to increase knowledge and understanding of the destination. These stages include:

♦ **Booking**: information on programmes that allow the visitor to connect with residents of the community before arrival such as home stay and volunteer opportunities

♦ **Pre-trip**: provision of a reading list, destination fact sheets, language classes and orientations, interactive opportunities with past visitors, advertising

♦ **Transportation to destination**: promotion of sustainable modes of transportation (hybrid cars, carbon-offset)

♦ **On-board transportation**: educational videos, destination-related activities, puzzles, colouring books relevant to destination, sampling of destination cuisine and cultures, destination-orientated reading materials

♦ **Arrival at destination airport**: adequate signage and information kiosks; provision of art, music, food that introduce soulful elements of the destination; use of volunteers to provide information and assist in interpretation

♦ **Transportation to lodging**: training taxi, limo and car rental drivers to be interpreters, videos or written material in transportation that tells a story of the destination

♦ **Arrival at lodging**: lodging as an opportunity for culture to be transmitted through facilities and staff; provision of FME and destination information packets in the lodge, introducing guests to aspects of the destination

◆ **Stay in destination**: introduction of visitors to volunteer projects, providing opportunities for and encouraging patronage of local establishments and the purchase of locally made arts and crafts

◆ **Departure**: departure orientation to provide information on what visitors can do when they return home to increase their knowledge of the destination.

These activities may lead to innovative ideas for marketing and public relations and enable visitors to truly experience a community's values, interests and aspirations.

A flexible approach to FME implementation

FMEs are based upon activities of different kinds, different sizes and duration, requiring sophisticated planning and administration to ensure their success. FME organisation is high pressure and needs to be managed with high precision. In broad terms, the management of FMEs can be divided into four main stages:

◆ Pre-planning

◆ Organising

◆ Operations

◆ Evaluation.

Whilst the balance and order of activities may change depending on the nature or purpose of the FME, all four stages need to be carefully managed. Table 9.3 provides examples of ways in which these stages may be managed in a sustainable way.

Table 9.3: Management stages of an FME

Pre-planning	
The idea	May come from public, private or interest groups. The focus here should be on co-operation and partnership between these groups: for example, sitting down with the stakeholders to develop common interest, vision goals and objectives; ensuring that all stakeholders are happy and ready to participate and there are no ambiguities as to what each will get out of the FME.
Aims and objectives	Incorporating a commitment to do well by the environment; to appreciate the social and cultural aspects of the community, and to have economic accountability.
Establishing a team of organisers	Represented by all the different interests of the community, including: local authorities, sponsors, community groups, firms, school, churches and service clubs, each representing different community perspectives and having responsibility for economic, marketing, financial and operational variables.
Feasibility study	Focusing on the WHO (participants), reaching those who are sensitive to the environmental, social and cultural values of communities; WHAT (activities), carefully choosing activities that will promote enjoyment whilst at the same time have the least negative impact; WHEN (timing), choosing a time that will benefit the host community economically, as well as allowing for the physical and social carrying capacity; WHERE (location), WHY (motive). WHAT needs to be sustained and how is this best achieved. Finally reaching a decision based on the overall good of all concerned for the proposed FME to achieve long-term sustainability.

Organising	
Location and venue	Considerations that need to be made are: size and capacity to suit activities; availability of services and facilities; capacity of infrastructure; location central to transport; business, leisure, and attractions; social and cultural acceptability; safety and security.
Timing	Considerations include: target audience availability, clash with other events, lead time for marketing and organising
Collaboration	Sponsors, transport, business, media
Consultation	Community groups, professional groups, local authorities and residents
Cost of entry	Considerations include cost of production, aims and objectives, market research, yield required. Community needs should also be considered, for example having concessional rates for families, seniors, minors and carers.
Finance	**Sustainable budgeting and controlling, including proper accountability**
Human resources	Providing quality with sufficient resources. Using local skills and knowledge of voluntary and paid staff. Providing training
Marketing	Commitment to reaching travel consumers that are orientated toward socio-cultural and environmental responsibility. Promotion, marketing and advertising of the event are sensitive to the host community. This is important in the pre-event marketing as well as during the event. Educating the proposed consumers on sustainable principles.
Procurement	Purchasing products that adhere to green principles and choosing suppliers that are environmentally responsible and source their products ethically. It is advisable to ask suppliers where they source their products. Where possible, use organic and locally sourced foodstuffs, and products with the Fair Trade mark, which guarantees a fair deal for disadvantaged producers.
Operations	
Communication	Conduct frequent communication with all stakeholders, monitor progress, revise details and confirm alterations. Use checklists and flowcharts to ensure everyone knows their responsibilities. Signage to be adequate to reduce congestion, traffic, litter, safety and security, to foster respect of local culture and natural movement of residents.
Crowd control	In an emergency, involving local authorities and volunteers in spreading people evenly, to constrain disorderly crowds. Adequate planning and training for emergency such as bomb, medical, terrorist risk, other contingencies.
Quality and value	Making sure that the products and services offered are delivered at the right time, to the right place, and that the needs of all stakeholders are met. Adoption of a positive culture that is adaptable to change. Offering a product and service that bring credibility and satisfaction at a price that is seen to be of value to stakeholders.
Waste minimisation	Set up effective waste minimisation and recycling facilities for your onsite contractors, delegates and audience. This also includes working with many recycling organisations who will pick up waste for recycling or distribution to charities.
Appropriate use of energy	Investigate whether green electricity can be bought in for the event.
Shutting down	Ensuring only footprints are left behind. Ensuring that the environment and the community have been left the way they were found. Thanking all relevant stakeholders.
Evaluation	
	Evaluation is to determine how well the FME was conducted in terms of the impact on the environment and economic, social and cultural considerations. It is essential that evaluation is considered from different perspectives: The FME organisation, staff and volunteers, sponsors, customers and the host community.

Source: Presbury and Edwards (2005)

It must be understood that the effort in attempting to implement sustainability is enormous and complex, and can be beyond the financial and technical means of a smaller FME organiser. However, organisers of small FMEs can begin by selecting a few priorities that are within their resources and expertise.

Industry insight: Marriott Green Meetings

The average three-day meeting at a Marriott hotel attended by 1000 people produces more than 12 tons of trash, uses 200,000 kilowatts of power and consumes 100,000 gallons of water. Marriott, JW Marriott and Renaissance Hotels and Resorts are introducing a series of eco-friendly meeting products that will help guests and meeting planners reduce their environmental impact. Products and services include:

♦ 100% post-consumer fibre writing pads
♦ Biodegradable pens made from recycled content (Marriott purchases 47 million pens per year)
♦ Access to recycling containers in or near meeting rooms
♦ Boxed lunch containers made of recycled content, including biodegradable cutlery kits and napkins
♦ Organic, sustainable and natural food and beverage options that include Fair Trade teas, coffee and chocolates
♦ Organic flowers
♦ Linen-less banquet buffet tables made of 49%-recycled aluminium
♦ Giving food that is 'safe-to-donate' to America's Second Harvest's network of food banks.

Our customers have been demanding greener meetings and we feel we can make a difference in the world by taking steps to reduce our footprint on the environment. . . As part of the program, event and sales managers will be trained on what makes a meeting environmentally friendly.

(http://www.marriott.com, 2010)

Monitoring and evaluation

Critical to any FME is the monitoring and evaluation of the possible outcomes and what has been learnt in the process, to ensure the festival's sustainability. Stakeholders have a right to know what the FME achieved. Reporting back to stakeholders is an important part of promoting the profile and acceptance of FMEs.

Monitoring and evaluating are essential components of FME sustainability, because they specifically aid in:

♦ The evaluation of FME economic, environmental and social effectiveness
♦ Determining the worth of the FME
♦ Identifying costs and benefits
♦ Providing information to assist with accountability and transparency
♦ Providing information for sensitive marketing and interpretation

 ♦ Providing information on negative impacts arising from FMEs
 ♦ Gaining acceptance/credibility/support; and
 ♦ Incorporating changes that may occur and from which others can learn for the future.

Monitoring

Monitoring is the systematic collection and analysis of information as an FME progresses. The aim of monitoring an FME is to ensure the FME is on track for meeting sustainability criteria and to let organisers know when things are going wrong. Monitoring provides a basis for evaluation and should be based on targets set and activities planned during the planning phases of the FME.

A monitoring programme should be established at the outset of FME planning, and it is critical that baseline information be developed on initial conditions allowing for early warning of future changes (Eagles *et al.*, 2002). A monitoring programme involves management and staff, visitors, suppliers and the community and should be undertaken in an organised and systematic manner.

Monitoring should:

 ♦ Contain meaningful variables that are useful in identifying changes in activity
 ♦ Be a reliable system that draws on accurate results to form reliable conclusions
 ♦ Be affordable – must be able to resource and carry out recommended procedures
 ♦ Be easy to implement – making sure that procedures are in line with the nature of the FME
 ♦ Be appropriate to capability – and implementable within the FME capacity
 ♦ Occur within the defined goals and objectives – social, cultural, economic and environmental goals
 ♦ Be established with clear measurement criteria – with appropriate benchmarks and thresholds which will be different for each FME activity; and
 ♦ Collect data that will effectively represent a continuous process.

Evaluation

Evaluation can be described as a 'process of critically observing, measuring and monitoring the implementation of an FME to assess its outcomes accurately' (Aller *et al.*, 2008: 530). Evaluation loops the management process back to the planning stage. It measures the proposed goals and objectives against the actual outcomes or results. It answers questions about: what was done? Who did it? How was it done? What worked, what didn't and what is recommended for next time? Evaluating an FME assists organisers in measuring the costs and benefits of the FME, celebrate the FME's achievements and, most importantly, promote achievements so others can learn from that experience.

It is important to note, however, that evaluation should occur not only at the end but also throughout the FME management cycle. In the pre-planning and research stage the costs and benefits of holding an FME are evaluated. During the organising stage the progress of the FME is constantly checked and adjustments made, depending on the circumstances.

Post FME evaluation, however, is the most common and comprehensive method, as this is the time that necessary data have been collected on the financial expenditure of the participants and stakeholders, as well as the community.

Methods for evaluation

Methods used for monitoring and evaluating FMEs include:

◆ Surveys that provide information on demographics, and spending and revenue patterns, not only at the event venue but the broader business community.

◆ Surveys to gauge the feelings and attitudes of various stakeholders, especially the human factors, that is, those that affect the quality of life and wellbeing of the individuals or groups within the community.

◆ Observation including visual inspections of the outcome of an activity, observation of performance and working methods, discussion of work practices and the generation of information on quality performance, audience reaction, crowd flow and behaviour, infrastructure and services capacity, effects on the community, as well as observed impacts on the environment.

◆ De-briefings with various stakeholders to discuss issues, initiatives, problems and possible solutions. This allows for the generation of new ideas, provides valuable feedback from different perspectives, and enables the entire team to have a sense of ownership of the process.

◆ Financial control measures, including scrutinising the expenditure and reviewing the use of the resources that have been consumed in achieving set activities. The expenditure would be compared to the budget, which was planned at the outset.

◆ Measuring usage of resources such as water and energy. Comparisons then need to be made against benchmarks, standards and resource indicators.

◆ Recording both positive or negative media coverage. Keeping a file of newspaper articles and summaries of radio interviews can offer important lessons for the future.

◆ Benchmarking, which involves identifying those who exemplify best practice and then comparing one's own performance to others.

The nature of the evaluation will be determined by the purpose and size of the FME, but one of the primary reasons for conducting an evaluation is to report back to stakeholders and summarise all the lessons learnt to make recommendations for future FME management. Evaluation steers the learning process, and should be used to improve effectiveness and efficiency, maximise the beneficial impacts, and formulate innovative ideas for the future.

Future challenges and issues

With the recognition of the benefits of FMEs, it is likely that this sector of the tourism industry will increase. Competition is likely to intensify with the growth of developing nations and their need to increase the economic wellbeing of their destinations. The increase in these activities puts pressure on the environmental, social, and cultural resources of destinations. Ensuring sustainability and protecting those resources is a key strategic issue facing the tourism industry. Successful FMEs require the active and concerted efforts of all stakeholders to maximise the economic contribution of FMEs, whilst at the same time abiding by the principles of sustainability. To this end, this chapter is a first step in equipping students with the necessary knowledge to plan, organise and implement sustainable FMEs.

Activity

Choose a FME in your community. Evaluate whether the FME meets the sustainability criteria outlined in Table 9.3. Develop a management plan for this FME in the future in a more sustainable way. Your plan should be divided into the following stages:

♦ Evaluation of the current practices of the event and whether it meets the sustainability criteria outlined in Table 9.3

♦ Preplanning

♦ Organising

♦ Operations

♦ Evaluation.

Your plan should reflect all the principles outlined in this chapter.

Useful websites

BS8901 Sustainable Event Management System   http://www.bsi-global.com/BS8901
Green events guide   http://www.oursouthwest.com/SusBus/gevents.html
Roskilde Festival   http://www.roskilde-festival.dk/uk/
Sustainable Events Summit 2009   www.citmagazine.com/news/895557
Sustainable Living Festival   http://festival.slf.org.au/
Sustainable Living Foundation   http://www.slf.org.au/

References

Allen, J. (2000) *Event Planning – The Ultimate Guide*, Mississauga ON: John Wiley & Sons Canada.

Allen, J. (2002) *The Business of Event Planning*, Mississauga ON: John Wiley and Sons Canada.

Allen, J., O'Toole, W., McDonnell, I. and Harris, R. (2008) *Festival and Special Event Management*, 4th edn, Milton, QLD: John Wiley & Sons Australia.

Andersson, T.D. and Getz, D. (2008) 'Stakeholder management: strategies of festivals', *Journal of Convention and Event Tourism*, **9** (3), 199-220.

Astroff, T.M. and Abbey, R.J. (1998) *Convention, Sales and Services*, 5th edn, Cranberry, NJ: Waterbury Press.

Burns, J. P.A., Hatch, J.H. and Mules, T.J. (1986) *The Adelaide Grand Prix: The Impact of a Special Event*, Adelaide: Centre for South Australian Economic Studies.

Clarkson Centre for Business Ethics (2000) *Principles of Stakeholder Management*, Toronto: CCBE.

Craik, J. (1991) *Resorting to Tourism: Cultural Policies for Tourist Development in Australia*, St Leonards, Australia: Allen and Unwin.

Crompton, J.L., Lee, S. and Shuster, T.J. (2001) 'A guide for undertaking economic impact studies: the Springfest example', *Journal of Travel Research*, **40** (1), 79-87.

Crompton, J.L. and McKay, S.L. (1997) 'Motives of visitors attending festival events', *Annals of Tourism Research*, **24** (2), 425-439.

Delamere, T.A. (1998) 'Development of a scale to measure local resident attitudes towards the social impact of community festivals', unpublished doctoral thesis, University of Alberta.

Douglas, N. and Douglas, N. (2001), *Special Interest Tourism*, Richmond VIC: John Wiley & Sons Australia.

Dwyer, L. and Edwards, D. (2004) 'Sustainable tourism planning' Business Enterprise for Sustainable Travel Education Network, CD Rom.

Dwyer, L., Mellor, R., Mistilis, N. and Mules, T. (2000) 'A framework for assessing "tangible" and "intangible" impacts of events and conventions', *Event Management*, **6**, 175-189.

Eagles, P.F.J., McCool, S.F. and Haynes, C.D. (2002) *Sustainable Tourism in Protected Areas: Guidelines for Planning and Management*, Gland, Switzerland: IUCN Programme on Protected Areas.

Formica, S. and Uysal, M. (1996) 'A market segmentation of festival visitors: Umbria Jazz Festival in Italy', *Festival Management and Event Tourism*, **3**, 175-182.

Friedman, S. (2003) *Meeting and Event Planning for Dummies*, Hoboken, NJ: Wiley Publishing.

Getz, D. (1997) *Event Management and Event Tourism*, Elmsford, NY: Cognizant Communication Corporation.

Getz, D. and Frisby, W. (1988) 'Evaluating management effectiveness in community-run festivals', *Journal of Travel Research*, Summer, 22-27.

Goldblatt, J. and Nelson, K. (2001) *The International Dictionary of Event Management*, 2nd edn, Missassauga ON: John Wiley & Sons Canada.

Hargreaves, A. and Fink, D. (2003) 'The Seven Principles of Sustainable leadership', International Centre for Educational Change Ontario Institute for Studies in Education/University of Toronto, found at http://www2.bc.edu/~hargrean/docs/seven_principles.pdf accessed 29 January 2010.

Harris, R. and Huysken, M. (2002) *Public Events: Can They Make a Contribution to Ecological Sustainability?*, Sydney: University of Technology Sydney, Australian Centre for Event Management.

Hassan, S.S. (2000) 'Determinants of market competitiveness in an environmentally sustainable tourism industry', *Journal of Travel Research*, **38** (February), 239–245.

Hjalager, A-M, (2009) 'The Roskilde Festival as a tourism innovation system', *Scandinavian Journal of Tourism and Hospitality Management*, **9** (3/4), 266-287.

Hoyle, H.L. (2002) *Event Marketing*, Mississauga ON: John Wiley & Sons.

International Institute for Sustainable Development (IISD) (1994) 'Principles for sustainable tourism, code of environmentally responsible tourism, and codes of ethics for tourists', available at http://www.iisd.org/sd/principle.asp, accessed 2 November 2009.

Jeong, G. and Faulkner, B. (1996) 'Resident perceptions of mega-event impacts: the Taejon International Exposition case', *Festival Management and Event Tourism*, **4**, 3-11.

Karl, M. (2000) 'Monitoring and evaluating stakeholder participation in agriculture and rural development projects: a literature review', November 2000, SD Dimensions, available at: Sustainable Development Department (SD), Food and Agriculture Organization of the United Nations (FAO), http://www.fao.org/sd/PPdirect/PPre0074.htm, accessed 12 October 2004.

Lee, H. and Graefe, A.R. (2003) 'Crowding at an arts festival: extending crowding models to the front country', *Tourism Management*, **14**, 1-11.

Liburd, J.J. and Derkzen, P. (2009) 'Emic perspectives on quality of life. The case for the Danish Wadden Sea Festival', *Tourism and Hospitailty Research* 9(2) 132–146.

Marriott Hotels (2010) http://www.marriott.com, accessed 29 January 2010.

Mayfield, T.L. and Crompton, J. L. (1995) 'Development of an instrument for identifying community reasons for staging a festival', Journal of Travel Research, Winter, 37-44.

McCabe, V., Pool, B., Weeks, P. and Leiper, N. (2000) *The Business and Management of Conventions*, Richmond VIC: John Wiley & Sons.

McCann, C. and Thompson, G. (1992) 'An economic analysis of the first Western Australian State Masters Games', *Journal of Tourism Studies*, **3** (1), 28-34.

McCleary, K.W. (1995) 'Applying internal marketing techniques for better festival organization and management', *Festival Management and Event Tourism*, **3**, 1-7.

Middleton, V.T.C. (1998) *Sustainable Tourism: A Marketing Perspective*, Oxford: Butterworth Heinemann.

Motloch, J.L. (1991) *Introduction to Landscape Design*, New York: Van Nostrand Reinhold.

Nelson, J.S., Jayanthi, M., Brittain, C.S., Epstein, M. and Bursuck, W.D. (2002) 'Using the nominal group technique for homework communication decisions', *Remedial Special Education*, **23** (6), 379-387.

Nicholson, R.E. and Pearce, D.G. (2001) 'Why do people attend events: a comparative analysis of visitor motivations at four South Island events', *Journal of Travel Research*, **39** (4), 449-460.

Pashiardis, P. (1993) 'Group decision-making: the role of the principal', International *Journal of Educational Management*, **7** (2), 8-12.

Presbury, R. and Edwards, D. (2005) *BEST Sustainable Tourism: Festival, Meetings and Events Management Module*, Business Enterprise for Sustainable Travel Education.

Reid, S. and Arcodia, C. (2002) 'Understanding the role of the stakeholder in event management' Conference Proceeding of Events and Place Making, Sydney: University of Technology Sydney Australian Centre for Event Management, 470-515.

Sharpley, R. and Tefler, D.J. (2002) *Tourism and Development: Concepts and Issues*, Bristol Channel View Publications.

Small, K. and Edwards, D. (2003) 'Evaluating the socio-cultural impacts of a festival on a host community: a case study of the Australian Festival of the Book', in Griffin, T. and Harris, R., *Current Research, Future Strategies: Bridging Uncertainty*, Proceedings of the Asia Pacific Tourism Association, July 2002, Sydney University of Technology, Australia.

Small, K. and Edwards, D.C. (2006) 'Residents' expectations and perceptions of the social impacts of community festivals', paper presented at conference Cutting Edge Research in Tourism, 6-9 June, Guildford.

Smith, M. and Duffy, R. (2003) *The Ethics of Tourism Development*, London: Routledge.

Tyrrell, T.J. and Johnston, R.J. (2001) 'A framework for assessing direct economic impacts of tourist events: distinguishing origins, destinations, and causes of expenditures', *Journal of Travel Research*, **40** (1), 94-100.

UNEP (2002a) 'Agenda 21', http://www.un.org/esa/dsd/agenda21/, accessed 2 November 2009.

UNEP (2002b) 'Biological diversity and tourism: international guidelines for sustainable tourism', http://www.biodiv.org/programmes/socio-eco/tourism/guidelines.asp, accessed 29 January 2010.

Uysal, M., Gahan, L. and Martin, B. (1993) 'An examination of event motivations: a case study', *Festival Management and Event Tourism*, **1** (1), 5-10.

Van de Ven, A.H. and Delbecq, A.L. (1971) 'Nominal versus interacting group processes for committee decision-making effectiveness', Academy of Management Journal, 14 (2), 203-212.

Watt, D.C. (1998) *Event Management in Leisure and Tourism*, Harlow: Addison Wesley Longman.

Weaver, D. (2002) *Tourism in the 21st Century*, London: Continuum.

Weber, K. and Chon, K. (2002) *Convention Tourism, International Research and Industry Perspectives*, Binghamton, NY: Haworth Hospitality Press.

Wills, J. (2001) *Just, Vibrant and Sustainable Communities: A Framework for Progressing and Measuring Community Wellbeing*, Townsville QLD: Local Government Community Services of Australia.

Wilmott, P. (1989) *Community Initiatives: Patterns and Prospects*, London: Policy Studies Institute.

WTO (1995) *What Tourism Managers Need to Know: A Practical Guide to the Development and Use of Indicators of Sustainable Tourism*, Ottawa: Consulting and Audit Canada.

WTO 'WTO Global Code of Ethics', found at http://www.bmwi.de/BMWi/Redaktion/PDF/G/global-code-of-ethics-englisch, accessed 29 January 2010.

Yeoman, I., Robertson, M., Ali-Knight, J., Drummond, S. and McMahaon-Beattie, U. (2004) *Festival and Events Management: An International Arts and Culture Perspective*, Oxford: Elsevier.

10 Volunteer Tourism

Stephen Wearing, Kevin Lyons and Suzanne Leigh Snead

Rationale

The aim of this chapter is to provide students with a critical understanding of the phenomenon of volunteer tourism. It will consider how volunteer tourism occurs in diverse community settings with a particular emphasis upon international contexts. It emphasises the potential volunteer tourism has as a transformative form of sustainable tourism that extends beyond the finite limits of a particular volunteering experience. In this chapter, students will develop a foundational understanding of how this transformation is best realised, and ultimately aims to lead both volunteer tourists and host communities toward responsible and continuing participation in local and global development.

This chapter begins by defining volunteer tourism and providing students with an understanding of its development and progression. Particular attention is paid to the way volunteer tourism has been conceptualised as an alternative form of sustainable tourism that is grounded in philanthropic and altruistic ideologies. It also critiques this viewpoint and encourages students to look at volunteer tourism as a reciprocal relationship between host communities and volunteer tourists. This reciprocity is explored by considering the needs of the host community by examining the principles of community planning that underpin quality volunteer tourism projects with particular emphasis upon the strengths and weaknesses of community development processes. The chapter then examines the needs of volunteer tourists, particularly those who are young adults. While volunteer tourism is increasingly being undertaken by a diverse range of individuals, its value as an educational tool for students studying sustainable tourism cannot be overstated. This chapter explores how hands-on volunteer tourism community work allows students to gain invaluable personal and career experience, as well as build powerful life and job skills that can be applied towards future community-building initiatives. This chapter also examines the principles of leadership and group dynamics that underpin successful volunteer tourism ventures.

Learning outcomes

On completion of this chapter the student should be able to:

+ Articulate what is meant by volunteer tourism and how it relates to sustainable tourism
+ Describe the development of volunteer tourism and the factors that have contributed to its proliferation
+ Describe who the major stakeholders are in volunteer tourism and the roles they contribute, as well as the benefits for each

♦ Critically discuss cross-cultural issues and contested meaning within volunteer tourism philosophies and behaviour

♦ Critically explain how volunteer tourism relates to the concept of community planning and community development

♦ Explain how clear ethical standards, leadership and community involvement are important components of successful volunteer tourism programmes.

Understanding volunteer tourism

'Volunteer tourists' have been defined by Wearing as tourists 'who, for various reasons, volunteer in an organized way to undertake holidays that might involve aiding or alleviating the material poverty of some groups in society, the restoration of certain environments or research into aspects of society or environment'(2001: 1). These holidays appear to be targeted at young adults who find time to give up work and study commitments for an 'experience'. Simpson (2004) equates volunteer tourism to that of volunteering by 'gap year' students in the UK which combine hedonistic tourism with altruistic development work. The activity is becoming even more popular with 275 organisations listed worldwide in the 2003 *Guide to Volunteer Vacations* by Bill McMillon *et al*. (Brown and Lehto, 2005).

Evolution of volunteer tourism

The intersection between volunteering and tourism falls broadly into two camps. The first is from a supply-side perspective where volunteers provide unpaid labour that supplements and supports the supply of tourism services. Volunteers are the backbone of many community festivals and mega-sporting events that attract thousands of tourists. They are also the unsung heroes behind the scenes supporting tourist attractions such as zoos, museums and heritage sites.

The second intersection, 'volunteer tourism' (also known as 'voluntourism'), is a form of tourism demand and is the focus of this chapter. Volunteer tourists are those individuals who travel to host communities in need, typically in developing countries, to volunteer their vacation time to work on a wide range of humanitarian or environmental restoration projects. Volunteer tourism developed in the 1990s as a way for non-government organisations (NGOs) to supplement their long-term international volunteers with short-term support. However, at the dawn of the 21st century, there has been a rapid rise in commercial tourism operators who specialise in providing a wide range of packaged experiences to those wanting to volunteer but who do not have the time or inclination to seek out volunteering experiences independently.

Volunteer tourism's ascendancy has coincided with the emergence of the 'new tourist' (Poon, 2003) – a more mature tourist who seeks personal development and authentic experiences through travel that are lacking in mass tourism. The new tourist avoids mass tourism and seeks to travel independently to less frequented destinations, or to engage on a deeper level with locals than the superficiality of transactional relations most often encountered in mass tourism (i.e. a tourism encounter with locals may only extend to waiters, tour guides or hotel staff in mass tourism experiences). This breed of tourist seeks purposeful travel and usually has an interest in nature, culture and personal development (Poon, 2003).

The explosion of volunteer tourism is also occurring within the larger environmental and sustainability concerns in Western society. Issues such as globalisation, climate change, destruction of natural habitats, endangered species, international relations and Western aid to developing countries pervade the news and public consciousness. Volunteer tourism fills a niche for those wishing for first-hand experience of the world in a way that is environmentally friendly, sustainable and politically correct. The invention of the term 'volunteer tourism' itself is the result of an increased recognition of, and reaction to, the negative impacts being caused by mass tourism and a recognition of the importance of conserving natural environmental quality. The underlying ideology of volunteer tourism represents a transition in society from 'travel to take' to a 'travel to assist' – putting something back while you travel.

Contexts for volunteer tourism

Volunteer tourism can take place in varied locations such as rainforests and cloud forests, biological reserves and conservation areas. Popular locations include countries in Africa, Asia and Central and South America. Activities can vary across many areas such as scientific research (wildlife, land and water), conservation projects, medical assistance, economic and social development (including agriculture, construction and education), and cultural restoration. Indeed, volunteers can find themselves anywhere between assisting with mass eye surgery operations, tree planting, conducting a health campaign, teaching English and improving village sanitation to constructing a rainforest reserve and assisting physicians and nurses with a mobile clinic. There is usually, however, the opportunity for volunteers to take part in local activities and interact further with the community. Hence the volunteer tourist contribution is bilateral, in that the most important development which may occur in the volunteer tourist experience is that of a personal nature, that of a greater awareness of self: 'When volunteers come back they feel empowered, knowing they have been able to make a difference … You come home feeling you don't have limits. You feel a lot more confident in your ideas and beliefs and that you can contribute to society' (Hill, 2001: 28).

The volunteer tourist

While anyone can be a volunteer tourist, there tend to be some commonalities among the kinds of people who engage in volunteer tourism. The overwhelming majority are from industrialised, developed nations (often seeking to volunteer in developing or 'Third World' nations), they are affluent and tend to be free (perhaps temporarily or longer term) from most typical life responsibilities, such as mortgages, parenting or employment, which allows them the time and money to engage in a volunteer tourism experience.

Even though they are volunteering, volunteer tourists will almost always pay in some way for the privilege of participating in the development, research or conservation activities of the host organisation. The funds are necessary for operations of the programmes and may or may not include lodgings and amenities for the volunteer tourist. The amount is usually more than an average tourist would expect to pay on a 'normal' holiday to a similar location. While there are some sponsorship programmes and alternative contribution arrangements provided by some organisations, the financial contribution required of the volunteer tourist is illustrative of the wider nature of the experience, of greater benefits for host and tourist alike.

Motivations and benefits

There have been a growing number of studies on volunteer tourists and the factors influencing their decision to volunteer. Brown and Lehto (2005) found that the three principal motivations behind volunteering were cultural immersion, making a difference and seeking camaraderie while Mustonen (2007) believes that the motivations fluctuate between altruism and egoism. Broad and Jenkins (2008) group motivations into four main categories: altruism, desire to travel, career development and personal interest/personal development.

Personal and career development

It has been suggested that from a personal growth perspective, volunteer tourism experiences instil openness to and acceptance of other cultures, and foster cultural sensitivity, cultural awareness and empathy towards others (Wearing, 2001). This openness is a product of self-growth.

Altruism is a common explanation used by volunteer tourists but self-development and adventure are also cited as strong motivators (Wearing, 2001; Pearce and Coghlan, 2008). However, despite their recognised potential to teach young people about themselves and their life directions, volunteer tourism and other forms of career break activity such as working holidays may be dismissed as a respite from the more serious concerns of adulthood such as life and career decisions, with only a vague concession that such experiences might look good on individuals' resumes (see Havenhand, 2000). Indeed, tourism and travel research has rarely considered the impact of travel experiences upon one's future life trajectories. Given that recent research and government reports argue that increasing youth unemployment rates are in part the product of a dearth of opportunities for young people to gain meaningful work experiences that enable them to build career goals (Bessant et al., 1998), it is important to pay more serious attention to the potential role volunteer tourism may play in providing career clarity to young people.

In a survey of young people's attitudes to post-compulsory education, work place experience was identified as the most useful source of information regarding career planning and development (Department of Employment, Education and Training, 1994). Peters and Waterman (1982) argue that many traditional approaches to career planning are overly prescriptive and inflexible primarily because too much emphasis is placed upon goal setting that is driven by external cues without allowing room for experimentation and self-directed learning. As an alternative, Peters and Waterman (1982) suggest a 'ready, fire, aim!' approach to career planning that allows individuals to experiment with a range of work experiences before committing to a particular career path. Volunteer tourism is an ideal context for such experimentation.

The volunteer organisation

A wide range of institutions and organisations do, and will continue to, play an important role in providing volunteer tourism experiences. The type of organisation varies considerably, and a number provide international support and sponsorship for the implementation of research projects and community development. These organisations facilitate the volunteer tourism process through provision of necessary resources that may not otherwise be available and objectives that move beyond the commodified process found predominantly in the tourism industry. The international scope of these organisations can prove invaluable assistance in terms of their accumulated knowledge and experience. These types of organisations provide a large number of recruits through volunteer tourism with free time and money to spend on sustainable development efforts (Whelan, 1991).

Organisations can operate with a focus on achieving such objectives as conservation, community development and personal development, offering a range of experiences that engage the tourist in events aimed at developing values such as stewardship, mutuality, knowledge and ethics: values that are not focused simply on the pleasure of the experience, or the desire to escape from day-to-day existence (Wearing and Deane, 2003). NGOs may range in scope, size and location. For example, small, locally developed organisations such as Pepy Ride Tours, a volunteer tourism non-profit organisation in Cambodia, focus specifically upon the progression of volunteer tourism development and delivery in countries throughout South East Asia while large international agencies such as Oxfam International include volunteer tourism-related services and activities as part of a much larger range of social service activities in countries around the globe.

Some examples of NGOs include Global Volunteers Network (*www.volunteer org.nz*), Voluntary Services Overseas (www.vso.org.uk), Rotary Youth Projects, Education International (www.ei-ie.org), Sustainable Travel International (www sustainabletravelinternational.org), the David and Lucile Packard Foundation (www.packard.org), Oxfam (www.oxfam.org.uk) and the Indonesia International Rural and Agriculture Development Foundation (www.iniradef.com).

Examples of research organisations include Earthwatch (www.earthwatch.org), the Centre for Global Development (www.cgdev.org), the British Schools Exploring Society (www.bses.org.uk), the Scientific Exploration Society (www.ses-explore. org) and the Dolphin Research Institute (www.dolphinresearch.org.au).

Examples of conservation organisations include Ngamba Island Chimpanzee Sanctuary (www.ngambaisland.org), Conservation International (www.conservation.org), the Nature Conservancy (www.nature.org), Orangutan Foundation International (www.orangutan.org), the International Rhino Foundation (www. rhinos-irf.org), Rainforest Alliance (www.rainforest-alliance.org) and the Wildlife Conservation Society (www.wcs.org).

Commercial operators and commodification

The rising interest in volunteer tourism has not gone unnoticed by the commercial tourism industry, with many commercial operators now offering volunteer tourism packages and products. Although there has been some progress in volunteer tourism through industry, government and association initiatives, the majority of effort by the mainstream tourism industry has been focused towards self-interest rather than through a true attempt to be sustainable. Volunteer tourism has caught the imagination of many local communities, governments, international organisations and the tourism industry. While volunteer tourism is increasingly being seen as a way to promote sustainable tourism, it is also seen as being able to provide valuable income. Modern tourism has created multinational economic investment, and the extent of tourism practices' impact on both the host and guest has been great in a relatively short period of time (Lyons and Wearing, 2008).

In principle, volunteer tourism as a leisure experience offers the potential for increased understanding between guest and host nations of the local community and economy in a decidedly decommodified manner. Commercial volunteer tourism creates an ironic oxymoron in which volunteer tourism experiences are being commodified into a market economy. Compared with experiences run by NGOs or research-based organisations, the volunteer experiences offered by many commercial tourism operators are inadequately designed and fall short of meeting the needs of host communities and the tourist, or create even greater negative impacts (Simpson, 2004).

The current pending issue is whether the philosophy of sustainable volunteer tourism in its true form can influence the mass practices of mainstream tourism, or whether volunteer tourism will be usurped and misrepresented as another form of economics-driven mass tourism. Volunteer tourism offers a model that challenges the commodified practices of global tourism. It may be unrealistic to expect that full-scale responsible tourism practices adopted by volunteer tourism organisations will be embraced or endorsed immediately by mainstream tourism. However, if volunteer tourism is effectively regulated and practices of sustainability established, a more viable and rich volunteer tourist experience is possible, as well as a potential positive influence on the tourism industry overall.

The host community

The host community is the place where and people with whom the volunteer tourists engage in their projects. 'Community' refers to a group of people who share a common identity, such as geographical location, class or ethnic background, or who share a special interest, such as a common concern about the destruction of native flora and fauna and are the community associated with the destination area of the tourist. These communities may be rural or urban, local or international.

The history of host communities and mainstream tourism has been an interesting, if not a controversial, one. Many of the ideas that have supported the development of a community-based approach to tourism have come about through the enormous impacts that tourism developments in the 1980s had on host communities. These communities often had little say and control in the development that was occurring. The social impact of unrestrained tourism developments caused upheaval in many communities.

Tourism planning often occurs without host community involvement at the outset. Many tourism projects are prepared by professionals or managers without input from the host community. When these projects are made available for community input, usually not until the final stages of development, they often fail to get support as they do not meet community needs or values. In addition, many social groups within the host community often feel helpless and frustrated because they are unsure about how to get their concerns addressed at any point of the development process.

Critics have pointed out that volunteers and the host communities they seek to help may be vulnerable to the potential problems that may arise when some profit-focused and unscrupulous commercial operators are not regulated. Reports of poorly planned volunteer projects that do little to benefit a community are emerging as a growing number of these commercial operators enter the market to capitalise on a lucrative form of niche tourism without regard for or involvement from host communities. Volunteer tourism offers potential for a new range of opportunities and a significant positive image for the tourism industry if a best practice community development approach is adopted – but could suffer from a backlash if approached unregulated and ad hoc. Important public, academic and industry debate is now underway around issues of accreditation to ensure that volunteer tourism grows to become a viable and ethically sound alternative to mass forms of tourism. This is further discussed below in the section on structuring volunteer tourism and ethics.

Cross-cultural issues

Multicultural understanding and exchange

Volunteer tourism is touted, both in academic literature and in popular commercial advertising, as a means to develop further cross-cultural understandings between people. The opportunity to volunteer in a setting or community different to the volunteer's home setting allows for opportunity to compare similarities and differences between the tourists and hosts through mutual interaction and work between people of multicultural backgrounds.

Global citizenship

Developing global citizenship is espoused as another benefit of volunteer tourism. The notion that globalisation has drawn the world closer together requires that people of all backgrounds and cultures broaden their world view beyond the borders of their own city, state, and nation. A culture of tolerance that is based on mutuality can be developed through interpersonal interactions between people of different backgrounds, nations and ethnicities, such as may be experienced between volunteers and hosts on volunteer tourism projects. This concept of the shared planet and international neighbours is driven by economic forces, environmental concerns and issues of national security. Carter (2004) draws parallels between the idea of global citizenship and the Greek concept of cosmopolitanism, a moral position that celebrates cultural diversity and human rights and an active concern for the needs of others (Carter, 2004). Cosmopolitanism, and the global citizenship it infers, requires an ability to at-once negotiate a world full of diverse interests and differences while developing a personal narrative that is inclusive of the 'other' thus internalising a sense of global homogeneity and shared humanity (Kramer, 1997).

Othering

According to McGehee and Andereck (2008: 20), 'Many volunteer tourism organisations cite the interactions between volunteers and their hosts as perhaps the most vital component of the volunteer tourism experience for both parties'. Volunteer tourists often are seeking meaningful and authentic encounters with new cultures and societies, to learn more about different cultures and to personally develop a greater sense of what it means to live in a multicultural, diverse world. Likewise, host communities can also benefit from cultural exchange in their interactions with the volunteers, through learning about new cultures and being exposed to new ideas via their guests.

However, there is also criticism that such interaction may result in reinforcing 'othering', particularly when volunteer tourists from affluent, mostly Anglo, developed societies volunteer in impoverished or indigenous communities. A preconceived stereotype of the members of the host community being less privileged or culturally primitive may be reinforced in the mind of the volunteer tourist when comparing the environment and lifestyles of the host community with the volunteer's own environment and lifestyle at home. The volunteer tourist may then adopt an unwittingly imperialistic attitude about how much the host community needs their help, and fails to view their hosts as members of a different culture with different perspectives to offer (Simpson, 2004). This 'othering' is enhanced by the tourist's displaced experience of 'culture shock'.

Culture shock

Culture shock is a phenomenon whereby 'the ebbing and flowing of exhilaration, anxiety, frustration, hostility, bewilderment, homesickness, denial, lethargy, and other reactions to situational stress, are supposed to subside and eventually settle into a calming sea of relative adjustment to, and acceptance of, the other culture as just another way of consuming reality' (Furnham and Bochner, 1986: xvi). Studies on culture shock have looked at the psychological adjustment of immigrants, workers and students to foreign environments. The concept has been looked at less frequently in the tourism literature, with Weaver claiming that 'tourists seldom experience culture shock because they are short-term sojourners who never actually enter another culture' (1987: 2). However, this idea is challenged by Pearce (1981).

More recently, studies have been undertaken to show that culture shock can take place when people return home. This has been referred to as 'reverse culture shock' (Mitchell, 2006), 'cross-cultural readjustment' (Ward and Kennedy, 2001) and 're-entry' (Mitchell, 2006). The result of such shock is 'when sojourners leave home, they often carry with them a static, mental and emotional snapshot of home; on some level, they expect home to stand still [and therefore,] they can be unprepared, then, for the changes that have occurred at home during their absence – changes that no longer match their image of home' (Mitchell, 2006: 5).

Structuring volunteer tourism experiences

Ethics

Volunteer tourism can be many things to many people. At the time of writing, there is no universal code of ethics to guide tourism operators in structuring the experiences for volunteer tourists. In looking at approaches to volunteer tourism, we must examine the values on which it is developed, the goals of its development, and how it impacts the host community.

If we consider volunteer tourism as a part of the idea of sustainable or alternative tourism, it can be seen as a growth area and has the potential to influence change in the tourism industry overall. Volunteer tourism may create an awareness of a need for the following:

♦ Tourist infrastructure which is sensitively developed where the tourism industry accepts integrated planning and regulation

♦ Supply-led (as opposed to demand-led) marketing by the tourism industry

♦ The establishment of carrying capacities (environmental and cultural) and strict monitoring of these

♦ The environmentally sensitive behaviour and operations of tourists and operators of all types of tourism.

For an ethical, sustainable volunteer tourism industry, we suggest the following must be present:

♦ A cultural and ethical framework that promotes host self-determination in the industry as central to the volunteer tourism experience

♦ Operators who are willing to be slow in developing a product that will then allow input from host communities and aim to have minimalistic impact by staying within the social and physical carrying capacities of an area

♦ Organisations who see their operations as a two-way interactive process between host and guest whereby the natural resource amenities, the local community and the visitor all benefit from the experience and the visitor can actually make a substantive contribution.

The achievement of these components will require strong, focused leadership and community involvement, discussed below.

Leadership

Leadership has been defined as the ability and desire to influence individuals in a specific setting so that they are able to reach a specific goal or outcome (see Edginton et al., 1998). However, leadership is dynamic and carries with it a range of potential meanings dependent upon the relationship between the leadership context, those who are being led and the personal characteristics of the leader. Leadership is also closely associated with the use of formal and informal power and its impact upon efficient and effective decision making.

In volunteer tourism contexts, leadership is typically associated with the formally sanctioned power assigned to those who make decisions about the organisation where volunteers work. This includes those in administrative and management roles such as policy makers and business owners as well as those who work directly with individuals as they participate in volunteer tourism activities. However, it is equally important to consider how leadership may emerge from the informal power exercised by volunteers and host community members and other interest groups such as transnational organisations who may not share the same interests as volunteer tourists.

Community involvement

It is one thing to talk about the ideas, values and principles of community and how they fit into the world in which we would like to operate; but it is another to actually do something about it. Most tourism is self-serving in the sense that what it creates in host communities is directed to benefit the tourist. Volunteer tourism seeks to provide resources that are directed toward the community and the needs they have identified as important for their development. But volunteer tourism is not just ideas, values and aspirations for a better world in a broad sense. In many circumstances it concerns itself with how tourism in destination areas can be used to support and enhance the local community. How should volunteer tourism operate within this context?

The first aim is to ensure communities in the wider sense have input into what happens with projects that are to occur (Dwyer and Edwards, 2004), be that in a destination or for conservation or scientific reasons. Tourism destinations are often made up of a series of separate 'places' such as landscapes, wildlife or specific activities. The people who best know and understand how these areas function are the people who deal with these places on a regular basis: members of the host community who use the area regularly, rather than the travel agencies or other transient organisations that bring people in and out of the area.

However, rarely are members of the community asked by private operators what their vision is for the area. Nor have members of the host community traditionally been part of the planning process. Likewise, planning decisions have often been made by people who do not understand the intricacies or functions of the destinations and attractions of the region. As a result, the tourism destination created does not suit community needs or use the resources to their best advantage.

Careful analysis, organisation and planning can help enhance the positive aspects of volunteer tourism development and alleviate the negative. Because each community is unique, each must make its decision based upon local circumstances. What has worked in one community may not apply in another. Likewise, not every community is suited for tourism development, nor is tourism suitable for every community.

There is a growing awareness within small communities of the benefits to be derived from developing volunteer tourism as part of their economics. Often this awareness comes on the heels of a declining traditional local industry such as agriculture or manufacturing. To be a truly successful part of a community's economy, tourism must be sustainable, even if only on a seasonal basis. To be sustainable, it must be properly planned and managed to ensure a continuing high quality experience for the visitor.

Community fieldwork describes a wide array of initiatives from grassroots activities associated with direct service in a community to engagement through policy and public debate. Volunteers engaging in such work may find themselves involved in direct aid work such as handing out food rations or helping to build a school or a bridge. While such activities are important, they describe only one aspect of a broader approach to assisting communities in need. This broader approach is best described as community planning. Community planning describes the systematic processes used by a diverse range of professions, institutions, organisations, groups and individuals to achieve identified outcomes associated with developing and enhancing communities and community life. These outcomes may be goal-driven, trends-driven, opportunity-driven, issue-driven, and/or vision-driven (see Kelly and Becker, 2000; Dwyer and Edwards, 2004).

The two major processes used in community planning are social planning and community development (see Edginton et al., 1998). Social planning is a task-focused process that emphasises efficiency and rationality and is well suited to large-scale planning. Community development is a community empowering process that identifies resources and services that enable community members to meet their own needs.

A major criticism of social planning is that it reinforces a provider–customer relationship that encourages communities to look to those outside the community to help meet its needs. Volunteer tourists entering a village to work on a particular project may in fact be a manifestation of a form of social planning. Ultimately this process is potentially disempowering as it breeds dependency rather than sustainable and self-sufficient communities. In contrast, community development recognises that community members are best positioned to identify and develop a plan for meeting their own needs and interests. Community development often involves a collaborative process where host communities engage in a range of community-building endeavours. The role of volunteer tourists in this model is one of facilitation, ultimately helping communities to help themselves. This may involve teaching community members specific skills they will be able to use to transform their communities once outside help leaves.

A criticism of community development is that the community organising process that is necessary for empowering communities to act on their own behalf is time consuming. Short-term volunteer tourism experiences of a week or two are often inadequate unless they are part of a coordinated and ongoing series of experiences that leave a community empowered. In addition, community development often involves competing interests and priorities and can ultimately result in factionalism. This raises the question: who speaks on behalf of a host community? Volunteer projects may inadvertently serve the needs of a vocal and powerful minority in a community while the majority may remain unserved.

Striking a balance between the efficiency and rationality of social planning and the effectiveness and empowerment of community development is one of the major challenges faced by those involved in organising volunteer tourism activities.

Future challenges and trends

The major challenge ahead for those involved in the development of volunteer tourism is its rapid growth. Volunteer tourism is no longer merely a by-product of NGOs' core business. It is now a legitimate form of tourism that is attracting interest from consumers who seek the opportunity to volunteer while also having a holiday. This development has led to the proliferation of commercial operators who seek to profit from the opportunities this demand has generated. However, this is not to say that the commodification of volunteer tourism cannot be managed in a way that ensures the mutual needs of volunteer tourists and host communities are both served. One approach that is beginning to be considered is to introduce guidelines or even accreditation standards for non-profit and commercial operators who provide volunteer tourism services. This would involve identifying those practices and policies that are already in place around the globe that lead to effective outcomes for both hosts and guest volunteers.

In recent years, a wave of ethics and responsibility has spread through the tourism industry, where operators and tourists alike appear to be in search of richer experiences (Fennell and Malloy, 2007). This finding is reported by Goodwin and Francis (2003, cited in Fennell and Malloy, 2007) in their summary of the work of the UK-based organisation Tearfund which found that, generally, tourism of an ethical nature adds value to tourism packages. The research concluded that operators seen to be more ethical gain a competitive advantage in the market by securing long-term relationships (Fennell and Malloy, 2007). Weeden (2002) states that responsible tourism now holds a key position in the tourism industry landscape, particularly from the consumer-demands perspective, where tourists are starting to make decisions based on the ethical qualifications of operators on issues related to tour operator–host community relations, treatment of employees, product marketing, and operators' actions and attitudes towards the natural environment (cited in Fennell, 2006).

It may be difficult to enforce such standards through administrative mechanisms alone. Additionally, the market itself may be able to enforce such standards through consumer choice. The growing power of the Internet allows potential volunteer tourists to do their own research on potential volunteer tourism opportunities through websites such as voluntourism.org, where information about volunteer tourism opportunities is posted and scrutinised. Through such services, the volunteer tourist consumers themselves can play a role in ensuring best practice in volunteer tourism occurs by avoiding those organisations that do not follow the principles of community development and provide services based on the needs of local communities. This would enhance the opportunity to ensure volunteer tourism is able to meet the expectations of a code of ethics and ensure that benefits 'for all' is not just a catch phrase.

Chapter review

Volunteer tourism developed in the mid-1990s from NGOs' recruiting volunteers to work on conservation, research and development projects in various locations around the world. This development coincided with the emergence of the 'new tourist', environmental awareness and globalisation concerns, leading to a market demand for more meaningful, sustainable tourism experiences, and a proliferation of commercial tourism operators producing excursions under the volunteer tourism banner. However, this growth has been haphazard and unregulated, and there are many critics who assert a large number of commercial operators are offering poorly structured experiences that do not benefit the tourist or the host community.

Proponents of volunteer tourism cite benefits for the volunteer tourist including engaging in intercultural exchange with members of host communities, self-discovery, skill development, and maturity of a personal understanding of diversity and multiculturalism. However, critics of volunteer tourism claim that neoliberalist ideology has perverted the altruistic intentions of the volunteer tourist, and that ultimately the experience may reinforce stereotypes of poverty in developing nations and foreign cultures as 'others', and reaffirm an imperialistic notion of Western ideologies and lifestyles for the volunteer tourist.

A consistent code of ethics needs to be developed and embraced by all participants of volunteer tourism to ensure its sustainability and legitimacy. Additionally focused leadership and involving host communities in planning are essential to structuring successful volunteer tourism ventures.

Review questions

1   What are some of the motivations and benefits of volunteer tourism for tourists? For host communities?

2   How has volunteer tourism positioned itself as an alternative to mass tourism? What factors threaten this positioning?

3   How can host communities be inadvertently disadvantaged by volunteer tourism? What proactive actions can be taken to mitigate negative and disadvantageous effects of volunteer tourism?

4   List and discuss the reasons why volunteer tourism needs a code of ethics for tourism operators.

Case study: Innovations in volunteer tourism and fundraising tours

The popularity of volunteer tourism as a form of alternative tourism has grown significantly over the past decade. Volunteer tourists can now be found throughout the world participating in a wide array of social, educational, political and environmental projects. While these projects continue to use volunteer tourists as a significant source of labour, the NGOs and community organisations that provide and support them have begun exploring other innovative ways to attract and engage volunteer tourists who may wish to provide their voluntary labour in less direct ways. As a result, programmes are now emerging that move beyond the convention established in volunteer tourism where participants travel to a destination community to volunteer their labour while simultaneously being a 'tourist' in the broadest sense of the word. Instead, these new programmes fuse adventure, volunteerism and philanthropy incrementally into an innovative tourism experience that challenges traditional debates about the decommodifying processes embedded in volunteer tourism. One example of this new type of volunteer tourism is the development and provision of fundraising adventure tours. Fundraising adventure tourism has been adopted by a number of NGOs who recruit participants willing to raise a predetermined sum of money, half of which is used to support the NGOs' core business and the remaining funds are used to fund an adventure tour.

Previous arguments have suggested that volunteer tourism does not fit into the commodified regime of mass and packaged tourism as its focus is not on the exchange value in the tourism system (Lyons and Wearing, 2008). This case study explores whether the act of fundraising as an act of volunteering, conducted prior to participating in an adventure tour, enabled participants to experience the decommodified frame of gift economy that has been heralded as the hallmark of volunteer tourism (Wearing, 2001) or whether this separation undermines this process. One of these innovative programmes developed and operated by Oxfam Community Aid Abroad Australia – Oxfam Challenge programme – is examined.

An analysis was conducted of the marketing materials of Oxfam and diaries and web-blogs of 25 individuals who participated in fundraising/cycling adventures with Oxfam Australia– Oxfam Challenge programme. The adventure fundraising tour conducted by Oxfam Australia is marketed as an adventure experience with a difference. Oxfam Australia recruits participants willing to raise $5000 which in part covers the cost of a two-week cycling tour through remote villages in China, Vietnam or Cambodia where they visit environmental and humanitarian projects and where the funds they raised are being used. While participants are recruited through Oxfam Australia, the adventure tour component of the programme is outsourced to a commercial travel service provider who provides a fully packaged programme including airfares, meals, a bicycle and a guide. This component of the experience is almost identical to any packaged adventure-based tour conducted by a wide range of operators globally.

There are four main themes that emerged from the findings of this case study. The first suggests that while the tourist gaze narrative dominated many of the blogs analysed in this study, a significant component of these narratives emphasised the altruistic experiences associated with volunteering, giving back and helping others through fundraising. The sense of giving was further enhanced when participants visited communities where the monies they had raised were being used. The second finding suggests that the market edge and the positioning of the fundraising adventure challenge as a unique product by Oxfam re-establish volunteer tourism as a commodified product within the rubric of de-commodification. The third finding suggests that the separation of the act of adventure from the act of giving appear to have had little impact upon the participants. This case study suggests that the motives and satisfactions of participants in this new form of volunteer tourism appear very similar to more traditional forms. However, the strong emphasises upon more hedonistic pleasures associated with the physical challenges of cycle touring suggest that altruism remained in the background while on tour and only emerged when participants visited the communities where the money they raised was used. This relates to the fourth finding of this study, that the physicality of adventure is closely associated with appeasement and a metaphorical approach to volunteer tourism. This study suggests that the commodified/decommodified aspect challenges the distinctions that have been made about volunteer and alternative tourism more broadly and considers whether the newer innovations in volunteer tourism are better viewed as a continuum of commodification.

Ideas for discussion

1   Does the case study suggest that commodification is an inevitability in volunteer tourism? What aspects contribute to its commodification? Is it possible to create a truly decommodified volunteer tourism 'product'? If so, how?

Further reading

The World Guide: Global reference, country by country, 11th edition, New Internationalist Publications Ltd.

DeGraaf, D.G., Jordan, D.J. and DeGraaf, K.H. (1998) *Programming for Parks, Recreation, and Leisure Services: A Servant Leadership Approach*, State College, PA: Venture.

Edginton, C.R. (1997) 'Managing leisure services: a new ecology of leadership toward the year 2000', *Journal of Physical Education, Recreation and Dance*, **68** (8), 29-32.

Edginton, C.R., Hanson, C.J., Edginton, S.R. and Hudson, S.D. (1998) *Leisure Programming: A Service-Centered and Benefits Approach*, Boston, MA: McGraw-Hill.

Ford, P. and Blanchard, J. (1993) *Leadership and Administration of Outdoor Pursuits*, State College, PA: Venture.

Ledwith, M. and Campling, J. (2005) *Community Development – A Critical Perspective*, Bristol: Policy Press.

Moore McBride, J.B., Menon, N. and Sherraden, M. (2006) 'Limitations of civic service: critical perspectives', *Community Development Journal*, **41** (3), 307–320.

Holmes, K. and Smith K. (2009) *Managing Volunteers in Tourism: Attractions, Destinations and Events*, Oxford: Butterworth-Heinemann.

Useful websites

Action and research: http://www2.fhs.usyd.edu.au/arow/o/m10/facilitate.htm
Australian APEC Study Centre: www.apec.org.au
Australian Department of Foreign Affairs and Trade: http://www.dfat.gov.au/
Australian International Development Assistance Agency: www.ausaid.gov.au
Australian-based site providing up-to-date news on relevant issues and provides access to a range of viewpoints: www.worldgrowth.org
Brookings Institution: www.brookings.org
Global exchange: www.globalexchange.org/
Globalisation: http://www.globalisationguide.org
Group facilitation skills: http://www.projectperfect.com.au/info_role_of_the_facilitator.php
Human Development Report Office: http://hdr.undp.org/

International Institute for Sustainable Development: www.iisd1.iisd.ca/
International Monetary Fund: www.imf.org
Life and Debt: http://www.lifeanddebt.org
New Internationalist website: http://newint.org
Open Democracy: www.openDemocracy.net
Oxfam Australia: www.oxfam.org.au
Oxfam's international 'Make Trade Fair' campaign: www.maketradefair.com
Sussex University Institute of Development Studies: www.eldis.org
Third World Network: http://www.twnside.org.sg/twr.htm
Third World Traveler: http://www.thirdworldtraveler.com
Training and mentoring skills: http://www.developmentgateway.com.au/cms
UK Department for International Development: www.dfid.gov.uk
United Nations Development Programme: www.undp.org/
World Bank: www.worldbank.org/
World Trade Organisation: www.wto.org/
ZNet: www.Zmag.org

References

Bessant, J., Sercombe, H. and Watts, R. (1998) *Youth Studies: An Australian Perspective*, Melbourne: Longman.

Broad, S. and Jenkins, J. (2008) 'Gibbons in their mist? Conservation volunteers' motivations at the Gibbon Rehabilitation Project, Phuket, Thailand', in K.D. Lyons and S. Wearing (eds), *Journeys of Discovery in Volunteer Tourism: International Case Study Perspectives*, Wallingford: CABI, pp. 72-85.

Brown, R.B. and McCartney, S. (1999) 'Multiple mirrors: reflecting on reflection', in D. O'Reilly, L. Cunningham and S. Lester (eds), *Developing the Capable Practitioner: Developing Capability through Higher Education*, London: Routledge, pp.16-32.

Brown, S. and Lehto, X. (2005) 'Travelling with a purpose: understanding the motives and benefits of volunteer vacationers', *Current Issues in Tourism*, **8** (6), 479-496.

Carter, A. (2004) *The Political Theory of Global Citizenship*, London: Routledge.

Department of Employment, Education and Training (1994) 'Young people's attitudes to post-compulsory education and training: follow-up study', Canberra: AGPS.

Dwyer, L. and Edwards, D. (2004) 'Sustainable tourism planning module', Business Enterprises for Sustainable Travel Education Network Australia: University of Western Sydney.

Edginton, C.R., Hanson, C.J., Edginton, S.R. and Hudson, S.D. (1998) *Leisure Programming: A Service-centered and Benefits Approach*, Boston, MA: McGraw-Hill.

Fennell, D. (2006) *Tourism Ethics*, Clevedon: Channel View Publications.

Fennell, D. and Malloy, D. (2007) *Codes of Ethics in Tourism: Practice, Theory, Synthesis*, Clevedon: Channel View Publications.

Furnham, A. and Bochner, S. (1986) *Culture Shock: Psychological Reactions to Unfamiliar Environments*, London: Methuen.

Havenhand, B. (2000) *Working Overseas: For Australians and New Zealanders*, Newcastle: Global Exchange.

Hill, S. (2001) 'Options for school leavers 2001', *Sydney Morning Herald* supplement, Sydney.

Kelly, E.D. and Becker, B. (2000) *Community Planning: An Introduction to Comprehensive Planning*, Washington, DC: Island Press.

Kramer, L. (1997) 'Historical narratives and the meaning of nationalism', *Journal of the History of Ideas*, **58** (3), 525-545.

Lyons, K.D. and Wearing, S. (eds) (2008) *Journeys of Discovery in Volunteer Tourism: International Case Study Perspectives*, Wallingford: CABI Publishing.

McGehee, N. and Andereck, K. (2008) 'Pettin' the critters: exploring the complex relationship between volunteers and the volontoured in McDowell County, West Virginia, USA, and Tijuana, Mexico', in K.D. Lyons and S. Wearing (eds), *Journeys of Discovery in Volunteer Tourism: International Case Study Perspectives*, Wallingford: CABI, pp. 12-24.

Mitchell, P. (2006) Revisiting Effective Re-entry Programmes for Returnees from US Academic Programmes, Washington, DC: AED Center for International Training.

Mustonen, P. (2007) 'Volunteer tourism – altruism or mere tourism?', *Anatolia: An International Journal of Tourism and Hospitality Research*, 18 (1), 97-115.

Pearce, P.L. (1981) '"Environment shock": a study of tourists' reactions to two tropical islands', *Journal of Applied Social Psychology*, **11** (3), 268-280.

Pearce, P. and Coghlan, A. (2008) 'The dynamics behind volunteer tourism', in K.D. Lyons and S. Wearing (eds), *Journeys of Discovery in Volunteer Tourism: International Case Study Perspectives*, Wallingford: CABI, pp. 130-143.

Peters, T.J. and Waterman, R.H (1982) *In Search of Excellence: Lessons from America's Best-run Companies*, New York: Harper and Row.

Poon, A. (2003) 'Competitive strategies for a "new tourism"', in C.P. Cooper (ed.), *Classic Reviews in Tourism*, Clevedon: Channel View Publications, pp. 130-142.

Simpson, K. (2004) '"Doing development": the gap year, volunteer-tourists and a popular practice of development', *Journal of International Development*, **16** (5), 681-692.

Ward, C. and Kennedy, A. (2001) 'Coping with cross-cultural transition', *Journal of Cross-cultural Psychology*, **32** (5), 636-642.

Ward, L. (2007) 'You're better off backpacking – VSO warns about perils of "voluntourism"', *The Guardian*, 22 August, 12.

Wearing, S. (2001) *Volunteer Tourism: Experiences that Make a Difference*, New York: CABI Publishing.

Wearing, S. and Deane, B. (2003) 'Seeking self: leisure and tourism on common ground', *World Leisure Journal*, **45**, 4-12.

Weaver, G. (1987) 'The process of reentry', *Advising Quarterly*, **2** (Fall), 2-7.

Weeden C. (2002) 'Ethical tourism: an opportunity for competitive advantage', *Journal of Vacation Marketing*, **8** (2), 141-153.

Whelan, T. (ed.) (1991), *Nature Tourism – Managing for the Environment*, Washington, DC: Island Press.

11 Crisis, Recovery and Risk Management

David Beirman

Rationale

Tourism is often the first sector that is impacted by crises and also the first sector that community leaders look towards in the recovery phase (Carlsen and Liburd, 2007). The significance of crisis and risk management in tourism is emphasised by the frequency, severity and global scale of crises which have disrupted and undermined the tourism industry during the first decade of the 21st century. Events including the terrorist attack on the World Trade Center and the Pentagon in September 2001, the Bali bombings of 2002 and 2005, the attack on the Taj Hotel, Mumbai in November 2008, epidemics or pandemics such as SARS in 2003 and H1N1 (swine flu) in 2009 and natural disasters including the Indian Ocean tsunami of December 2004 had a widespread impact on the tourism industry. In late 2008 the onset of a global economic recession generated a significant downturn of international tourism movements during 2009. This was a global version of the Asian Financial Crisis of 1997–98 which impacted heavily on tourism in East and South-East Asia during the late 1990s.

The tourism industry is paying increasing attention to the issue of crisis and risk management. In September 2009 the UN World Tourism Organisation released its sos.travel web site (UN World Tourism Organisation, 2009) integrating crisis management knowledge with day-to-day destination and tourism business management on a global level. At the industry level, tourism businesses and tourism industry associations are approaching the issues of crisis and risk with growing emphasis and professionalism. The key outcome of this trend is that destinations and tourism businesses will require informed knowledge and employees who are increasingly risk aware and able to assist businesses and destinations to implement crisis and risk contingency plans and recover from crisis events.

Crisis and risk management have only emerged since the mid-1990s as related fields to the broader body of tourism management and sustainability research. Devastating as they can be, crises and risks require government and non government entities to respond in a sustainable manner and offer destinations the opportunity to 'build back better' to a more resilient and sustainable tourism sector.

Learning outcomes

After completing this chapter, students should be able to:

◆ Define crisis and risk as they apply to tourism

◆ Examine the development of risk, crisis and recovery management methodologies in the tourism and hospitality industry since 2000

◆ Examine key crisis and risk typologies in tourism

◆ Discuss means to measure the severity of a crisis event

◆ Assess the role of perception as a factor in the definition and actuality of tourism crisis and risk

◆ Develop a contingency plan through the application of the five Rs of crisis and risk recovery to facilitate sustainable tourism development.

Defining crisis and risk in tourism

Academic literature on tourism crisis and risk offers a wide range of definitional options. Joan Henderson (2007) in her book *Tourism Crises: Causes, Consequences and Management* claims that there is no single universally accepted definition. However, she states that three elements must be present: a triggering event which causes significant change, a perceived inability to cope with that event and a threat to the existence of the foundation of the organisation. Henderson cites Hermann's definition (Hermann 1972) in which a crisis contains the three elements of unexpectedness, urgency and danger. Laws *et al.* (2007) observe that in a crisis situation participants are taken by surprise and have little time to make difficult decisions under circumstances of tension and instability. Crises under these circumstances are catalysts for change. The oft-quoted definition of the word crisis based on its Mandarin root encompasses the concepts of danger and opportunity.

Pforr and Hosie (2009) analyse the literature on tourism crisis management and concur with Henderson, that there is no stand-out definition of tourism-related crises. As Ritchie(2004) and Prideaux (2007) have stated, many crisis events are unforeseen but this has to be countered by stating that while the extent and timing of a crisis event may be unpredictable, the risk of a negative event occurring is at least measurable according the laws of probability.

An event which illustrates the distinction between crisis and risk is the October 2009 earthquake near Samoa which generated a tsunami which struck the southern coast of the Samoan island of Upolu. The tsunami destroyed many coastal villages and tourism resorts and resulted in the deaths of 142 people including at least ten tourists. Since the Indian Ocean tsunami of December 2004, risk preparedness levels for tsunamis in coastal regions worldwide have been enhanced. However, the quake which triggered this particular tsunami was very close to the affected coast. Residents and visitors had literally minutes to evacuate when the tsunami struck at 0645. The Samoan tsunami conformed to the definition of crisis which stresses unpredictability, severity, urgency and danger. The tsunami clearly impacted on the viability of Samoa as a tourism destination (especially the affected coastal area).

From the recovery perspective, Samoa's tsunami forced Samoa's tourism marketing authorities to radically change their marketing approach for the destination from an idyllic paradise to a destination which is resilient.

Tourism crises necessarily involve cause effect, severity and response. Faulkner and Russell's (2000: 333–334) definition of a 'disaster', focused on unpredictability and catastrophic changes which were beyond immediate control. This led to this author's own definition of a tourism crisis: 'a crisis is a situation requiring radical management action in response to events beyond the internal control of an organisation necessitating urgent response of marketing and operational practices to restore the confidence of employees, associated enterprises and consumers in the viability of the destination or enterprise' (Beirman, 2003: 4). It is appropriate to add that a crisis severely undermines the viability and marketability of a tourism destination or enterprise. This definition can also be adapted to include management failure. The term 'crisis', by necessity, must also include a concept of impact severity. A tourism crisis severely impacts on tourism. Conversely a hazard or cyclical slump may cause a measurable loss in demand for destinations or tourism businesses but does not compromise the viability of a destination or business. A 5% decline in business does not constitute a crisis.

The 2009 outbreak of H1N1 (swine flu) is a clear example of a situation which commenced as a tourism crisis and evolved into a hazard. When the initial cases of H1N1 occurred in Mexico in March and April of 2009, they generated a great deal of fear which led to destination Mexico virtually becoming a tourism pariah. This was at a time when the number of cases were measured as a few thousands and deaths related to H1N1 numbered less than 200. The World Health Organization's definition of H1N1 as a global pandemic exacerbated the perceived fear factor associated with the virus although the mortality rate barely exceeded 1%.

In discussing tourism risk, the core definition necessarily involves an assessment of the potential of specific threats to destinations or businesses from various sources. In essence, risk refers to the possibility or probability of a negative event occurring. In the Asia Pacific Economic Cooperation (APEC) guide to risk management (APEC 2006), tourism risk is divided into four key categories:

- ♦ **Natural hazards** which include climatic events, floods, earthquakes, tsunamis, volcanic eruption, wildfires, mudslides or avalanches
- ♦ **Technological hazards** which can include failure of technological systems, industrial sites, buildings, transport systems or infrastructure
- ♦ **Biological hazards** which can include diseases and environmental contamination
- ♦ **Civil/ political hazards** which can encompass, crime, terrorism, political unrest and violence and economic shocks.

Increasingly, public and private sector tourism organisations and enterprises are developing risk management strategies as core elements of their overall management policies and practices. By 2009, most major international tourism associations including the UN World Tourism Organisation (UNWTO), Pacific Asia Travel Association (PATA 2003 and 2009) and APEC (2006) have developed crisis and risk management training modules which are freely available to their members and a wider audience of tourism professionals and students. Additionally, many national tourism organisations and associations conduct specialised training and publish manuals for their own members and stakeholders. Insurance companies base their entire business model on the assessment of risk.

Global e-dailies including Travel Mole and E Turbo News have promoted webinars and teleseminars in the field. Progress in the dissemination of crisis and risk management expertise within the travel industry is considerable in view of the fact that in 2002, IATA (International Air Transport Association) was the only major international tourism association which had taken crisis and risk management seriously enough to share crisis and risk management expertise with its constituents.

Tourism crisis typologies

Henderson (2007) identified eight key tourism crisis typologies, all of which contain subsets. The significance of the typologies is that some crises result from acts of nature and some are influenced by human activity. A breakdown in economic, social or environmental sustainability can be a contributing factor to all crises typologies. Most tourism crisis events simultaneously reflect a diminution of sustainability.

Economic and commercial tourism crises

The Asian financial crisis of 1997–98 and the global financial crisis (GFC) which began in late 2008 are two of the more prominent examples in which economic downturns have resulted in significant declines in tourism over a large region. Tourism, generally regarded as a discretionary expense, is vulnerable to significant shifts in economic confidence. During 2009 global international tourism visitation declined by 8% compared to 2008 (UNWTO 2009). Declines are variable with the GFC impacting variably on countries. So dramatic has been the global impact that in October 2009 the UNWTO (2009) released a detailed 'Roadmap for global tourism recovery' which was drawn from successive deliberations of the UNWTO's Tourism Resilience Committee which was formed in mid-2008. In the case of the UNWTO the emphasis of its recovery strategy sought the involvement of government backed and funded stimulus measures designed to support domestic, inbound and outbound tourism.

On a smaller scale, the collapse of key individual businesses as a result of management failures have had a widespread impact on tourism. In September 2001 the collapse of the Australian domestic airline Ansett led to massive disruption of domestic air services within Australia. Industrial action by transportation workers (e.g. pilots' strikes) have the potential to cause massive disruption to tourism.

Political tourism crises

There is a fine line between political tourism crises and terrorism. In defining political tourism crises, Henderson (2007) focuses on tourism crises stemming from internal political conflicts which occasionally manifest themselves through terrorist attacks. Coups, civil conflict, anarchy and disorder, and corrupt, extremist or repressive regimes individually or in combination all contribute to a destination being perceived as unattractive to foreign tourists. In recent years, Burma (Myanmar), North Korea, Iraq, Somalia, Zimbabwe, Kenya, Thailand and Fiji are just a small representation of countries in which potentially lucrative tourism income has been lost due to the political factors mentioned above. In the case of Burma (Myanmar), there has been an extensive campaign among some tourism professionals to boycott travel to the country as an expression of opposition to the regime.

In late 2008 and early 2009 a series of massive political demonstrations in Bangkok led to the closure of the main international airport (which had been occupied by anti-government demonstrators) for over a week in December 2008. Although the demonstrations were largely non-violent, they caused massive disruption to inbound and outbound tourism in Thailand and presented one of many recent challenges to the Thai Tourism Authority.

Terrorism and politically motivated violence targeting tourism

Terrorists have generated many crises for tourism destinations and enterprises in recent years. Terrorism as distinct from criminality consists of acts of violence, extortion and theft as part of a political agenda. A core motivator of terrorist activities is the intention to generate international publicity. There is a growing trend during the 21st century for terrorists to target tourists as this internationalises the publicity of their actions and cause.

The Bali bombings of October 2002 and October 2005 which targeted foreign tourists severely compromised tourism to Bali specifically and Indonesia generally. Egyptian tourism took over a year to recover from the 1997 Luxor massacre in which 55 tourists from 12 countries were killed. The November 2008 terrorist attack against the Taj Hotel in Mumbai, India has been a major challenge for Indian tourism. Terrorist groups have targeted Western hotels in Pakistan, Indonesia, Jordan and Egypt in recent years. As the tourism and hospitality industry and governments implement new and upgraded security measures, terrorist groups develop new tactics to circumvent them. In addition to attacks which are designed to kill and maim, terrorist groups are employing cyber terrorism as a new form of attack on tourism businesses. Acts of terrorism, especially those which target tourism, are a major challenge to business and national tourism offices as they require a lengthy and expensive process of rebuilding confidence and addressing the security threat.

Socio-cultural conflicts and crime

There are many countries where social inequalities, in which socially unsustainable tourism is a contributing factor, generate crime. Tourists who are perceived to symbolise the wealth locals lack, have been targeted in some countries. Some societies and communities regard foreign tourists with either suspicion or hostility, offended by the dress, behaviour or appearance of foreigners who are deemed insensitive to the local culture or religious traditions. Crime is a two-way transaction. There have some been cases in which tourists have been guilty of crimes against local cultures and communities. Invasions by football hooligans in Europe are recent examples.

The dissonance between the behavioural and cultural expectations of the host destination and tourists occasionally triggers a tourism crisis in which tourists avoid destinations where they feel unwelcome or are targets of criminal behaviour. This has been an overriding theme in several Caribbean Island nations.

A specific problem which applies to many Caribbean destinations (but not unique to the Caribbean) is the development of coastal resorts by either local or multinational operators which create tourist ghettos. The physical and economic barriers built up between tourists and locals breed resentment which is sometimes manifested in crime directed at tourists and tourist property. In Jamaica, Diana Macintyre Pike has fought hard to bridge the gap between tourists and Jamaicans in her campaign to develop a community tourism programme (Hawkes and Kwortnik, 2006).

Environmental tourism crises

Environmental tourism crises can be divided into three specific categories.

Natural disasters

These arise from earthquakes, volcanoes, tsunamis, extreme climatic events such as storms (typhoons, cyclones, hurricanes, tornadoes and dust storms), floods, mudslides and avalanches. There is little humans can do to prevent the occurrence of these natural forces but there are actions which government authorities and business can take to minimise exposure to and the impact of these events. In recent years the Indian Ocean tsunami of 26 December 2004 had a massive impact on tourism. In Thailand, half of the 11,000 people who died as a result of the tsunami were foreign visitors from over 80 countries. While tourists overall represented a small proportion of the 300,000 people who were killed by the 2004 tsunami in Indonesia, Thailand, India, Myanmar, Sri Lanka, the Maldives and East Africa, a regional natural disaster became a global tourism crisis.

Climate change

This is the subject of intense political debate but the implications of possible rising sea levels and rising global temperatures are significant for the tourism industry. Marginal ski resorts could be without snow and low-lying coastal or maritime resorts areas face the threat of inundation. Climate change is generally a gradual process but ignoring the threat is not a solution. Desertification or prolonged drought can lead to catastrophic consequences for regions once deemed as attractive tourism destinations. The February 2009 bushfires in Victoria (Australia) caused massive damage and loss of life in a region long regarded as an attractive tourism destination.

Human-generated environmental pollution and degradation

This is a widely acknowledged problem in both urban and rural regions. Poor air and water quality in cities and industrialised regions can create discomfort and illness for locals and tourists alike. One of the key issues which is set to have implications for all business including tourism is the concept of carbon (or emissions) trading in which there will be a globally recognised cost imposed on businesses which pollute. The airline industry which carries a large proportion of the 900 million+ international tourists who travelled in 2008 (UNWTO 2009) is actively researching and implementing measures to enhance fuel efficiency and reduce the level of emissions. Carbon trading will be factored into the cost of a wide range of tourism and hospitality services from 2010 onwards.

Tourism and health crises

In recent years there have been a number of health-related events which have generated tourism crises as defined earlier in this chapter. Since 2000 there have been three which fit the definition.

Foot and mouth disease, UK 2001

The outbreak of foot and mouth disease among livestock in the UK in 2001 did not result in any medical impact on either local or visiting human beings. However, in order to prevent the spread of the disease, the British agricultural and health authorities closed off large tracts of rural Britain to visitation, including many regions popular with domestic and international tourists. Frequently distressing media images of vast pyres of slaughtered animals being burned and the well-publicised closures and access limitations created negative images of Britain and obliged the British Tourism Authority (now known as Visit Britain) to conduct a massive recovery marketing campaign to reassure its key source markets that Britain was worth visiting (Beirman, 2003). The foot and mouth outbreak did result in a serious loss of visitation to rural Britain.

SARS, 2003

The outbreak of Severe Acute Respiratory Syndrome in February 2003 generated a major tourism crisis throughout Eastern Asia and Canada between March and July. The virus infected about 8000 people in 35 countries and resulted in 800 deaths. This was a high mortality rate for a respiratory disease, and the combination of a lack of knowledge of the disease and media coverage verged towards hysteria. SARS generated panic beyond the severity and scale of the epidemic. At its height, during the second quarter of 2003, international tourism arrivals in some Asian countries, notably Hong Kong and Singapore, fell by 90% compared to the corresponding months of the previous year. In Thailand, which had 12 cases (2 of which were fatal), tourism in 2003 fell by 1.5 million compared to 2002.

SARS is a classic example of a perceived health crisis which impacted heavily on tourism to countries in South-East Asia irrespective of the extent or the prevalence of the disease. Media images which suggested the whole population of Hong Kong and Singapore were wearing surgical masks remain enduring images of the disease. In fact in Hong Kong over 90% of SARS cases were confined to the residents of five large apartment blocks (Chiu, 2007). Canada which experienced over 140 cases of SARS and 44 deaths (mainly in Toronto) was the only major non-Asian country exposed to SARS (Wall, 2006).

In 2003 the Pacific Asia Travel Association spearheaded a recovery campaign for tourism in affected countries. Project Phoenix involved a recovery marketing campaign involving government tourism boards and the private sector backed by positive media coverage and advertising generated by the CNN and BBC. It became a template for many subsequent post-crisis recovery campaigns through its successful addressing of the factual and perceptual elements of a crisis. By late 2003 tourism activity had recovered throughout Asia and Canada to pre-SARS levels.

H1N1 (swine flu), 2009

The initial outbreak of the H1N1 strain of influenza occurred in Mexico in March 2009. From the outset, a media panic was generated which exaggerated the severity of the condition. Initially it was claimed that within a month over 170 Mexicans had died from swine flu but on closer examination many of those who died were found to have multiple health problems. There was concern that H1N1 would become another SARS for global tourism, and tourism to Mexico clearly suffered in March and April of 2009. H1N1 spread globally during 2009.

Between the beginning of March and September 2009, over 300,000 people in 100 countries contracted H1N1 and the mortality rate associated with the virus was just over 4000 or about 1.3% (roughly double that of standard influenza). Most of the people who died with H1N1 suffered from other health problems (WHO, 2009). There is no doubt that H1N1 has become a condition worthy of concern and close monitoring because of the very real risk of viral mutations. However, during 2009 despite the spread of the disease it rapidly descended from a tourism crisis to a health hazard.

Technological failures and tourism

Technological failures apply to all sectors of the tourism and hospitality industry. Failures in air traffic control technology have been a contributing factor in air crashes, rail traffic control failures have contributed to rail disasters and failures in ship construction have led to sinkings which resulted in heavy loss of life. Road transport is dangerous for both private users of the road system and tourist coaches. In hotels, failures in fire alarms and warning systems have proven fatal to guests.

Although commercial airlines have an excellent safety record compared to all other modes of powered transport, airline crashes (especially on international routes) when they do occur, generate massive publicity largely because they involve a large number of victims of many nationalities. The International Air Transport Association has long had a crisis communication unit, and most major international airlines have well-developed crisis management units and crisis management procedures. Central to the management of airline-related crises has been the appointment of a single spokesperson to brief the media and relevant stakeholders. Rapid response with a focus of concern on victims and their immediate families is integral to airline crisis management. For airlines and other transport providers which do experience crashes, reputation management of the company or provider becomes a core issue.

A growing threat to all businesses including tourism is the growth of cyber crime and cyber terrorism which have the potential to disrupt computer systems, extract confidential information from databases or even shut down command and control systems of airlines, air traffic control, railway systems, tour operations and booking records and communications systems.

Technological failure tends to impact on individual tourism enterprises and service providers, and as such, a crisis event is generally limited to that enterprise. However cyber destruction in a computer-linked business world has the potential to trigger a tourism crisis on a far wider scale.

The role and significance of perception in tourism crises

There is a growing recognition among tourism academics and practitioners of the significance of perception as an element in tourism crises and the importance of perception in the management of crises. Avraham and Ketter (2008) and Nielsen (2001) examine the role and management of media coverage in the creation of and amelioration of tourism-related crises. In today's instant, globalised media, the coverage of events and interpretation by the reporters colour their public perception. As mentioned earlier in this chapter, the coverage of the 2003 SARS outbreak and the early phase of H1N1 in 2009 created a sense of fear and panic. In the case of H1N1 the use of the WHO's definition of a pandemic was legitimate, and the issue of responsibility for creating an apocalyptic perception of H1N1 may be more properly directed at WHO than either CNN or Fox Media.

Negative news reports of events in a country will often colour perceptions of that country as a travel destination. Israel regularly features in news reports because of ongoing conflicts on its border with Lebanon and with Palestinian factions in Gaza and the West Bank. While these conflicts are very real and sometimes very violent, they rarely impinge on tourism destinations in Israel or tourists.

Since 9/11, there has been an enhancement of the profile of government travel advisories in shaping perceptions about destinations. This occurred in part because the Internet reduced the cost of mass communications and travellers are demonstrating a growing concern about safety. Many believe governments are in a position to provide credible advice relating to safety of their citizens. In most Western countries a four- or five-level security threat assessment can influence a traveller's decision to visit a given destination. Generally speaking, government travel advisories err on the side of caution based on the assumption that they are an extra territorial security measure to protect a nation's citizens (Beirman, 2006).

Destination marketing organisations (DMOs) and the broader travel industry spend millions of dollars to influence perception. Journalist familiarisation tours, travel agency hosting and the subsidisation of TV crews from lifestyle and travel shows are just a few of the measures the tourism industry takes to influence favourable coverage of destinations and travel products. DMOs sometimes subsidise the inclusion of destinations in wholesale product brochures and governments sometimes offer incentives for airlines to fly to a destination or for hoteliers to develop accommodation. DMOs are heavily engaged in developing interactive websites and destination brochures for widespread distribution to the pubic and travel sellers. Most DMOs and travel companies are aware of the importance of balancing their push and pull marketing programmes. DMOs run promotional activities targeted at travel agents, integral to their push marketing campaigns while seeking to raise the profile in pull marketing activities of their destination to either a broad or targeted consumer market.

There has also been a growth of blogs on the Internet in which tourists themselves influence perceptions. Sites such as Trip Advisor and Lonely Planet invite travellers to assess destinations, tours, airlines and accommodation, As these assessments are assumed (not always correctly) to be free of commercial bias, many travellers use these sites when planning and researching a trip.

The management of perception has become an integral part of crisis and recovery management practice. As mentioned earlier in this chapter, PATA's Project Phoenix, the recovery campaign to restore confidence in Asian and Canadian tourism following the SARS outbreak of 2003 (Yates, 2006), is widely regarded as a global template for managing a perception-based crisis. While national tourist offices and individual tourism and hospitality companies spent large sums of money developing marketing campaigns to entice tourists back to SARS-affected destinations and businesses, PATA solicited the support of major global news networks, specifically the BBC and CNN, to run campaigns designed to restore confidence in these destinations. Tourism businesses were able to use their considerable advertising strength as negotiating leverage with these networks. In response to SARS, over 30 countries simultaneously combined single country marketing campaigns with a broader Asia/Pacific regional message. The intensity of this campaign resulted in a recovery of the market to SARS-affected destinations within six months.

In Israel, where regional support from neighbouring countries was minimal, recovery from the tourism downturn resulting from the Intifada of 2000–04 was conducted on a step by step basis. The Israeli strategy centred on building a staircase of confidence initially targeting Israel's stalwart market (travellers with a high level of affinity and commitment to Israel). As this market solidified it then focussed its attention to the waverers and finally the discretionary travel market. Unlike the SARS recovery campaign which generated rapid results, Israel's recovery took three years from the end of the active phase of the Intifada in 2003 to approach pre-Intifada (September 2000) levels of tourism.

Effective crisis communication addresses perception. The literature and best industry practice stress the importance of honesty in dealing with perceptual issues. Countering false negative perceptions with false positive perceptions may serve as a short-term panacea but is not a viable strategy for managing perceptual issues.

Measuring the severity of a crisis and the analysing key security issues

Tourism crises can occur on scales ranging from specific business or localities to a crisis which impacts on the viability of global tourism. There is a wide range of measuring devices employed by tourism academics and practitioners.

The author's book *Restoring Tourism Destinations in Crisis* (Beirman, 2003) introduced a ranking of crisis severity dubbed DESTCON (Destination Condition). The ranking is used refer to the intensity of a crisis in tandem with geographic impact:

◆ DESTCON 5 refers to normal conditions.

◆ DESTCON 4 refers to a crisis event which affects either a limited number of tourism businesses in a limited area.

◆ DESTCON 3 refers to a crisis event which affects a large number of tourism businesses in a single country. An example of this could be a natural disaster which impacts on a specific area of coastline affecting tourism to the area and businesses in that area.

♦ DESTCON 2 refers to a crisis event which affects destinations and businesses in a region which could involve more than one country. SARS is a good example of this.

♦ DESTCON 1 refers to a crisis situation which impacts on global tourism. In recent years the 9/11 attack which stimulated a fear of flying on commercial aircraft and the global financial crisis which has generated a downturn in global tourism are two examples.

Chatterjee and Pearson (2009) distinguish between crises resulting from internal and external causes. They also discuss the severity of a crisis in terms of recovery times and the systemic competency and resources of the destination or organisation to recover. This is a classic strategic management approach to crisis and contingency management.

After the 9/11 attack in 2001, the US Government's Department of Homeland Security developed an advisory system focusing on threat levels which applied to security threats specifically based on the risk of terrorism.

Figure 11.1: US Government Homeland Security threat advisory levels

Security threats have been discussed at length throughout the literature and practice of tourism crisis management. Tarlow (2001) and Pizam and Mansfeld (1996, 2006) have written extensively on the security threats to tourism.

The nature of security threa ts and preventative measures is a dynamic process. Western-owned hotels have been increasingly targeted by terrorist groups since 2001 culminating in the attack on the Taj Hotel in Mumbai in November in 2008. Many of the major hotel chains upgraded security to deal with external threats. In July 2009 a suicide bombing of the JW Marriott Hotel in Jakarta was constructed by a terrorist, a paying guest of the hotel who assembled the bomb in his room with the help of accomplices. When he moved to self-detonate at a hotel restaurant he was unchallenged by hotel security staff. This was one of many examples in which the tactics of terrorists and criminals constantly change when security measures are introduced, and the challenge to security professionals is to anticipate and prioritise security risks.

As Figure 11.2 demonstrates, there are several key elements of the tourism security cycle and all have their vulnerabilities and security challenges. From a crisis management perspective, the primary challenge is to develop risk assessment and contingency management procedures to minimise the most likely threats at each link of the security cycle. Tourism authorities are increasingly co-operating with police and government security agencies. This is especially apparent during

Figure 11.2: Tourism security cycle

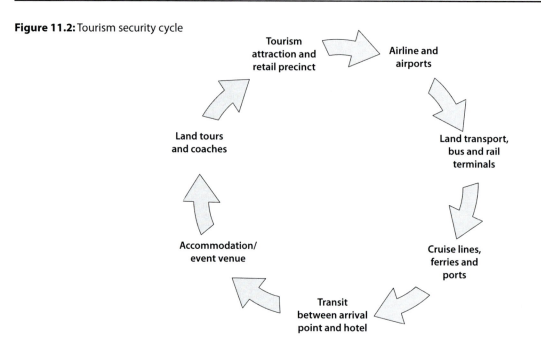

the organisation of mega events where security has taken on an increasing level of importance. Attacks on well-publicised mega events have the potential to envelop a destination and its tourism industry in a crisis.

There is also a gradual engagement between the tourism industry and government in consulting on the issue of government travel advisories. In 2003 the Australian Department of Foreign Affairs and Trade became the world's first foreign ministry to establish a formal consultative arrangement with the national travel industry leadership. This was followed by similar agreements in the UK (2004) and Canada (2005).

Tourism risk, crisis and recovery management in action

The appropriate management of tourism crises is important for the sustainability of tourism in the destination and can present the opportunity rebuild the destination more sustainably through the use of low- or zero carbon buildings, sustainably sourced products and materials and high quality green space. As Carlsen and Liburd (2007, p. 274) state,

> "Socially desirable outcomes including the introduction of more ethical marketing practices and increased corporate social responsibility may emerge from a tourism crisis. Governments, DMOs and tourism stakeholders may demonstrate increased concern for the welfare and security of visitors and all those involved in tourism after a crisis. They may also demonstrate greater awareness of the environment in the wake of natural disasters, and undertake demarketing of certain areas to facilitate environmental rehabilitation".

Figure 11.3: The five Rs of crisis management.
Adapted from Gurtner, 2007

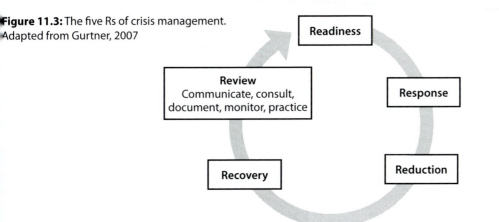

The five Rs of crisis and risk management – readiness, response, reduction, recovery and review can assist entities to have in place the sustainable strategies to deal with a crisis or risk. As the figure below illustrates there is an integral linkage between contingency management (risk awareness) and the ability to respond to and recover from a crisis event. The TEFI values of knowledge, ethics, professionalism, mutuality and stewardship are incorporated within the five Rs.

Readiness

Many crises send out early warning signals that if picked up on and responded to prior to the occurrence of the crisis then the crisis may be minimised or prevented before it happens – provided there is a contingency plan in place. Contingency plans are well-prepared documents which can cover the most likely risks and threats to a tourism destination from a range of perceived threats.

A contingency plan should contain the following elements:

♦ Nature or typology of the crisis

♦ Identify potential early warning signals

♦ Identification of the risk environment: socio-physical, planning and economic

♦ Development of a SWOT analysis to assess the vulnerability of, and risk to the enterprise or destination, and identify weaknesses that require attention and management.

♦ Integration with other organisational plans

♦ A hazard assessment checklist for a specific property type (i.e. hotel, resort, park, attraction) followed by a site visit and assessment of a property

♦ Logistics of essential services such as food and water

♦ Assignment of management and staff roles to deal with the specific threat and their emergency contact details

♦ Training in the expertise and duties required to fulfil specific roles

♦ Scenario training and drills for managing the onset of a crisis event that enable employees to test and refine their newly acquired skills

♦ A crisis communication plan

- ♦ Appointment of spokesperson, back-up and team to manage crisis communication and an evaluation of key messages
- ♦ Back-up procedures and personnel
- ♦ Sources and readily available contacts for external emergency assistance
- ♦ Contacts of critical stakeholders
- ♦ Use of tools such as automated and on-demand research services for example eWatch, National Earthquake Information Center (NEIC), CustomScoop.com, Incorporated Research Institutions for Seismology (IRIS) and Factiva.

Contingency plans should be available in hard copy and e-manual form available to all relevant management and staff. However contingency plan/s require simulation, and drills to be conducted at regular intervals.

Readiness should include an enterprise being adequately covered by insurance policies which include insurance coverage for property, data, professional and public liability and accident insurance for personnel. Data should be backed up and stored in alternative location. In locations which require ongoing power such as hotels, auxiliary power should be available. Clearly defined evacuation procedures and signage should be in place. The high dependence on IT of many tourism and hospitality businesses requires training in manual procedures in the event of a power outage or IT breakdown.

Stakeholders are an important element in the contingency plan and it is necessary to involve a broad range of internal and external entities in cooperating and sharing crises plans, in order to realise an effective response (Mitroff and Anagos, 2000). Stakeholders can include employees, other businesses and community, state, national, and international parties, such as police departments, fire departments, aid agencies and electricity and water authorities. It is necessary to allow plenty of time to involve stakeholders, so that relationships can be developed, cooperation gained and capabilities can be built (Mitroff and Anagos, 2000).

Response

Response includes actions that are taken before the actual crisis (for example when a hurricane warning is received), in response to the immediate impact of the crisis, and as sustained effort during the course of the crisis. Timing and establishing clear lines of communication are critical elements of response which affect the efficiency of dealing with the crisis and managing internal and external interests. The International Air Transport Association maintains that the first hour after an event has occurred is critical. PATA maintains that there is an immediate need to establish to stakeholders and the media that the enterprise or destination management is aware of events and in the process of managing the situation even if all facts are not immediately available. Establishing a clear line of communication is critical.

There are a number of key points in the effective response to a crisis situation:

- ♦ Provide consistent truthful messages throughout the organisation
- ♦ Briefing of key stakeholders and staff
- ♦ Identify needs of stakeholders including current guests, employees, prospective customers, local community, volunteers

♦ Demonstrable concern and action to tend to victims as the top priority

♦ Avoidance of blame transference

♦ Honest assessment of damage and casualties

♦ Maintenance of an ethical approach and honesty in all dealings with staff, stakeholders, victims and their families and media and, where possible, stress on positives

♦ Utilisation of the website as a primary form of external communication and updating information

♦ Contextualisation of the crisis in terms of its impact and anticipated time line of recovery

♦ Establishment of an emergency hotline

♦ Priority to recovery over budgetary considerations

♦ Seeking and welcoming of help from and offers of support to other organisations which may have been similarly affected

♦ Development of a timetable for recovery

♦ Maintenance of contact with relevant rescue, medical, emergency services, police services and local government authorities and maintenance of lines of communication with diplomatic legations in the event of victims from foreign countries

♦ Initiation of contact with media as facts are confirmed to minimise the risk of speculative and inaccurate reporting and media recovery.

Reduction

The concept of reduction in tourism crisis management is part of the process in which the enterprise begins the process of resuming operations and implementing strategies which protect and rebuild the destinations image as a safe and attractive place to visit. At the reduction phase there should be a full assessment of damage, casualties and loss and the beginning of marshalling a recovery alliance. In the case of a destination which has experienced a crisis event, government will usually take a lead role with the support of the tourism industry. An integral part of the reduction phase is the delineation of truth (the extent of damage to destination or reputation) from speculation and downright fiction.

During the reduction phases of a tourism crisis, services may be limited in the most affected zones and it is important to explain what damage has occurred, what attractions and services are open or operating and what is not. Provided that the community and tourism industry agree that tourism can resume, then it is important to communicate this to tourism consumers and sellers and point out that tourists are welcome.

The Samoan Tourism Authority successfully carried out this phase within two weeks of the 29 September 2009 tsunami and used their web site to deliver the message. This strategy can be referred to as the 'isolation strategy' in which the problem areas or access restrictions are clearly identified and explained within a broader context that tourism can proceed normally. Many businesses may use this phase as a limited or *soft* re-launch of their business activities. During this phase there are some key actions and messages:

♦ Positive focus on stewardship, reconstruction and rehabilitation

♦ Announcements of attractions, hotel and resorts re-opening

♦ Enactment of business continuity plan

♦ Communication of an anticipated time line of recovery

♦ Plans for new initiatives and measures which would minimise repetition of the circumstances which led to the crisis

♦ Preparation of a full recovery plan and incentive marketing plan for major source markets

♦ Ensuring that any actions involve due concern for victims and engage the local community in the process of recovery.

Recovery

Infrastructures and superstructures of destinations are often in ruin after a crisis which requires the future assessment of the socio-economic development of the destination (Carlsen and Liburd, 2007). A central element of the UNWTO's recovery plan following the Indian Ocean tsunami of December 2004 was a review of coastal hotel and resort design and construction specifications such that future developments would meet sustainability requirements to ensure that buildings and occupants would be less vulnerable to a tsunami or sea surge in the future. The Japanese authorities have consistently toughened building regulations after successive earthquakes during the twentieth century.

Most tourism crisis recovery strategies correctly emphasise the importance of employing a well-targeted marketing campaign but modern tourism recovery needs to address triple bottom line sustainability standards. These oblige tourism stakeholders to enact a recovery which is economically, socially and environmentally sustainable. Earlier in the chapter, the definition of the word *crisis* incorporated the concepts of danger and opportunity. Recovery from a crisis event presents the opportunity to re-image or redefine a tourism business or a destination.

Following a crisis the tourism industry may be keen to resume tourism activity. However 'ripple effects' of crises require careful consideration of the implications of allowing or encouraging tourism activity at a site of a crisis or disaster. The after shocks that continue to hit cities and resort towns in Chile following the February 2010 earthquake demonstrate that dangers can continue well after an initial event. In the case of health outbreaks it can be some time before it is truly known whether the real threat has passed.

A prevalent error made by tourism businesses and DMOs when seeking to lure back business is the promotion of a range of unsustainable discounts on air fares, hotel rates and tours which may succeed in attracting bottoms on seats or backs on beds but at a financial loss to businesses. Incentives are a legitimate tactic to lure tourists back to a destination but value-added inducements which have high perceived value to consumers and low cost for enterprises are far more sustainable forms of marketing incentive than massive discounts which benefit consumers but compromise the financial viability of a business which has already endured losses from the crisis event.

The essential elements in a post crisis tourism recovery campaign include:

♦ The establishment of key recovery objectives and a time line

♦ Involvement of tourism industry stakeholders and the local community in a recovery alliance

♦ Stratification and prioritising of target markets (the Israeli method of targeting its post-Intifada recovery campaign at stalwarts, waverers and discretionary travellers in that order is workable for many recovery campaigns)

♦ Ensuring that key opinion leaders in target markets are in a position to witness and communicate the fact that the destination/enterprise is open for business. Testimonials from credible opinion leaders are a key element of rebuilding confidence

♦ Identification of negative and false perceptions and targeting them in any advertising or marketing campaigns with the rider that rebuttals must be demonstrably truthful. Crisis management should minimise the use of media spin and focus on facts. A core element of recovery is the rebuilding of trust and confidence. Lies should not have any part in the recovery equation.

♦ Involvement of the media as an ally to a marketing campaign

♦ Regarding a crisis as an opportunity to completely re-image a destination during the recovery phase

♦ Ensuring there is a high level of consultation between destination marketing authorities and tourism industry stakeholders

♦ The application of the maxim 'build back better' to the environmental, economic, and socio-cultural elements associated with the destination.

Review

Contingency planning is only a means to an end and the continuous capture, processing and dissemination of tacit and explicit knowledge by stakeholders in tourism destinations is important (Carsen and Liburd, 2007). The process of sustainable crisis and risk management should involve an extensive consultation and debriefing process involving all key stakeholders, analysing lessons learned during the crisis management process and sharpening contingency plans to ensure that mistakes made in managing a specific crisis will be minimised or avoided in future. In common with all aspects of management, crisis and risk management involves a dynamic learning process in which organisations should plan for how to adapt to future crises while learning from the past.

Crisis and risk – future challenges

Previously this chapter discussed the way in which tourism can be impacted by technological failures. This continues to be one of tourism's biggest challenges. Technological crises can threaten the integrity and performance of critical tourism information infrastructure. Improved knowledge on how this infrastructure can be better protected is required to mitigate future crises. Tourism is made up of many small to medium enterprises who struggle to digest enormous amounts of information, which is continually being augmented and updated. How can these users query diverse information sources and effectively manage the information they receive to support their activities in the lead up to, during and post a crisis?

A fundamental goal of the use of information systems in crisis and risk management is the ability to supply decision makers at all levels with the information they need when they need it. The information users who must be served during a crisis are diverse and require varied formats of communication and ethical decision making. Therefore understanding how both old and new technologies can assist information communication to get the appropriate messages between the right people is a constant challenge. Improved knowledge in this area will assist in managing the crisis, minimising damage and improve the coordination and timely execution of the contingency plan.

Conclusion

Crisis and risk management has undergone a major shift from a peripheral issue of tourism management to a core issue during the first decade of the twenty-first century. Crisis management is increasingly a core issue of discussion among tourism academics and tourism professionals. Academically, sustainable crisis management in tourism is a relatively new field and while the body of research is growing rapidly the field is relatively open. The five Rs were presented as framework to assist entities to have in place the sustainable strategies to deal with a crisis or risk affecting tourism.

International and national tourism associations around the world are taking the issue of crisis and risk seriously while enterprises and destination managers are beginning to incorporate crisis management and contingency planning within their armoury of management skills. There is no standard recovery timetable from a crisis because the extent and intensity of damage caused by a crisis to tourism destinations and enterprises are subject to infinite variables. Yet it is evident that as the global tourism industry becomes more skilled at managing crisis events recovery times from comparable crises are reducing. In those situations where an enterprise or destination is prepared for a crisis they can not only recover faster but with significantly less damage. What this chapter has argued for is that crisis management should be underpinned by a philosophy of sustainability demonstrated in action to 'build back better'.

Review questions

1   What are some of the major elements involved in building back better?
2   Discuss the role of information technology in the crisis management.
3   Discuss the role of the media in the creation of perception of tourism crises by referring to at least one recent example of a tourism crisis.
4   Explain the nature and role of government travel advisories in destination perception. Are they, as is sometimes claimed, a form of political interference in another country or are they a constructive assessment of risk?

5   How might the application of the five Rs differ between a five star hotel, a golf resort and a national airline?

6   How can tourism organisations develop and implement a post-crisis recovery marketing campaign which is free of spin? Refer to a recent tourism crisis event.

7   Discuss the role of the media in the creation of perception of tourism crises by referring to at least one recent example of a tourism crisis.

References

APEC (Asia-Pacific Economic Cooperation) (2006) *Tourism Risk Management – An Authoritative Guide to Managing Crises in Tourism*, Singapore: APEC International Centre for Sustainable Tourism APEC Secretariat.

Avraham, E. and Ketter, E. (2008) *Media Strategies for Marketing Places in Crisis*, Oxford: Elsevier.

Beirman, D. (2003) Restoring Tourism Destinations in Crisis, Crows Nest NWS: Allen and Unwin, pp. 20-90.

Beirman, D. (2006) 'A travel industry perspective on government travel advisories', in J. Wilks, D. Pendergast and P. Leggat (eds), *Tourism in Turbulent Times*, Amsterdam: Elsevier, pp. 309-319.

Carlsen, J. and Liburd, J.J. (2007) *A Research Agenda for Tourism Crisis Marketing Recovery and Communications.* Journal of Tourism and Travel Marketing Vol. 21, no. 3, 265-276

Chatterjee, S.J. and Pearson, C.A.L. (2009) 'From conception to implementation: towards a crisis management framework', in C. Pforr and P. Hosie (eds), *Crisis Management in the Tourism Industry*, London: Ashgate, pp. 23-36.

Chui, L. (2007) 'Presentation on SARS in Hong Kong in 2003', paper presented at the conference APEC Tourism Forum , 15 May 2007, Surfers Paradise.

Faulkner, B. and Russell, R.(2000) 'Turbulence, crisis and complacency', in B. Faulkner. B. G. Moscardo and E.Laws (eds), *Tourism in the Twenty First Century*, London: Continuum, 328–349.

Glaesser, D. (2006) *Crises Management in the Tourism Industry*, Oxford: Elsevier

Gurtner, Y.P. (2007) 'Tsunami and tourism- a preliminary investigation', E. Laws, B. Prideaux and K. Chon (eds), *Crisis Management in Tourism*, Wallingford: CABI Publishing, pp. 217-233.

Hawkes, E. and Kwortnik, R. (2006) 'Connecting with culture: a case study in sustainable tourism', *Cornell Quarterly*, **47** (4), 369-380.

Henderson, J. (2007) *Tourism Crises: Causes, Consequences and Management*, Amsterdam: Elsevier.

Hermann C.F. (1972) *International Crises: Insights from Behavior Research*, New York: Free Press.

Holway, S. (2007) 'The ten commandments of tourism recovery', keynote address presented at the conference APEC Tourism Forum, 15 May 2007, Surfers Paradise.

Laws, E., Prideaux, B. and Chon, K. (2007a) 'Crisis management in tourism: challenges for managers and researchers', in E. Laws, B. Prideaux and K. Chon (eds), *Crisis Management in Tourism*, Wallingford: CABI Publishing, pp. 1-12.

Laws, E., Prideaux, B. and Chon, K. (eds) (2007b) *Crisis Management in Tourism*, Wallingford: CABI Publishing.

Mansfeld, Y and Pizam, A. (eds) (1996) *Tourism, Crime and International Security Issues*, New York: John Wiley and Sons.

Mansfeld, Y. and Pizam, A. (eds) (2006) *Tourism Safety and Security, From Theory to Practice*, Amsterdam: Elsevier.

Nielsen, C. (2001) *Tourism and the Media*, Melbourne: Hospitality Press.

Pacific Asia Travel Association (2003) *Crisis, It Won't Happen to Us*, Bangkok: PATA.

Pforr, C. and Hosie, P. (eds) (2009) *Crisis Management in the Tourism Industry*, London: Ashgate.

Prideaux. B. (2003) 'The need to use disaster planning frameworks to respond to major tourism disasters in 2001', *Journal of Travel and Tourism Marketing*, **3** (1), 281-298.

Tarlow, P. (2001) *Event, Risk Management and Safety*, Camberwell VIC: John Wiley and Sons.

UNWTO (United Nations World Tourism Organisation) (2009) *Tourism Barometer October 2009*. Madrid: UNWTO.

Wall, G. (2006) 'Recovering from SARS: the case of Toronto tourism', in Y. Mansfeld and A.Pizam (eds), *Tourism Security and Safety. From Theory to Practice*, Amsterdam: Elsevier, pp. 143-167.

Wilks, J. and Page, E. (2003) *Managing Tourism Health and Safety in the New Millennium*, Amsterdam: Elsevier.

Wilks, J., Pendergast, D. and Leggat, P. (eds) (2006) *Tourism in Turbulent Times*, Amsterdam: Elsevier.

World Health Organization (2010) Swine Flu Update: www.who.int.csr/disease/swineflu/en/, accessed 26 February 2010.

Yates, M. (2006) 'Project Phoenix: A Benchmark for Reputation Management in Travel and Tourism', in J. Wilks, D. Pendergast and P. Leggat (eds), *Tourism in Turbulent Times*, Amsterdam: Elsevier, pp. 263-276.

Industry e-publications recommended for updates on tourism crisis events

E Turbo News	http://www.eturbonews.com/
Travel Mole	http://www.travelmole.com/signout.php
E Hotelier Com	http://ehotelier.com/

12 The future of sustainability

Janne J. Liburd and Deborah Edwards

Introduction

Tourism constitutes exceptional opportunities as a phenomenon, industry, career and lifestyle. Sustaining the economic, social and environmental elements of tourism will be essential to maintaining a phenomenon that can support communities, provide employment and meet the experiential needs of customers. Thus, it is vital to provide the tourism managers of tomorrow with an explicit understanding of, and the capability to effect creative and innovative solutions for the sustainable development of tourism. Aiming to effectively enhance the understanding of sustainable tourism development through information sharing and social interaction, BEST EN has been producing educational modules since 2001.

BEST EN is guided by a strong belief that sustainable tourism principles should be practised in all aspects of tourism operations on a daily basis and that sustainability should be treated as a managerial philosophy rather than a subject matter, which is taught in one comprehensive course. This collection of chapters embodies the collective work of a group of volunteers composed of the academics of BEST EN and industry practitioners of the tourism industry worldwide. The conceptual point of origin reflected throughout the book is that tourism students, as future professionals, should be intimately aware of the values underpinning sustainability and be able to critically reflect upon desirable futures in order to pursue creative and sustainable vistas. Each of the chapters takes the view that sustainable tourism management needs to be seen as a dynamic process of change, rather than a static goal to be achieved, and therefore must be tackled with ever-evolving, flexible strategies.

Reporting on the opportunities and challenges for a transition towards more sustainable practices, relevant theories and concepts have been linked to practice through case studies or exercises. The chapters have also exposed how management strategies and leadership beyond narrow sectoral concerns are of pivotal importance to understanding the contribution tourism can make to sustainable development. Throughout this volume self-centred, short-term practices and linear thinking in causes and effects have been rejected in favour of a holistic understanding of stewardship, which should be exercised throughout the value-chain and in mutual collaboration with relevant stakeholders. These are practices that lead to a more comprehensive understanding of sustainable tourism as a complex adaptive system where social, cultural, environmental and economic goals are at stake.

In this final chapter we begin by addressing the interrelated values of knowledge, ethics, professionalism, mutuality and stewardship proposed by the Tourism Education Futures Initiative (TEFI) by highlighting some of the central implications and issues addressed in the individual chapters, and consider possible future directions. In the second half of this chapter we provide a commentary on sustainability and collaboration in tourism.

TEFI values and sustainable tourism development

Knowledge

Having knowledge and ongoing knowledge acquisition about sustainable tourism development, as addressed in Chapter 1 may appear to be a patently obvious value. Without sustainability knowledge, tourism will continue to leave permanent, undesirable footprints on the physical, social, cultural and economic environments of destinations. Chapter 2 illustrates how inappropriate types and scales of development may result from laissez-faire tourism policies and a lack of national, regional or local planning and regulation. Chapter 9 explains that poorly managed festivals can lead to negative outcomes such as noise, overcrowding, and increased pressures on services and infrastructure.

The value of knowledge is more complex than individual acquisitions and summary descriptions of principles and practices in the world around us. Valuing knowledge means understanding how new knowledge connects to existing knowledge that exists in both explicit and tacit formats. This understanding is exemplified in the approaches to corporate social responsibility (Chapter 6), triple bottom line reporting (Chapter 7), innovation (Chapter 8), festival and event management (Chapter 9), crisis and risk management (Chapter 11) and volunteer tourism (Chapter 10). Knowledge is created through processes of critically selecting, connecting and reflecting in multiple contexts. Critical thinking calls for an unrelenting examination of any form of knowledge and the knowledge creation process to recognise the existence (or non-existence) of the use and power that supports it and the further conclusions to which it tends. Critical thinking is not only about criticizing but being critical of the constitution of knowledge and underlying dogmas which must be extended beyond the confines of disciplinary knowledge towards the self and the world. We further address the reflection of self and the world in the interrelated value contexts below.

The dissemination and development of knowledge takes place both in solitude and in social environments that are characterised by information sharing and social interaction, which are clearly evident in this book. Access to social, economic and educational networks can create or assist in refining the use of knowledge. Increasingly, problem solving and innovation take place through sharing and cooperation in open knowledge systems, where providers and users of knowledge meet, exchange and co-create solutions for sustainable tourism (Chapter 8) through understanding that many views of the world are different from our own. The sustainable development of tourism requires a process of planning, innovation and management that brings together the interests and concerns of a diverse group of stakeholders in a sustainable and strategic way (Chapters 2, 3, 5, 6, 7, 9 and 10). It is this complexity that demands a planning approach which is multidimensional and is purposely integrative and adaptive. Herein lies the need for ongoing monitoring, evaluation and recognition of the role of stakeholders, which have been argued throughout this volume as prerequisites for successful adaptation and strategy implementation. Readers are referred to the BEST EN wiki to engage in further discussion of individuals and groups influencing sustainable tourism development (http://www.besteducationnetwork.org/besten_wiki/).

Ethics

As the basis for good action, ethics provides a framework for judging sustainability actions. Striving for actions that are deemed 'good' and are based on sustainability principles and values are a measure of ethical behaviour. Ethics also involves making such principles and values explicit and rendering the decision-making processes in tourism transparent through corporate social responsibility (Chapter 6) or reporting mechanisms such as triple bottom line accounting (Chapter 7). Codes of conduct can assist in delineating appropriate behaviour within a firm or an organisation which is why chapters in this volume have referred extensively to the UN World Tourism Organization's Global Code of Ethics for Tourism, (http://www.unwto.org/ethics/index.php). The set of ten principles setting the frame of reference for responsible and sustainable tourism was developed by UNWTO in consultation with stakeholders in 1999 and ratified by the UN in 2001. While the Global Code of Ethics for Tourism is not legally binding, one of its articles provides for a voluntary mechanism of dispute conciliation through a World Committee on Tourism Ethics.

Recognising that good actions do not occur in a vacuum but are derived from specific values requires further understanding and respect for actions based on different systems. The relationship between understanding and respect and different systems was explored in the contexts of volunteer tourism (Chapter 10) and corporate social responsibility (Chapter 6). The ethical principle of intergenerational equity in sustainable development sees everyone as impartially situated as equals, which can be exercised in the workplace through human resource management (Chapter 5) and supplier-driven innovation (Chapter 8). Making the ethical principles of operation transparent (Chapter 3) by adaptation into triple bottom line reporting (Chapter 7) and as a central pillar of social responsibility (Chapter 6) opens up for competitive advantage in the market (Chapter 11) by securing long-term relationships with the growing expectations and demands of consumers who are concerned about the impact of their purchase decisions and travel behaviour (Chapters 4 and 9). Accountability in all aspects of operation is of pivotal importance to avoid 'green-washing' (Chapter 8) as claims to ethical business practice lends themselves to increased media and stakeholder scrutiny. In other words, evoking ethical action moves beyond critical thinking by including ethical self-monitoring in sustainable problem solving and reflective tourism practice.

Mutual respect

Mutuality is seen as a process that starts from the self and is extended to others in an equitable and respectful manner. Described as a transition from 'travel to take' to 'travel to assist', the phenomenon of volunteer tourism (Chapter 10) is illustrative of critical action based on mutual respect and reciprocity. While motivations for engagement may fluctuate between altruism and personal development, the activity fosters openness, sensitivity toward others and imbues the potential to enhance sustainability at multiple levels (self, community, business, organisation, the destination). Adopting fair trade practice as a measure of sustainability in tourism, mutual respect can also be demonstrated in corporate social responsibility in pricing and labour practices. Similar principles of equity and mutual respect are also espoused in the context of poverty alleviation set by the Millennium Development Goals, by the UN Global Compact (Chapter 6) and by the universal Human Rights. Working with internal and external stakeholders require different opinions, philosophies of life and cultures to be met with tolerance and mutual respect in innovation processes (Chapter 8), festivals, meetings and events (Chapter 9), community engagement in sustainable tourism planning (Chapter 2) and crisis recovery (Chapter 11).

Sustainable human resource practice in tourism pays attention to the quality of working life and competitive performance. Long and unsocial working hours, low pay and often low status of some tourism jobs that may be prone to seasonality mean that tourism is an industry that does not easily attract new, or retain existing, staff (Deery, 2002). By considering improvements to working conditions, training and organisational performances, sustainable human resource practices and work/life balance can be addressed. Findings by Deery and Jago (2009) indicate that while employees may have substantial concerns regarding negative impacts of their work on their home life, they still indicate an overall level of satisfaction with their work/life balance. Clearly this is an area in need of further research. These sentiments do not appear consistent with the summation of the individual components of satisfaction, such as personal attributes, mutual support, industry norms and the way these components are managed whereby the sustainability of tourism and hospitality operations can be maintained.

Professionalism

New ways of thinking about the professions are essential. Higher educational institutions must prepare tourism students to become practitioners, researchers, philosophical scholars and knowledge brokers throughout their studies and in their subsequent careers. Encompassing ethical leadership, practicality, attention to services, critical reflexivity, proactivity, teamwork and partnership building skills, sustainable tourism managers must provide vision and management beyond the individual tourism firm or organisation. Students as future tourism professionals must appreciate the ethical dimension of innovation and creativity for sustainable tourism development; there is ample historical evidence of innovations that have led to ethically disastrous consequences. It is often useful to explicitly distinguish between creativity and innovation. Creativity is typically used to refer to the act of producing new ideas, approaches or actions that are appropriate to the problem at hand, while innovation often begins with creative ideas and involves a process of both generating *and applying* such creative ideas in a specific context for human, cultural or economic purposes.

Chapter 8 suggests that improving the links between tourism firms and their value chains at a destination and beyond can lead to new innovations through knowledge sharing and acting as role models. Realising sustainability also lies in changing the mindset of enterprises and destination managers away from 'competitiveness' to 'diversity and attractiveness'. Focusing on attractiveness rather than competition may reduce the incentive to pursue maximum growth and dominance and thus lead to more sustainable resource use. Placing corporate social responsibility (Chapter 6) and triple bottom line accounting (Chapter 7) at the core of operations enhances accountability through transparent and thereby more trustworthy practices. The need to create a concerned demand for sustainable tourism poses a professional challenge to future managers. Understanding the importance of strategic communication, social acceptability and social learning for a sustainable tourism transition represent areas in need of further research. The position of the media has been emphasized in the context of risk and crisis management (Chapter 11), addressed in relation to the effectiveness of marketing (Chapter 4) and as stakeholders in festivals, meetings and events (Chapter 9). The role of the media as a potential driver for sustainability must be examined in more detail with an emphasis on opportunities afforded by new social media for influencing behavioural change and learning and real-time communication.

Stewardship

As sustainability requires us to think about desirable futures there is a need to move beyond mixed-use planning purely in terms of supplying spatial diversity for potential uses, to interweaving cultural and place-specific elements into the physical form of such developments whether in urban or natural environments. Chapters 1, 2, 9 and 10 emphasize a need for a more dynamic understanding of local communities in the sustainable development of tourism. The local context, local cultures and the interests of the residents, workers and environment who are at the centre of the rich milieu that characterises the tangible and intangible features of destinations should be brought closer to the concerns of visitors. To belong to a place is informed not only by particular modes of localised cultural knowledge, but shared through associated symbols and imaginations that inform social practice. Communities should be made sufficiently aware of and brought to understand the tourism industry and its impacts, as well as the various processes to integrate and engage in participatory planning, consensus building and conflict resolution among all stakeholders. Students must be mindful that notions of local participation and local communities should not assume they are homogenous groups of people that easily reach consensus. The range of stakeholders, networks and actors in tourism destinations are multiple as are their aspirations, needs and quality of life. A place-based approach towards sustainable tourism development should be underpinned by identification and monitoring of the socio-cultural, environmental and economic changes that are acceptable for the destination community whose habitat it is, or may become, the object of tourism development (Liburd, 2007).

The dynamics and unpredictability of complex systems amplify the importance of tourism crisis and recovery management, as argued in Chapter 11 and further illustrated in the context of festivals, meetings and events (Chapter 10). Optimising recovery from crisis and building resilience can lead to maintaining attractiveness in the global marketplace, just as failure to monitor, act and communicate effectively may have detrimental effects for tourism businesses and the destination overall. Crises require government and non-government entities to identify stakeholders needs, including current guests, employees, prospective customers, local community and volunteers, to ethically respond and offer destinations the opportunity to 'build back better' to a more resilient and sustainable tourism sector (Chapter 11). It may well be that resilience at the individual firm level, which can be substantiated through stakeholder relationships and innovation can become a potential indicator of systems resilience at the destination level.

Dealing with complex adaptive systems, where future insecurity and uncertainty are implicit forces, 'thinking outside the box' is required to look at existing domains and problems from new angles in addition to having confidence in venturing off the beaten path. Promoting such a collaborative culture of creativity in tourism that acknowledges and seeks to learn from failure encourages students to move from hypothesis and conventional knowledge towards possibilities and originality. Understanding what works also means understanding the 'othering' of things and those who are made absent through exclusion from the network and thus silenced in the process. Chapter 1 reflected on issues of power. It is not surprising that the engagement of multiple stakeholders is susceptible to individual agendas, which can result in inequitable balances of resources. In short, relations of power must be integral to critical enquiry about how systems and networks are connected, released and reorganised.

Sustainability and collaboration in tourism

The chapters in this volume indicate that there are still many gaps in our understanding of the sustainable development of tourism. Dresner (2008, p. 160) argues that 'sustainability is trapped between the reflexivity of the world (which is how we got into this mess) and the need to be able to transform and control the direction of human society, which reflexivity implies is impossible'. A first step is asking questions at the local level. Can tourism practices continue indefinitely or will they destroy the local resource base and environment? If at the local level, tourism is dependent on external non-renewable resources how long might they last before being exhausted? How can one tourism region contribute to the knowledge, organisational and technological bases of other regions, nations, or through international relations? How can sustainable tourism assist in the preservation of living culture while facilitating dynamic understandings that embrace contemporary cultural appropriations and practices?

Attention should also be directed towards governance. Sovereign governments have the obligation to guarantee equality, safety and democracy, and to enable its citizens to fulfil individual potentials and enhance the quality of their lives. Governments at all levels have the tools to facilitate and substantiate changes towards sustainable development (Chapter 1). Regrettably, governments at the national level still tend to pay scarce attention to tourism as they are more occupied with other areas of public life (Miller and Twining-Ward, 2005). At the regional and local levels tourism is frequently afforded priority in government institutions, but it is poorly understood, especially as a driver for sustainable development (Cheong and Miller, 2000). This is in dire contrast to the recognition of government as a stakeholder acknowledged throughout this volume, demonstrating that future research attention needs to be paid to government as a driver for sustainable tourism.

Non-governmental organisations (NGOs) have been described as stakeholders in sustainable tourism development (Chapter 2, 9 and 10), which is another illustration of how governance is exercised in society. NGO involvement often fills or reduces the gap between the 'top' and 'bottom' of society by campaigning, lobbying, through press relations, educational material and networking, and deliberate targeting of marginal population segments in their work. Through dedicated advocacy, 'participative development' (Burns, 1999) promotion of sustainability (Mowforth and Munt, 1998), fair trade and ethical forms of tourism (Tourism Concern, 2010), the inclusion and diversity of approaches by the NGO sector are well-established. On the other hand, rather than promoting civic activism and deep-rooted changes NGOs are easily accused of preserving the status quo by setting up systems of patronage that not only undermine but also depoliticise social movements and other grassroots organisations (Gardner and Lewis, 1996; Brennan and Allen, 2001; Liburd, 2004). As a total social and economic phenomenon (Theobald, 2005) students are encouraged to reflect upon how to enhance political visibility, beyond public initiatives limited to marketing and institutional structures, in order to address the fundamental elements of sustainable tourism planning and overall governance. Moreover, students should be critical about the effectiveness and improvements of participatory methods and systems of governance while considering new and desirable modes of stakeholder involvement.

Adaptive management differs from conventional management practice by its insistence on processes of experimentation, monitoring and adaptation as part of a continuous social learning process (Miller and Twining-Ward, 2005, p. 285). The industry is ingrained in networks, collaborative practices and competition. It is easy to focus on competitiveness because it promises easy answers to complex problems. It suggests that we have to export as much as we can, repeat what others are doing – rather than make for ourselves. The result of this focus can be misallocated resources, homogenisation, and often more of the traditional medicine: more tax reliefs, more money for destination promotion, and more short training courses. The impacts of such 'treatment' programmes on innovation and human capacity building are – if ever assessed in depth – not very convincing (Baum, 2007), and may at worst, run counter to sustainable development.

Chapter 11 highlighted the ways in which tourism is impacted by technological failures. The World Business Council for Sustainable Development (WBCSD) stated that at the beginning of the new millennium, a global 'technosphere' is being created as communication infrastructure develops and as economic systems become more interdependent. The components are linked together in innumerable different inter-connections changing 'the speed with which knowledge is transferred and problems are perceived – but not the speed with which these problems are being solved' (WBSCD ND, p. 14). The diversity of tourism's dependence on technology in the absence of solutions will continue to create the potential for more and different kinds of crises. Yet, the same technology allows enterprises to respond faster, more efficiently, and with instant, worldwide impact. Students should be challenged to critically reflect upon how the tremendous amount of information on the Internet can be utilised by tourism enterprises when they need it, and made available for trustworthy content generation by the teams of stakeholders.

BEST EN – collaborative enterprise at work

The importance of effective networking and collaboration for sustainability in tourism cannot be overstated. BEST EN itself is an amalgamation of inter-disciplinary and multi-disciplinary knowledge and collaboration – specifically for larger, collective gain – with the associated norms of reciprocity and mutual respect. This book is principally a product of equitable participation in knowledge creation processes at annual, BEST EN Think Tanks by academics and industry professionals who are engaged in learning together. Knowledge about sustainable tourism development is employed as a process and activity, i.e. as use, evaluation, transformation, reuse of materials and development of new knowledge. These processes and activities have generated educational modules, research agendas and industry case studies. The rich materials have been distributed through BEST EN's website, as a community of practice, and through dedicated special journal issues and two book publications, including the present volume. In order to generate collective knowledge, participation is based on a variety of methods that allow for individual reflection on both subject matters and methodology.

Striving to identify knowledge gaps, provide vision and cutting-edge insight to topics relating to sustainable tourism, the nominal group technique (NGT) has been successfully applied at a number of Think Tanks. Its structural usefulness is found in idea generation, identification of key objectives and democratic decision making (Jurowski and Liburd, 2002). Box 12.1 describes the NGT process.

The bulk of the published tourism research looks primarily to the past with little attention paid to the generation and analysis of future scenarios. At the 8th BEST EN Think Tank, a combination of methods was applied. By generating and exploring possible futures through Futures Wheels and back casting (see Box 12.2), current trends and important relationships were identified, which effectively opened up for consideration, the potential consequences of current decisions and unsustainable practices (Benckendorff, 2007).

Box 12.1 Nominal group technique

The nominal group technique (NGT) encourages the development of individual views that are debated and given consideration by the group (Chapple and Murphy, 1996). It was developed by Delbecq and van de Ven in 1968 who synthesized studies related to social psychology, management science, and social work (Ho, Lai, and Chang, 1999). Within the highly structured technique are elements of brainstorming and brainwriting, as well as voting techniques that balance participation among group members.

The NGT begins with the articulation of the problem or question by a facilitator. It is important that the problem be a distinct task that gives the participants a specific question to which they can respond (Roth et al., 1995). Once all group members clearly understand the question the process proceeds through five distinct steps:

1. Silent generation of ideas
2. Reporting of generated ideas
3. Clarification of ideas
4. Ranking of ideas
5. Presentation and discussion of the results of the voting process.

Box 12.2 Futures Wheel

The Futures Wheel is a structured mind-mapping technique developed by Glenn in 1971 (Glenn, 2003). Its most common use is as a graphical tool to explore the impacts or consequences of trends, events or decisions (Deal, 2002). The wheel organises these impacts or consequences as a series of concentric rings or circles centred on the specific trend, event or decision being explored (Glenn, 2003). In the first or innermost ring are the most immediate or primary consequences. Leading on from each of these are secondary consequences arranged in a second ring, with a third ring of tertiary consequences (Glenn, 2003).

The three key strengths of the Futures Wheel technique are:

♦ The production of a visual or graphic representation that allows for both the sequencing of events/actions across time and the display of complex relationships

♦ Its flexibility and ease of use, and

♦ The encouragement of systems thinking among the participants in the exercise (Benckendorff, 2007; List, 2004).

The key challenge in using the Futures Wheel is the need for discipline on the part of the facilitator to ensure that the primary, secondary and tertiary levels are clearly maintained and that the suggestions provided by participants are linked directly to the items already identified in the wheel. Without such discipline the wheel can become too complex to be useful (Benckendorff et al., 2009).

Attempting to develop dynamic and open knowledge bases to assist sustainable tourism teaching and research, the BEST EN wiki on Sustainable Tourism was launched, as mentioned above (http://www.besteducationnetwork.org/besten_wiki/). Wikis allow students to be online and work with semester topics in social and multi-media settings combining text, images, audio, video files, and so on (Christensen, 2009). In anticipation that the wiki will become a dynamic and organic record of the latest concepts and ideas in sustainable tourism development it is a means to facilitate collaborative learning uninhibited from the limited timeframe of the annual Think Tanks. This ambition is further supported by an open innovation platform in tourism, entitled INNOTOUR (http://www.innotour.com) to maximise student relevance and learning, research collaboration and industry innovation. The integration of Web 2.0 tools and methods in BEST EN's collaborative knowledge generating activities are underpinned by the values of mutuality, equity, professionalism and stewardship. Web 2.0 represents an entirely novel perception of knowledge – not just as a state possessed by the individual – but as process and activity, which may conflict with academic tradition (Dohn, 2009). These conflicting yet interacting demands on the students is an area in need of further research to assess the quality and outcome of utilising Web 2.0 learning in tourism education.

Increasingly, students insist on relevance and perspectives for their studies based on a comprehensible and logical integration of theory and practice. The argument for a more comprehensive understanding of tourism and its contribution to sustainable development is not confined to the academic setting. The majority of tourism enterprises are small, have limited resources for comprehensive turnarounds and new entrants may – or may not – bring with them strategic capabilities and capital for needed, sustainable investments (Thomas, 2004; Moscado, 2008). Knowledge transfer is seriously constrained. The European University Association's Creativity Project (2006-07) explicitly encouraged universities to transcend the conventional position between the 'ivory tower' and the world around it by balancing active engagement in society with a certain distance from the world, thus transforming the ivory tower into a 'watch tower'.

There is an obvious need to search for new possibilities to assist the tourism industry to not only overcome barriers towards innovation but to facilitate much wider capacity building through education (Airey, 2008). We argue that an epistemological space exists within studies of tourism for post-disciplinary approaches based on even greater flexibility, plurality, synthesis and synergy (Coles et al., 2006), which must be subjected to ongoing experimentation. While there is still a lack of evidence to support the hypothesis, Web 2.0 opens opportunities for the rethinking and reorganisation of knowledge interaction and dissemination between industry, education and research (Liburd and Hjalager, 2010). Miller et al. (2010) argue that social networking tools can help encourage sustainable behaviour through connecting people and overcoming the sense of disempowerment. Moreover, findings by Cooper et al. (2007) indicate that graduates may find that their degrees only offer a few years of currency rather than a lifetime of expertise. This raises the need to understand and promote lifelong and self-directed learning to underpin professional expertise.

With the present configuration of the tourism world reflected in the topics addressed in this book, such as marketing (Chapter 4) and operations (Chapter 3), universities are called upon to produce human resources that can help solve these problems. The urgency of the day-to-day inevitably competes for space with the equally urgent, but never quite so pressing issues of the future. Giddens (2009) captures the predicament of acting now for the future in the context of climate change. Giddens notes that since we are not currently unduly affected by the outcomes of climate change we fail to act. But when we are finally pressed into action by its consequences it will be too late to do anything about them. Based on reflexive, critical thinking and deep understanding of the values of the sustainable development in tourism, students and educators are strongly encouraged to engage in visualising desirable, sustainable futures within and beyond the classroom setting, mindful that 'dreams require optimism and a sense that one's hopes can be fulfilled' (Rifkin, 2005 p. 348). Reflection upon the grounds, theoretical foundations and thereby also upon the values we apply when making our decisions for sustainable tourism development should take us to applicability and ethical action.

In acknowledgement of all the resourceful individuals who have participated in the collaborative, knowledge generation processes at BEST EN Think Tanks over the past decade we dedicate this volume. We are grateful to each and everyone as they exemplify how people can come together to co-create solutions to understand the sustainable development of tourism for students, academics and the tourism industry. At BEST EN we look forward to continuing these collaborations in the anticipation that the 'sustainable tourism conversation and collaboration' will continue to introduce new ways of thinking and acting.

References

Airey, D.W. (2008) 'Tourism education: life begins at 40', School of Management, University of Surrey. http://epubs.surrey.ac.uk/cgi/viewcontent.cgi?article=1039&context=tourism accessed 12 September 2009

Baum, T. (2007) 'Human resources in tourism. Still waiting for a change', *Tourism Management*, **28**, 1383-1399.

Benckendorff, P. (2007) 'Envisioning sustainable tourism futures: an evaluation of the Futures Wheel method', *Tourism and Hospitality Research*, **8** (1), 25-36.

Benckendorff, P., Edwards, D., Liburd, J.J., Jurowski, C., Miller, G., Moscado, G. (2009) 'Exploring the future of tourism and quality of life', *Tourism and Hospitality Research*, **9** (2), 171-183.

Brennan, F. and Allen, G. (2001) 'Community-based ecotourism, social exclusion and the changing political economy of Kwa-Zulu Natal, South Africa', in D. Harrison (ed.), *Tourism and the Less Developed World. Issues and Case Studies*, Wallingford: CABI Publishing, pp. 203-221.

Burns, P. (1999) 'Tourism NGOs', *Tourism Recreational Research*, **24** (2), 3-6.

Chapple, M. and R. Murphy (1996) 'The nominal group technique: extending the evaluation of students' teaching and learning experiences'. *Assessment and Evaluation in Higher Education*, **21** (2), 147-160.

Cheong, S. and Miller, M. (2000) 'Power and tourism: a Foucauldian observation', *Annals of Tourism Research*, **27**, 371-390.

Christensen, I-M. (2009) 'How can examination practice reflect the use of collaborative Web 2.0 courses?', in *Book of Abstracts. 15th International Conference on Technology Supported Learning & Training*, Berlin: Online Educa, pp. 334-337.

Coles, T., Hall, C.M. and Duval, D.T., (2006) Tourism and post-disciplinary enquiry, *Current Issues in Tourism*, **9**(485), 293–319.

Cooper, T., Hofheinz, P. and Purdy, M. (2007) *Skills for the Future*, London: Accenture.

Deal, W.F. (2002) 'Making the connection: technological literacy and technology assessment', *Technology Teacher*, **61**, 16-25.

Deery, M. (2002) 'Labour turnover in international hospitality and tourism', in S. Watson, N. D'Annunzio-Green and G. Maxwell (eds), *Human Resource Management: International Perspectives in Hospitality and Tourism*, London: Continuum, pp. 51–63.

Deery, M. and Jago, L. (2009) 'A framework for work–life balance practices: addressing the needs of the tourism industry', *Tourism and Hospitality Research*, **9**, 97-108.

Dohn, N.B. (2009) Web 2.0: Inherent tensions and evident challenges for education, *International Journal of Computer-Supported Collaborative Learning*, **4**(3) accessed 2 May 2009 from http://www.citeulike.org/journal/springerlink-120055

Dresner, S. (2008) *Principles of Sustainability*, 2nd edn, London: Earthscan.

European University Association (2007) *Creativity in Higher Education. Report on the EUA Creativity Project 2006-2007*, Brussels: EUA Publications.

Farrington, J., Bebbington, A., Wellard, K. and Lewis, D.J. (1993) *Reluctant Partners? Non-governmental Organisations, the State and Sustainable Agricultural Development*, London and New York: Routledge.

Gardner, K. and Lewis, D. (1996) *Anthropology, Development and the Post-modern Challenge*, London and Chicago: Pluto Press.

Giddens, A. (2009) *The Politics of Climate Change*, Cambridge: Polity Press.

Glenn, J.C. (2003) 'The Futures Wheel', in J.C. Glenn and T.J. Gordon (eds), *Futures Research Methodology Version 2.0*, Washington, DC: American Council for the United Nations University, pp. 1-15.

Ho, E.S.S.A., Lai, Y. and Chang, S.I. (1999) 'An integrated group decision-making approach to quality function deployment', *IIE Transactions*, **31**, 553-567.

Jurowski, C. and Liburd, J.J. (2002) 'A multi-cultural and multi-disciplinary approach to integrating the principles of sustainable development into human resource management curriculums in hospitality and tourism', *Hospitality and Tourism Educator*, 13 (5), 36-50.

Liburd, J.J. (2004) 'NGOs in tourism and preservation – democratic accountability and sustainability in question', *Tourism Recreation Research*, **29** (2), 105-110.

Liburd, J.J. (2007) 'Sustainable tourism, cultural practice and competence development for hotels and inns in Denmark', *Tourism Recreation Research*, **32** (1), 41-49.

Liburd, J.J. and Hjalager, A-M (forthcoming) Changing approaches to education, innovation and research – student experiences', *Tourism Journal of Hospitality and Tourism Management*, **17**.

List, D. (2004) 'Multiple pasts, converging presents, and alternative futures', *Futures*, **36**, 23-43.

Macbeth, J. (2005) Towards an ethics platform for tourism, *Annals of Tourism Research*, **32**(4), 962–984.

Miller, G. and Twining-Ward, L. (2005) *Monitoring for a Sustainable Tourism Transition: The Challenge of Developing and Using Indicators*, Wallingford: CABI Publishing.

Miller, G., Rathouse, K., Scarles, C., Holmes, K. and Tribe, J. (2010) 'Public understanding of sustainable tourism', *Annals of Tourism Research,* doi:10.1016/j.annals.2009.12.002, accessed 25 March 2010.

Moscardo, G. (2008) 'Sustainable tourism innovation: challenging basic assumptions', *Tourism and Hospitality Research,* **8** (1), 4-14.

Mowforth, A. and Munt, I. (1998) *Tourism and Sustainability: New Tourism in the Third World,* London: Routledge.

Rifkin, J. (2005) *The European Dream: How Europe's Vision of the Future is Quietly Eclipsing the American Dream,* New York: Penguin Group.

Roth, P. L., Schleifer, L.L.F. and Switzer, F.S. (1995) 'Nominal group technique – an aid in implementing TQM', *CPA Journal,* **65** (5), 68-69.

Theobald, W.F. (ed.) (2005) *Global Tourism,* Burlington, MA: Elsevier Butterworth-Heinemann.

Thomas, R. (2004) 'International perspectives on small firms in tourism', in R. Thomas (ed.), *Small Firms in Tourism. International Perspectives,* Amsterdam: Elsevier, pp. 1-12.

Tourism Concern (2010) http://www.tourismconcern.org.uk, accessed 13 March 2010.

WBCSD (World Business Council for Sustainable Development) (n.d.) 'Global scenarios 2000-2050: summary brochure', retrieved from http://www.wbcsd.ch/DocRoot/dtntHdPTlkbR35KCK6NF/exploringscenarios accessed 14 March 2010.

Glossary

Baseline indicator: a measurement, calculation, or location used as a basis for comparison.

Benchmarking: the use of information about competitors in the same industry used for comparisons and to set standards and goals

Best practice: the measurement of an organisation's specific tasks and activities against best-in-industry or best-in-world performers

Brainstorming: a process of generation of ideas in individual ways or in a group, avoiding immediate evaluations

Career mobility: The upward or downward mobility in an occupation or the change from one occupation to another.

Commodification: the process in which the final outcome of a product is solely defined by its economic value.

Community development: an empowering process that identifies resources and services that enable community members to meet their own needs.

Community profiling: activity that seeks to understand the current social condition of a destination and the people in the community who are likely to be affected by a proposed development.

Conservation: planned management of natural resources to prevent exploitation, destruction or neglect

Corporate citizenship: – often used as synonym to Corporate social responsibility; concerning the role of the enterprise as 'good citizen' in its interactions with the community.

Corporate social responsibility (CSR): – is a concept whereby companies integrate social and environmental concerns in their business operations and in their interaction with their stakeholders on a voluntary basis.

CSR integration in tourism: – the process by which tourism enterprises integrate the CSR concept into their business, by voluntarily implementing social and environmental responsibilities into their operations, and by interacting with their stakeholders.

Cultural resources: includes heritage, museums, zoological and botanical gardens, literature, libraries and archives, music, performing arts, visual arts, film, radio, video, television

Culture shock: the ebbing and flowing of emotions in reaction to situational stress, brought on by being placed in a context different or unfamiliar to the one a person is used to.

Destination marketing organisation (DMO): any organisation at any level which is responsible for the marketing of an identifiable destination excluding separate government departments that are responsible for planning and policy

Economic accountability: the liability to shareholders and stakeholders for corporate performance and action

Environmental management system (EMS): an integrated system which incorporates ISO 1400 and ISO 14001.

Environmental practices: practices which reduce negative and promote positive outcomes on the environment

Ethics: the systematic study of value concepts, 'good', 'bad', 'right', 'wrong' and the general principles that justify applying these concepts.

Evaluation: the process of critically observing, measuring and monitoring the implementation of an FME to assess its outcomes accurately

Facilitation strategy: creating marketing collaboration bridges between DMOs and individual travel and tourism firms and between the umbrella campaigns organised by the DMOs and industry marketing expenditure

Global citizenship: the concept that citizenship is not bound by nations, but that people of all nations and cultures need to develop a culture of tolerance based on our shared humanity and peaceful co-existence.

Globalised tourism: There is a growing trend for airlines, cruise companies, travel agents, tour operators and accommodation providers to agglomerate on a global scale. This is reflected by the growth of global tourism associations including the UN World Tourism Organization, the World Travel and Tourism Council, the International Hotels and Restaurants Association and the United Federation of Travel Agents just to name a small number of global tourism organisations.

Green jobs: Broadly, a green job is one that reduces negative impact on the environment.

Heritage resources: includes any relict physical survival of the past, idea of individual and collective memories in terms of non-physical aspects of the past when viewed from the present, accumulated cultural and artistic productivity, natural environment and industrial heritage

Host community: the place and people with which the volunteer tourists engage in their projects. 'Community' refers to a group of people who share a common identity, or who share a special interest.

Human factors: the role of humans in man–machine systems and how systems can be designed to work well with people, particularly in regard to safety and efficiency

Impact assessment: to predict the likely economic, social, and environmental effects of alternative tourism plans

International community: Sustainable human communities meet their current needs without compromising other species and future generations. Cities and counties make day-to-day decisions affecting the sustainability of both their community and the planet.

International Institute for Sustainable Development (IISD): A policy research institute dedicated to effective communication of their findings. They engage decision-makers in government, business, NGOs and other sectors in the development and implementation of policies that are simultaneously beneficial to the global economy, the global environment and to social well-being.

Marketing: a social and managerial process by which individuals and groups obtain what they need and want through creating and exchanging products and value with others.

Master marketing strategy: a strategy that reviews the strengths, weaknesses, opportunities and threats of the business and shapes its long-range marketing objectives.

Monitoring: (1) the evaluation of tourism plans against key criteria to determine the extent to which they continue to promote sustainability including: ecological integrity; social integrity, cultural integrity; economic contribution; equity; community participation; and visitor satisfaction.

Monitoring: (2) the systematic collection and analysis of information as an FME progresses

Natural resources: include topography, climate, water, wildlife, vegetation and location.

NGOs: non-government organisations

Othering: a process of focusing on the differences between the self and other people or cultures, regarding the culture, beliefs, a features of the self to be normal, and the differences in others to be alien, deficient or of less worth.

Sense of place: the mental construct of the temporal–spatial experience that occurs as an individual ascribes meaning to settings, through environmental perception and cognition

Shareholder activism: – a way in which the shareholders of a company can assert their influence as co-owners in order to influence and modify its behaviour. It can cover a wide set of activities, from selling the shares, private or public dialogue with the managing board, putting forward shareholder resolutions and ultimately replacing individual directors or the entire board.

Social planning: a task-focused process that emphasises efficiency and rationality and is well suited to large-scale planning.

Socially responsible: a strategy that seeks to achieve social as well as financial returns by functioning ethically.

Stakeholder group: Groups of constituents for an organisation who affect or can be affected by an organisation's actions

Stakeholders: all individuals who have an interest in the event, such as the various business organisations, guests, vendors, media, the community, etc

Strategic marketing system: the open system of strategies that flows from the corporate mission or vision through each level with two feedback control loops

Strategic marketing: all the decisions and actions used to formulate and implement strategies designed to achieve the marketing objectives of an organisation or a destination

Sustainable tourism: tourism which leads to the management of all resources in such a way that economic, social and aesthetic needs can be fulfilled while maintaining cultural integrity, essential ecological processes, biological diversity and life-support systems

Tourism audit: a demand- and supply-side analysis of a destination to assess its capacity to both host tourism and attract tourists.

Tourism crisis: an event or a set of circumstances which severely undermines the viability and marketability of a tourism destination or a tourism enterprise

Tourism operators: private sector firms which supply good and services to tourists

Tourism planning: is about determining 'what should be as well as what is'.

Tourism security: Each element of the tourism industry is vulnerable to varying security threats. Some are physically obvious including terrorist attacks. Others are less obvious including cyber crime or cyber-terrorism. Each element of the tourism industry has varying areas of preparedness. Airlines and airports have a high level of security consciousness and have increasingly become harder targets. On the other hand, restaurants and tourist attractions have little defence and minimal security presence and have increasingly become targets for both terrorism and crime.

Value-added: the enhancement added to a product or service before the product is offered to customers

Visioning: the task of planning to visualise the area, that is the product, as visitors and managers and the community wish it to be in the future

Volunteer tourist: tourists who, for various reasons, volunteer in an organised way to undertake holidays that might involve aiding or alleviating the material poverty of some groups in society, the restoration of certain environments or research into aspects of society or environment.

Volunteering: an activity that takes place in not-for-profit organisations or projects and is of benefit to the community and undertaken of the volunteer's own free will, without coercion; for no financial payment; and in designated volunteer positions only.

Work intensity: An increase in workload usually attributed to efficiency measures, and shortages of trained staff.

Work/life balance: broad concept including proper prioritising between career and ambition, compared with pleasure, leisure and family.

Index

05802168